THE SULTANS CAME TO TEA

THE SULTANS CAME TO TEA

JUNE KNOX-MAWER

ALAN SUTTON
1984

Alan Sutton Publishing Limited
17a Brunswick Road
Gloucester GL1 1HG

Copyright © 1961 June Knox-Mawer

First published 1961 by John Murray
This edition published 1984

British Library Cataloguing in Publication Data

Knox-Mawer, June
   The sultans came to tea.
   1. Aden (Yemen)—Social life and customs
   I. Title
   953'.35   DS247.A24

ISBN 0-86299-121-8

Printed in Great Britain
by Redwood Burn Limited, Trowbridge

TO RONALD

Contents

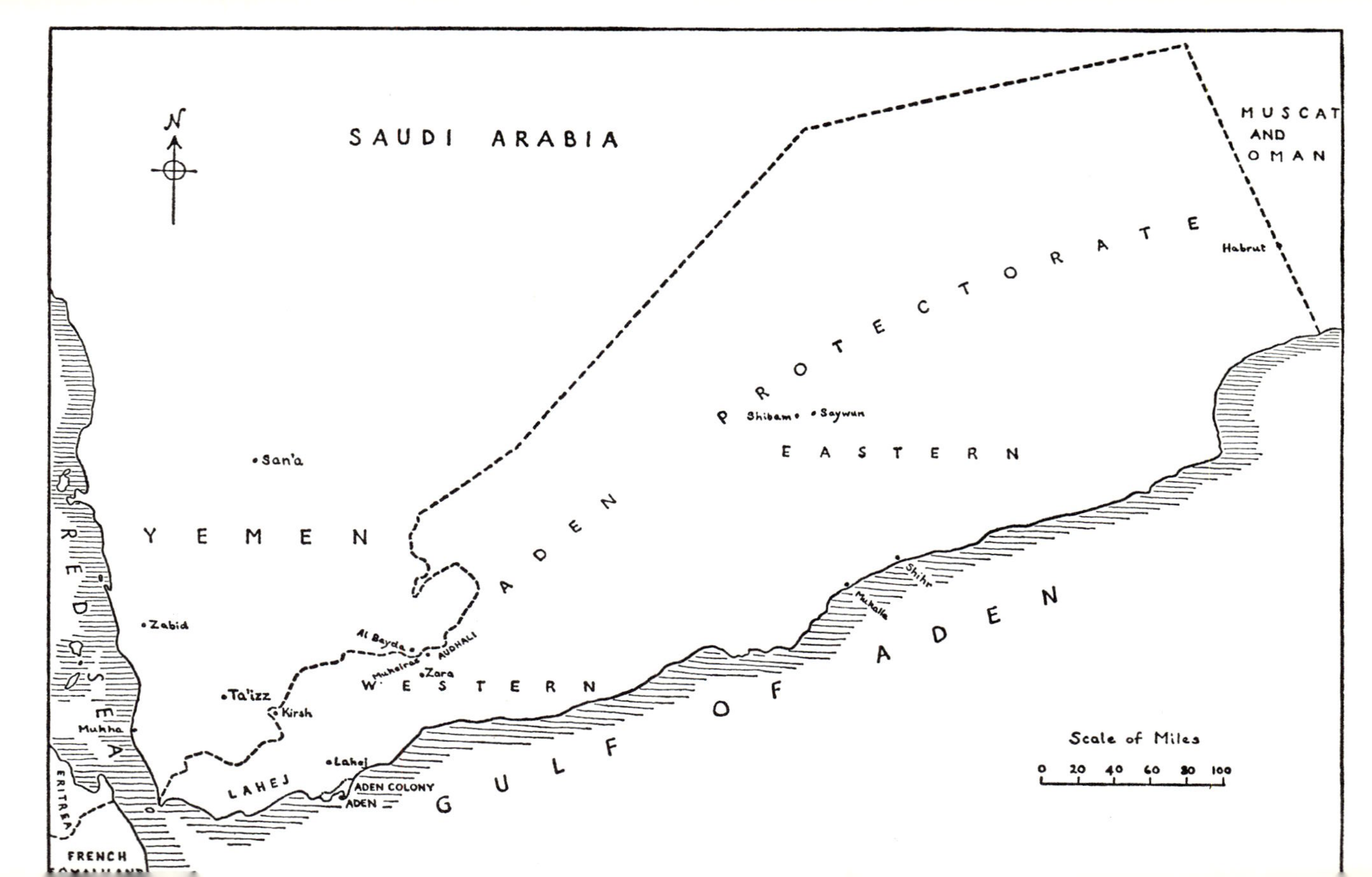
N
SAUDI ARABIA
MUSCAT AND OMAN
PROTECTORATE
EASTERN
P
Shibam
Saywun
Habrut
YEMEN
ADEN
San'a
Zabid
Al Bayda
AUDHALI
Muheiras
Zara
WESTERN
Ta'izz
Kirsh
Muhha
Lahej
LAHEJ
ADEN COLONY
ADEN
GULF OF ADEN
Shihr
Mukalla
RED SEA
ERITREA
FRENCH SOMALILAND
Scale of Miles
0 20 40 60 80 100

Frockcoats, Frankincense and Myrrh

'I'm sure you'll be very happy here,' said my hostess. Her gaze wavered slightly to my left where a diminutive Arab servant, obviously new, was pouring out coffee in a nervous trickle just over the brim of each cup.

'I love it already—it's all absolutely wonderful!'

The glassy surface of the polite coffee morning atmosphere trembled at these vibrations of enthusiasm. I subsided, embarrassed, feeling uncouth. Perhaps learning to pitch the right key came with experience. The half-dozen other women in the room scrutinised me more closely. They were mostly around the age of forty. All of them looked well-preserved for their years, but with that faintly creased, slightly yellowing, over-travelled appearance which I had noticed about the English goods sold in the local shops.

'Of course, you're very young, aren't you?' enquired the formidable-looking lady of a senior Government official sitting opposite.

'Twenty-one.' I forced an apologetic smile.

'And you've been married . . .?'

'Six months,' I replied, feeling more than ever like the newest recruit before the examining board of the Order of British Colonial Wifehood.

'Heavens, what a baby!' cried the wife of the Resident Naval Officer in jollying tones.

There was a short preparatory silence. Then, almost simultaneously, a chorus of warnings broke out from all sides, like the off-stage wailings of the Trojan women.

'Of course, you're bound to be home-sick—the first tour is always the worst.'

'It's the dampness more than the direct heat really.'

'Amoebic dysentery is the *big* pest, you see.'

We were in the large and handsome house of a leading oil company official. Persian rugs soaked up the slats of white tropical sunlight that pierced through the Venetian blinds. Arab servants, wearing turbans in the Company's colours and snowy linen jackets and trousers, padded barefoot in and out with the trays—an older boy and a positively octogenarian 'boy' with wrinkled features, a neat grey beard and an air of patriarchal authority, had joined the new recruit. Otherwise this elegant mahogany and chintz room could have been set down, sporting prints, family silver, cut-glass decanters and all, in any piece of English countryside within Humber Super Snipe distance of town.

Very different were the scenes I had envisaged when the letter stamped 'Colonial Office' arrived at our Chester flat three months ago, appointing my husband Chief Magistrate, Aden.

'Ah, Africa . . .' I murmured.

'Arabia, you mean,' corrected my husband in a shocked undertone.

'Arabia then, even better! . . . Sheikhs on horseback, black tents against a desert skyline, exotic harems, camels . . .'

Well, perhaps all these would appear eventually. After all, it was only twenty-four hours since we had arrived, taking in for the first time through a glitter of reflected heat the bizarre crescent of high, wrinkled rock shelf and crowded buildings, the sprinkling of surrounding islands like fallen crumbs of ash, the whole Gothic, pinnacled coastline that is Aden from the sea. Naturally, all we had seen of the place so far was the inside of a couple of English houses and a few postcard views from open windows. Also, some of the Steamer Point shops catering for Europeans. Still, one would have expected a hint here and there of the Arabia surrounding us. And the European settings themselves were very unexpected. Well steeped in Somerset Maugham, I felt thwarted. No one-storey shacks with matted undergrowth festooning the broken-down verandah, no ancient mail-order catalogues lying open under a smoky swinging lamp, no bead curtains over mysterious doorways, no mosquito nets, no empty gin bottles under the table, no well-polished revolver, I felt sure, in the right-hand desk drawer, and obviously, no Vice anywhere. Instead, large Georgian-style white houses and blocks of modern flats overlooking the busy town and harbour, electricity and running water, cocktail cabinets, glossy magazines, and a general atmosphere, carefully insulated, of that well-known western product, gracious living. And the Arabs, always referred to as 'the locals' and never, of course, 'natives', were so far represented by these smooth-faced, impassive figures who pattered demurely around us as though with no other thought in their heads but the ritual service of English sahibs and memsahibs within the house.

Mrs Cunningham, the wife of the Government official with whom we were staying, arrived. She had come to take me off on the tour of inspection she had promised me. She laughed in her vague, charming, middle-aged way, her mind obviously occupied in selecting the most reliable-looking taxi in sight. We were now outside in the streets of the main European shopping centre, Steamer Point. The sun hammered down almost visibly, like tropical rain, with an intruding force that I had never before connected with sunshine. It scorched the bare arms of English women out shopping, drenched down on the few drooping trees in the children's playground, seeped through the corners of dark glasses, bounced off the glossy new backs of American cars, warmed the glass of the rickety showcases outside the shops and the silk scarves hanging in rows like flags above them. The heat even resurrected itself again through the soles of our shoes on the baked paving-stones.

We turned into one of the shops for a minute—Mrs Cunningham wanted to ask about a dress she was having made. The notice above the door announced 'Mayfair Elite Tailor'. Underneath in smaller letters was printed the legend 'M. Billaljee And Son, Gents Suites and Ladies Gowns constructed to immediate satisfaction. Welcome inside.' Inside, apart from the welcome extended by Mr Billaljee himself, a brown nut-like little man with an ancient pair of pince-nez embedded across his nose and long grey hairs growing out of his ears, there was also a compounded smell of burning incense, moth-balls and betel-nut (chewed by the proprietor), and a variety of goods wedged together ranging from Indian bracelets to American chewing-gum. On the white-washed walls faded prints of straight-limbed English sahibs in topees and dress uniforms, 1920 striped suits and trilbies, rubbed shoulders with highly-coloured portraits of Gandhi and Pandit Nehru. In the place of honour an Indian pin-up girl in a pink sari sipped coyly at a Coca-Cola on a trade calendar, alongside a representation of a Hindu goddess glittering with gummed-on sequins and a framework of tinsel. Mrs Cunningham disappeared beyond a bead curtain to try on the dress. Somewhere in the room above an Indian song quavered in and out on an ancient wireless set, a baby cried, and a woman shouted something which made both sounds stop almost at once.

Meanwhile I sat on an emaciated little chair and waited, watching an excessively thin young man, obviously the 'And Son' of the legend, selling a pair of brass gongs to two Australian ladies, Both wore hats and showed signs of battle fatigue. Although I was a novice I recognised them as visitors to Aden off a passing ship, or as the Aden residents called them, tourists, or even trippers. Their purchases completed, they sank into the other two chairs and unloaded themselves of a small mountain of duty-free trophies. In a final spasm of energy they fanned themselves with their new scarves while And Son brought them a fizzy drink each, obviously all part of the Mayfair Elite service.

'Well,' said the stouter and more flushed of the two, 'this seems to be about all. We'd better be getting back.'

'Do you think we've done everything?' enquired the other anxiously.

'A new camera for George, a wrist-watch for Edith's twenty-first, three pounds' worth of cosmetics and perfume—and the gongs—what more do you want?'

'I only thought there might be something we ought to see while we're here.'

'What, in this place? In Aden? Come on—we'll just be in time for second coffee-sitting if we hurry.'

As they rose to leave, re-loading themselves with parcels, I was back again on the ship that had brought us to Aden—all those swaying vistas of glass and chromium plate, mazes of hospital-like rubber-floored corridors, the loudspeaker *purées* of Schubert with the morning ices, *Lilac Domino* with afternoon tea, the false holiday-camp geniality exuded over the pre-lunch gins—and always the polite query—'and where are you bound for?'

And the same kindly dismay at the answer, 'Aden.'

'Oh dear, you'll certainly be hot enough there. Next thing to Hell, isn't it?' Or:

'Looks a bit grim, doesn't it—the barren rocks and all that?' Or again:

'Good Lord! Used to be a punishment station, didn't it? What have you two been up to?'

But the first sandy bays that glided into sight the morning before our arrival—could it only be three days ago?—had glittered enchantingly, scattered grains from the great desert beyond. The early sun was mild on our shoulders. We scoffed at the sceptics as all that day we watched the South Arabian coast float by like a succession of ruined castles on the horizon. Tapering volcanic crags, gaunt as a lunar landscape under the midday heat, dissolving to spires of dusty violet, silver and rose in the web of sunset; a cardboard romantic-opera backcloth, black and jagged, against a rising moon.

In the night the intervening distance vanished. All too quickly the dream became reality, to the clank and rattle of embarkation. The narrow lens of the cabin porthole had settled on a view of white houses, tall buildings, streets, even people, swarming in the shadow of yesterday's barren rocks. The sea beneath was alive with circling launches and boats and voices shouting to one another. We had arrived, and all the nightmare details of arrival crowded on us—the uncloseable suitcase and the unprintable adjectives, the vital missing key, the feverish trickle of perspiration between the shoulder blades, the carefully chosen hat-of-arrival that suddenly looked grotesque, the unaccountable dearth of all small change for impatient outstretched hands—and that strange smell! Was it the harbour or could it conceivably be the whole place?

And then Mrs Cunningham herself had appeared, accompanied by a delegation of court and police officials under whose magic influence all difficulties disappeared, including our immense mountain of 'baggage', leaving us free to gesture an elegant farewell from beneath the white fringed canopy of the police launch to the fast-receding figures on deck. No doubt they were shaking their heads sadly as they watched this light-hearted departure to our doom, but we were too far away to see—or care.

I was just trying to remember what it was Mrs Cunningham had been wearing that made her look so right and me feel so wrong, when she reappeared in person from Mr Billaljee's fitting salon, flushed in the face and somewhat worn-looking. The aged Mr B. pranced behind her, firmly in the grip of creative frenzy.

'I understand exactly, memsahib,' he piped tremulously, his mouth full of pins. 'I know new English fashion better than any-one—I *feel* what is looking good. The collar like this, the waistline so——' He fluttered both spidery hands in an agitated mid-air pattern of loops and curves and then dropped them again to his sides as Mrs Cunningham put in, 'You will try to remember blue thread with blue material, not red like last time, won't you?'

'Oo-oh, Mrs Cunningham,' was all he could murmur reproach-fully as we left. 'Surely you are trusting Billaljee——'

His last words were lost in the muted roar of a great yellow beast of a taxi which sprang at us, radiator teeth bared, as we emerged on to the pavement again. At first we ignored it and walked on. Slowly it dogged our footsteps along the pavement edge with the sinister, persistent stealth of an American gangster limousine.

'You want ride, memsahib?' came a voice from behind. A smiling face peered out. The back door swung open invitingly. We gave in and got in. Inside I leaned back luxuriously and sprang forward again twice as quickly. My piercing cry seemed to startle

Mrs Cunningham. Obviously she was long accustomed to the experience of being welded by white-hot leather to the seat of a car.

'Anything wrong?' she asked. But far be it from me to complain. I was fast learning the stiff upper-lip, British-abroad attitude.

'Just a bit warm,' I said, forcing a smile and telling myself the smell of scorched flesh was pure imagination anyway.

'They do get a bit hot when they've been standing in the sun.'

'Where to, memsahib?' enquired the chauffeur, a small lean-faced character with a top-heavy yellow turban and a wolfish grin.

'Crater, please. Just to have a look round.'

Immediately the taxi sprang into a series of actions which seemed to have nothing to do with the languid figure in front of us, idly touching the wheel from time to time with the first finger of his right hand. From his left hand, stretched along the back of the seat, hung a half-smoked cigarette, and his jaw champed regularly on some unknown substance.

'You've seen Steamer Point—there's nothing of real interest here,' continued Mrs Cunningham evenly as we spun round in a complete circle and charged down the other side of the street, leaving behind us a confused knot of hooting vehicles. 'Unless you want to stop anywhere.' But we had already flashed past the long crescent of European shops, the smooth-turreted block of the main hotel, Queen Victoria unamused among the dust and the oleanders of the public gardens, and were on our way.

'You seen the mermaid, memsahib?' asked the voice in front.

'Mermaid?' I gasped. Whatever next?

'Just a Doo-gone,' said Mrs Cunningham looking rather embarrassed.

'Doo-gone?' I repeated even more foolishly.

'Dugong. Sort of sea mammal—horrible-looking thing. It's stuffed, in one of the shops here, but hardly anyone goes to see it. It's more a local joke than anything else.'

I repressed any further interest in something that was just Not Done, but made a mental note of the doogone-mermaid just the same for future reference.

We were speeding along a broad road with the sea on our left. 'Ma-alla,' announced our driver, with a wave of his hand, breaking up the name into two syllables in the local way and making it sound exactly like the bray of a hungry Aden goat.

A paragraph from the guide-book sprang into my mind and I peered eagerly out at the strip of reclaimed land, bristling with the factory buildings and machinery of industrial Arabia. I tried hard to picture Noah launching the Ark here, as the legend said, and failed dismally. The disillusionment of the deprived tourist swept over me until further ahead a cluster of tall masts crowded over the warehouse roofs. As we turned a bend there was a glimpse of half a dozen definitely ark-like boats, with thick-ribbed, paint-encrusted prows jostling their reflections in the water as they stood at anchor beyond the wharves. One of them lay stranded on the beach, half completed, like some strange dynosauric skeleton, and two turbaned Arabs were hammering the curved beams into place in a leisurely antique sort of way, while the sun glittered down and the dust spun from the wheels of passing cars.

'The famous dhows,' said Mrs Cunningham, and I smiled and nodded back, more than satisfied.

Along the opposite side of the road the doors of the go-downs stood half open to reveal shadowy bales of dried skins, stacks of oozing dates swathed in hessian, Somali girls in bright African cottons squatting on the floor, unexpectedly white-faced under what I later learned to be a mask of powder to protect their skins from the gums they were sorting. Enticing whiffs of coffee and spices floated in through the open windows of the car as we passed. From the direction of the wharves came newly-arrived live cargo, flocks of black and white sheep from Somaliland nudged into shape by the long canes of the Somali shepherds in their flowing toga-style shawls and *futahs*, making a pastoral frieze of an urban roadside.

Progress up the hairpin-bend hill into Crater came to a sudden halt behind a tail of three stationary cars. Leaning out to investigate, our driver announced enigmatically, 'Hold-up, memsahib.'

We leaned out too to investigate and saw at the top of the hill an ancient-looking lorry slewed completely across the road, neatly bridging the pavement edge and the central island. Beneath the lorry lay stretched a number of Arab bodies, not fatally injured as my lurid imagination first announced but merely seizing the opportunity for a quick nap under the shade of the wheels. At the other end the driver ruminated over an open bonnet, tapping thoughtfully with a spanner at the interior workings of the vehicle. All this quite alarmed me.

'Whatever can have happened?' I asked excitedly.

Mrs Cunningham merely leaned back with a sigh and remarked, 'Oh dear! This sort of thing always seems to happen just here.'

Down the other side of the road a steady stream of cars rolled past with hundreds of smiling, interested faces pressed to the windows to survey our misfortune. Through a brief gap I glimpsed a sight of something even more alarming beyond, where a battered lorry hung in drooping ruins over the edge of the steep bank on the opposite side.

'This sort of thing too?' I asked, pointing weakly to the hideous scene.

'Oh yes—that was yesterday, wasn't it?' Mrs Cunningham enquired of our driver.

He nodded back laconically.

'And were they all killed?' These people were really too heartless. Sentences such as 'Human life has little value in the teeming East', flashed through my mind.

'Oh no, memsahib!' the driver said, most surprised. 'All coolies very good jumping down quickly round here.'

A timeless silence set in again, or rather a silence punctuated by a sporadic chorus of hooting horns, sounded, one felt, not out of impatience but pure love of the special music contributed by each car owner. At one point our driver stuck his head out of the window to engage an oncoming driver in what seemed to be a bloodcurdling stream of abuse.

'What was the matter?' I asked foolishly.

'Just my best friend, Abdu, memsahib. He is also the brother of my aunt's cousin.'

'It's the gutteral sound of the language I always think,' commented Mrs Cunningham dreamily.

Apparently hours later, the lorry that was blocking the road snorted into life and the sleeping coolies reluctantly stirred themselves to swing up on to the back again as it moved away. A young policeman who had just arrived to direct the traffic stream smiled happily and turned back in the direction from which he came. As we proceeded up the hill again Yellow Turban in front of us let fly an even harsher-sounding stream of language—no relative this time but the 'no-good driver' of the taxi behind us which scraped past us with an accelerating scream to overtake. We just managed to get our request in edgeways for him to stop for us to admire the view at the top. Below us shimmered the bizarre crescent of wrinkled rock shelf and crowded buildings, the small ships of the bay pinned like moths on watered silk, and far away, beyond the isthmus, the yellow sands and blue hills of Arabia Felix.

'Now we're going into Crater,' announced Mrs Cunningham as we climbed back into the yellow monster and drove on through a narrow pass of rock bridging the road. There was a sinister Jules-Verne ring about this remark, but in actual fact Crater itself looked less dramatic than it sounded. There it lay in its valley of grey rock, a spreading crowded confusion of flat rooftops, narrow streets and alleys, washing-festooned balconies and verandahs and obviously, despite the pseudo-sophisticated shop-front of Steamer Point, despite the big glossy ships in the harbour, the pulsing centre of the real Aden. Once inside 'the Crater' one forgot the extinct volcano it actually is, the volcano destined to erupt, so legend says, one last time on the Last Day of Judgment. This was a town—people lived here. The encircling ring of frozen lava became mere rugged background.

As we drove down into the *suk*, chaos assaulted us—and smells. It was the height of the day and the traffic had to elbow its way through an undulating sea of humanity; people walking, not in the European way, brisk and detached, but with the slow, gesticulating expansive progress of the East; people standing, clustered in gossip at the entrances of coffee houses, against a doorway or a shop pillar; people sitting on pavement edges and doorsteps to sell something, to beg anything, or merely to take the weight off their feet. Some people even slept, stretched out blissfully immune on a handy packing-case or charpoy.

As our car wound its way through, isolated scenes stamped themselves on my sentimental European eye. A genuine knife-grinder bent over his wheel under a peeling Egyptian film poster. Just outside my window a row of catches lacquered in the sun swung from a fisherman's wooden shoulder-yoke and, on the pavement opposite, what was obviously a real live weaver stranded together a length of striped material on an ancient machine that looked like a dismembered harpsichord. At this point I begged to get out and walk for a closer investigation.

'Walk?' queried Mrs Cunningham, amazed at such a bizarre suggestion. 'But it's so hot,' and then, relenting, 'Well, I did want to buy one of these local mats as a matter of fact.'

Along the pavement the small open shop-fronts unfolded bright as a string of paper flags. The only establishment that boasted a pane of glass was a toyshop on the corner and with their noses pressed against it stood three magnificent figures. Black-bearded tribesmen, picturesque in the best cinematic tradition, complete with bright ragged waistcloths, silver-hilted daggers and sprigs of wild herb in their turbans, they were gazing enraptured at a display of toy double-decker buses. Like everyone else they turned and looked at us with interest—obviously the sight of English-women on foot in the *suk* was fairly infrequent—but there was a special intensity about their scrutiny.

'They're from up-country,' explained Mrs Cunningham, forging ahead through the crowded pavement with a pleasant, generally-directed smile. 'They may never have seen a European female before.'

In that brief second I had a glimpse of ourselves through their eyes—strange creatures with immodest white legs, uncovered heads and painted faces, moving among men as equals and obviously, therefore, women of bad repute—although they did say these Christians gave their women extraordinary freedoms.

At that second too I experienced a new sensation that was to become familiar; a sense of the pressure of isolation among a crowd from whom one was divided by invisible barriers. Walking in streets like these, one was no longer merely oneself. One's skin made one the representative of a whole group, the outsider looking patronisingly in at what was for these people the everyday life, for us an exotic piece of local colour to be trapped in the camera lens or dashed off in the next letter home. The role of British memsahib was a stock one, and to be a Government wife, especially a judicial wife, restricted the part almost to a classic mime. I recalled the warning uttered before I left England by an elderly retired Colonial lady—'Remember, the natives are always watching you!'

Not that those who watched us did it in anything but the friendliest way. The time of what is politely known in official circles as 'trouble' had not yet come. Groups of helpful counsellors and interpreters gathered whenever we stopped at a stall. Soon a miniature procession had formed around us, headed by an important small boy, with one very old man bringing up the rear. All of them insisted on escorting us to a seller of *tayib katir* mats ('very good', was the translation given me, and I carefully impressed my first Arabic phrase on my memory for future use). This proved to be quite a long way but not too long for me. The shops we passed were fascinating, each one a single narrow crowded room leading directly off the street. Most of them seemed to sell cloth, bales of silks and brocades in stained-glass colours glowing from the depths of each well-like interior. Enamelled saucepans, giant decanters of cheap perfume, ropes of amber prayer beads, doormats and rolls of linoleum rubbed shoulders under the awnings, even—surrealist touch this—a drooping row of second-hand frock coats.

'From London, memsahib—it gets very cold at night in the Yemen,' explained the bearded shop-owner with dignity as though it were the most natural thing in the world. And perhaps it was!

Real yellow-gold glittered in the shabby doorways of a jeweller's shop where a cluster of Arab ladies, swathed from head to foot in the black silk cocoons of strictest *purdah*, were conducting a hasty shopping transaction, chattering like magpies over an ornate pendant necklace.

Apparently the frankincense and myrrh were there too, behind the shuttered doorways of the warehouses which lined the back streets we were now passing through. Here, white-robed merchants flitted like cabbage butterflies in and out of hot sleek Cadillacs and the air was full of the smells of burning incense, coffee beans, moth-balls, roasting corn on smoky braziers—and goats, goats, goats. Over and above everything the sun hammered down and the noise rose upwards like steam—clattering of dishes from the eating houses, a tangle of taxi horns, people clamouring in half a dozen languages and children crying in one universal tongue. Not far away someone was beating a drum. There was the busy insect whirr of sewing machines outside the tailors' shops, clank and rumble of trucks and camel carts, an Indian song and an Arabic voice throbbing and mingling, magnified by fifty different radios.

Eventually we found the mat-seller. He was an extremely fat gentleman reclining at ease with the inevitable glass of virulent coloured fruit squash at his side, an Arabic newspaper in his hand. The shop was small and dim, full of bags of grain and ancient brass scales. There were no mats in sight. We were waved to be seated on two uncertain-looking upright chairs while the necessary introductions were performed by our escorts and two more glasses of squash were brought in. About ten minutes passed in general sociability—exclamations as to the heat of the day, enquiries into the health of the Chief Justice.

'I do not have the privilege of knowing His Lordship personally,' admitted our host, brushing the remains of a past meal from the front of his robe with a plump beringed hand. 'But all speak of his wisdom—he is like a brother to us.' He gestured expansively, with a roll of a lustrous liquorice eye in the direction of his audience who stood absorbed around the doorway. There was a general murmur of agreement. One or two other members of the establishment had emerged from the back-quarters and it promised to be quite a party. This was obviously a merchant of some standing despite the dusty setting. Also a man of tact—two large framed portraits of the Queen and Colonel Nasser hung side by side above a pile of old ledgers on a corner table. There was an air of comfortable languor about the assembly quite different from the rapid chivying of the Indian shopkeepers who had been urging us to 'Come in and have look-see!' ever since we got out of the car. Just when I was beginning to wonder if the whole business of mats wasn't a sort of mirage, never to become reality, our host began to recall a certain cousin of his who, as it happened, had a case coming in front of the Chief Justice next week. This made Mrs Cunningham hastily remember that it was about mats she had come to see him—or rather a mat.

The plump one shook his head sadly. Good Persians were very hard to come by at the moment. A friend of his however had a couple of fair quality Indians which——

'No, no, local mats I mean—the Beihani strips.' A look of startled distaste passed over the gentleman's features. Rough Bedouin floor-coverings for the residence of the Chief Justice? 'Just something for the back verandah,' lied Mrs C. smoothly. 'But perhaps you have nothing—I don't see——'

But the mats were there. Holding up his hand for silence our friend rose slowly to his feet to reveal a pile of splendid specimens slightly indented by the rotund form which had been reclining on them. No less than half an hour later the top one was ours. The price settled on was exactly half-way between Mrs Cunningham's original offer and our host's first demand, a traditional solution, obviously, which seemed to please everyone. But the performance, watched closely by connoisseurs on both sides of the counter, was an exhausting one. Tottering out into the sun again with the mat cradled proudly in my arms and cries of congratulation ringing in our ears, I wondered if it could be lunch-time yet.

Mrs C. however, had not quite finished with me. Briskly unloading me and folding me back into the car, which by some miracle had trekked us down again, she whisked me off on a final kaleidoscopic tour which included, in rapid succession, the Tanks, the museum, the minaret and the lighthouse. I can remember that the Tanks, those outsize stone bowls for collecting rainwater which are every tourist's memory of Aden, were so much bigger than one had thought, like the Pyramids. Again like the Pyramids they impressed as a system but failed to communicate any sympathetic thrill with the past, although the popular legend crediting the Queen of Sheba with a hand in them added a touch of glamour to their somewhat blurred history. This theory somehow seemed right. They have a certain methodical, feminine look about them, those Tanks.

I remember too the scent of jasmine that drifted up from the surrounding gardens and the thickly-woven oleanders and hibiscus, white and pink, encircling the small one-storey building known as the museum. There was no one about and the green door was locked until an aged caretaker suddenly appeared from nowhere, stretching his arms and yawning. He unbolted the entrance with a flourish and went ahead to flick the dust from the first exhibits. It was an unassuming collection of traditional local craft in leather and clay and small relics from the Arabian hinterland, with the sunlight slanting through the windows on to the rickety glass cases and the hand-printed notices, but it moved me more than a number of great museums. I stood by myself, touching a delicate bronze statuette of Cupid, a stone charm of a sacred bull, the sadly graceful alabaster head of some young girl, with the sightless eyes of classical sculpture, 'blind with gazing on eternity'. Each piece was veined and whittled by the anonymous pressures of time and the tides of the moving desert sands. To myself I repeated the names of their places of origin—Shabwa, Qataba, Nuqub—and immediately loved a country that could produce such things out of its past. The coffee party seemed worlds away, unreal and meaningless, part of the terrifyingly superfluous veneer of European social life. Yet Aden contained them all—the sporting prints and the memsahibs, the *suk* and the sacred bull. Framed in glass on the opposite wall only a few feet away was the link between them, a tattered ensign flag 'first planted on the shore of Aden by a Mr Rundle, Mate, after the siege by the British in 1839'.

At the Cunninghams' house I had come across an old book on Aden, full of insect borings and photographs in faded sepia of canopied horse-cabs and Bedouin football teams. Sport being the best possible form of discipline, according to the author, a certain Colonel Harold F. Jacob—I knew from my colonel that the actual captor of Aden was Captain S. Bettesworth Haines. So I peered out with interest when, in the car once more, we passed his original residence, the first-ever Government House. It was a humble grey-stone relative of the present impressive building tucked away at the bottom of Khusaf Valley. 'Government office now,' said Abdu—we had learned the name of our chauffeur. I looked in vain for a stalwart, bearded ghost on the verandah, and for those parts of the building which Colonel Jacob asserted used to fall down regularly on the concussion of the 8 p.m. gun. But it wasn't hard to imagine it all. Along the walled fortifications of Crater, the garrison camp, rising high out of the rocks above us, the red jackets of the British soldiers would be moving at the gun sites, the sun striking like fire through the heavy uniform. Their families were quartered in huts along the isthmus below. I thought of the harassed wives in voluminous Victorian skirts shepherding the children into the shelter of the hillside caves in hot weather, while block-boats and brig-of-wars patrolled the coastline close to shore. Now all that remained were the walls and the watch-towers, a residue of cannons stranded in various gardens and public places, a few graves and wall-plates and a memorial plaque in a cemetery we had passed earlier, dedicated 'To the memory of the brave men of the First Bombay Fusiliers who fell at the capture of Aden'.

No doubt, at the top of the Main Pass, these visitors of the past were, like us, invited to gaze up at a certain inaccessible socket of rock where the remains of Cain are said to rest. And probably were equally sceptical. According to Abdu, the Moslems have a Cain too, by the name of Kabil, to rhyme with Habil, or Abel his brother.

As for the famous minaret, this turned out to be a delicate wedding-cake tower rising out of the modern banks and offices and flats, and the circling traffic of Crater's centre. Mrs Cunningham produced the facts with the patient facility of one long used to the assaults of avid newcomers and transit 'friends' off the plane or the ship for a few hours. The minaret was in fact the last relic of Aden's oldest mosque. It had been built by a certain Caliph some time before A.D. 718 and stood on what was then the sea front, before all the surrounding ground was reclaimed.

My impressions of the light-house were slightly blurred by its nerve-racking approach which had the effect of even bringing Abdu's second hand to the wheel from time to time. For light-house connoisseurs it looked an interesting model. Striped black and white, it perched on the edge of the Marshag peninsula like an overweight Belisha beacon. Its illumination was a giant oil-lamp with an ominous-looking hood arrangement which at night-time would rise and fall to blot out the yellow glow at the prescribed regular intervals.

Driving back through Steamer Point the heat was at high tide, lapping over deserted pavements and shop-fronts already shuttered for the afternoon siesta, sucking the last inches of shade from under the awnings and arcades. The only thing that moved was a thin buzzing line of cars returning lunchwards along the opposite side of the road. The line emerged from the hive of the Secretariat, an unpretentious, rambling verandahed building next to the Prince of Wales pier. As each car flicked past us a white-jacketed figure at the wheel, masked in sunglasses, raised one hand like a robot at Mrs Cunningham who returned the gesture with the promptness of a reflex action. As she did she smiled a split-second smile and between her teeth spoke her thoughts in a fascinating series of asides. So that recorded conversation might have run something like this!

'Anyway, I'm sure you'll get used to the climate.' Wave. Smile. *'That ghastly Wellington-Gimble—tight already.* Once you've had a month here you'll take it for granted.' Wave. Smile. *'Hm—dear David giving little Mrs Wagstaff a lift again—is it really wise of Molly to spend so much time in England I wonder?* And of course it's the people that make a place.' Wave. Smile. '*We really shall have to ask that man to our next drinks party, even if he does have tattoo marks on both arms,*' and so on.

The parking ground at the Club was empty. In the porchway—where only the Governor's car was allowed to draw up, so the rules said—the red-turbaned chowkida on duty dozed on a discarded dining-room chair. From the topmost Edwardian-Gothic pinnacle a Union Jack, bleached by the sun to a mere ghost of itself, drooped at the flagstaff. For a brief moment the miniature Big Ben at the top of the famous Clock-Tower Hill registered the right time at five minutes past one where it had stopped apparently two weeks ago. Up the hill, past the cluster of tin-roof huts at the bottom, past the fishermen squatting cross-legged in a crescent to mend an outspread canvas sail, toiled three dignified black-beetle cars. They were wending their way in order of protocol to the three senior residences thereon—the Chief Secretary's, the Attorney General's and the Financial Secretary's. We tagged on at the end, Abdu attacking the fantastic incline with the reckless verve of a wall-of-death rider, roaring past on to the highest pinnacle of all where the Chief Justice lived. It was the archetypal Colonial house, expansive and shabbily elegant, with a mixture of eighteenth-century English and traditional Moorish about its tall arched doorways and trellised front. As we stepped out of the car the sun quivered directly overhead like the sword of Damocles. Somewhere out in the glitter of the harbour a departing ship hooted a jaunty farewell to the Barren Rocks, taking the visitors with it. I thought again of Colonel Jacob and his austere comment, 'To the trippers Aden is a sealed book—they have not seen the soul of Aden,' and felt a glow of virtue at being received into that elect body, the residents of the Colony. But when and how was the book to be unsealed—if ever?

2

Downing Street

On the other side of Aden, out along the Khormaksar isthmus, is suburbia. Incongruous in the middle of the sand as a flock of prim white English sheep, disdainful but complacent, lie the R.A.F. and Government housing estates, each concrete box tucked securely around by the low walls of its compound. On either side the fringes of the Red Sea shimmer through the heat haze. The outline of the desert hills rises beyond them and overhead the Arabian sky burns with a steady white-blue flame.

With ineffectual thoroughness suburbia insulates itself against all this. Air-conditioners hum from the upstairs rooms and in the kitchen, dwarfed by a gleaming 'fridge, the cookboy wields a mixer-beater to the tinkle of Victor Sylvester. Jet planes sear across the airport runways, over the flat rooftops. But the hawks fly lower with neatly-numbered regulation dust-bins for their prey —big ragged-looking hawks free-wheeling groundwards to meet their shadows with a tremulous whistle, slow and detached as leaves from a tree.

Some of the houses have gardens. Here a tenderly-watered and watched-over cluster of creepers around the porchway, there a patch of sunflowers sprouting high with febrile intensity in the shade of a verandah, and everywhere those familiar lawns of sand, shell and stone. Grass, real grass, was Aden's rarest commodity. So far I had seen it only in the grounds of Government House, devoutly tended by half a dozen magicians in turbans and overalls and gazed on with a kind of superstitious awe by every homesick English visitor.

The houses of Government officers in Khormaksar are grouped together under the impressive title of Downing Street. There is no notice to this effect but Everyone Knows. Most coveted residence is, of course, No. 10, whose inhabitants bask in a faint reflected glory and like to tell improbable stories about indistinctly addressed letters from friends in England reposted in London with a scrawl across the envelope of a secretary—perhaps even the P.M. himself—remarking '*Not Known Here*'. The street itself is an arena of sand criss-crossed only by the tracks of dogs, small children and those odd vehicles which have floundered off the encircling strip of asphalt which links the houses together.

We had been allocated No. 1. As we drove up that hot windy morning a week later we approved of the cool airy lines of the grey stone and white plaster front. But our first impressions of the house were dominated by the stately figure standing motionless as a statue in an attitude of welcome on the topmost step. As we drew up alongside the statue sprang into life, performed a smart British Army salute and gravely descended the steps with outstretched hand and the never-to-be-forgotten announcement, 'I am Aboker.'

'Splendid,' I replied, bewildered but truthful, surveying the broad ebony Somali features, shining like an old-fashioned kitchen range, the wide gold-and-ivory beam, the orange embroidered shawl and cotton *futah* in Scots type plaid pattern which swathed his stout form. A gold signet ring flashed on the hand which grasped the ceremonial Somali staff and from the other swung a string of amber prayer beads. Standing there he emanated dignity, integrity and abundant self-confidence, and a wave of relief swept over me. Everything was going to be all right. Here in person was the answer to all our domestic problems, the obvious remedy for my distressing ignorance on all matters concerning Colonial housekeeping.

'I come to be your bearer, I see to everything,' he added by way of explanation. But it wasn't necessary. I hadn't for a moment thought otherwise. In a kind of happy dream we watched him marshal into order the lumbering procession of lorries which had followed us in through the gates, with our crates of luggage and belongings and items of extra household furniture supplied by Government.

Last but not least, winding up the parade came a lorry of a very special type. 'A sort of cage on wheels,' I reflected idly to myself, then blinked in disbelief at the throng of passengers in arrow-marked suits who pressed to the iron mesh at the back with cheerful waves and grins and cries of greeting. Out of the front jumped an Arab police officer with a bundle of papers in his hand. 'Oh dear, more warrants to be signed,' sighed Ronald. This was my first direct contact with my husband's work, and an almost unforgettable one.

Inside the house, Aboker had obviously been organising preparations. Honey-coloured tiled floors shone with polish, windows were open to the breeze and shutters closed to the glare. We liked the very long, high-ceilinged living-cum-dining-room, flanked by a verandah of almost the same size. It was all very modern, and in the stock, new-Colonial design, yet it had a certain older local atmosphere about it, with its generous excess of space, its extra-thick walls to insulate against the heat, the tall wood-raftered ceilings, and rough-cut grey stone of the outside pillars and lower walls. The furniture was in the best Government-issue traditions. There were solid teak bookcases, tables, desk, cane-backed chairs and sofa, all guaranteed indestructible against the ravages of time, climate, child or death-watch beetle. Some of the pieces were obviously new. But the design remained staunchly Indian-mutiny period, untouched by the least trace of any modern airy-fairy Swedish nonsense. The chairs were notice-ably huge, for use only by mahogany-limbed, square-shouldered, pipe-smoking Empire builders, giants among men, sprawling after the day's labour amid clouds of tobacco smoke with a stiff double whisky and a month-old copy of *The Times*. The little helpmeet was obviously expected to be of similar proportions—though there was a frivolous concession to femininity upstairs in the form of a dressing-table and even a dressing-stool, also very large. Like every other piece of furniture it was clearly marked on an uppermost corner with the mysterious initials 'G.F.' and a number. At first I was quite thrilled to think it was the genuine signature of the individual maker—one of the gentlemen in arrow-marked suits no doubt—and sadly disillusioned to learn, of course, it merely stood for 'Government Furniture'.

Leading me through the house on a tour of inspection, Aboker came to the closed door of the kitchen quarters. Here he paused significantly. Then, with a climactic flourish, he flung it open with the words, 'De other servants for de memsahib.' Inside, a roomful of Somalis and Arabs of all ages and sizes shuffled into line to be introduced, straightening their turbans and fishing in their shirt pockets for the 'chitties' or credentials from their last employer. Wildly I searched in my mind for the facts in the Aden handbook—the figure for the maximum number of servants needed was five and not fifteen? What about Mrs Cunningham with her three? Taking a deep breath I murmured to Aboker, 'Only two, of course.' 'Oh yes, of course, memsahib,' he replied surprised. 'These people only come and try!'

Sadly we turned away the taxi-driver whose licence had just been removed for dangerous driving and whose heart was now set on culinary achievements (including cocktail-mixing); the second night-watchman from the leading Indian stores who wanted to sweep and clean; the stonecutter with a sudden passion for gardening. Also a band of various small Aboker sons and nephews whom he was anxious to 'knock into de shape'—a phrase of which he was rightly proud—and many others. This left us with one very small middle-aged Arab, who announced himself as 'Abdu sweeper', and another Somali of more advanced years who stated himself to be able to cook 'anything, memsahib'.

Starting to organise the unpacking, I carried a trayful of brand-new wedding-present wineglasses over to the cupboard. 'Now be careful with this glass—very good glass,' I said sternly, just before tripping on a loose tile and sending the whole lot flying. It somehow seemed a good omen that not one of them so much as grinned.

And so, with food in the kitchen, cushions on the chairs, rugs on the floors and books on the shelves, Constable prints on the walls to remind us of the greenness of England, we settled down with our household. In a surprisingly short time we became accustomed to the new daily routine. This consisted of breakfast at 7.30 a.m., before my husband left for the court, lunch at 2.30 when he came home again for the day; afternoon sleep until 4 p.m.; then drinks and dinner at home or with friends after most of the men (and some of the women too) had conscientiously exercised themselves under a waning sun on the golf-course, the tennis court, the riding-field or swimming-pool. Daily market shopping was done by Aboker in the bazaars—the stalls piled high with multi-coloured fruit and vegetables, dates, roasted nuts, newly-ground coffee. A permanent item was the inevitable Somali mutton, and good fresh fish which was better.

In an equally short time we also became accustomed to the fact that our cook could (or would) produce nothing but stews for every meal except breakfast. There were, however, four variations on the stew theme. 'What today, memsahib?' he would query slowly. 'Da brown stoo, da Irish stoo, da hotpot stoo—' then, with a sudden flash of inspiration—'or da beef stoo?' Whatever one ordered, the dish which arrived on the table was, in some mysterious manner, inevitably stew. He was a rather old man, a little uncertain in his movements. Whenever he had produced what he considered to be a masterpiece he always insisted on by-passing Aboker and serving it himself. Because of his obvious shaky determination to get the dish safely to the table by hook or by crook, we christened him 'So-help-me-God'. 'So help-me's' real name was Charlie and he had spent most of his life in ships' kitchens—whether he had ever risen to the rank of cook is not recorded. His most treasured possession was a battered gold watch, long since stopped, which he used to wear on a chain suspended across some long-forgotten sahib's grey pin-striped waistcoat. He completed the outfit with a pair of white cotton pyjama trousers, a khaki army jacket (for street-wear only, this) and a pair of immense white-rimmed sunglasses. These last he brought out and put on as a source of inspiration while creating in the kitchen. The sight of this apparition brooding in a smoky corner over a charcoal cooking-stove which resembled a disused Wellsian time machine was truly remarkable.

Once or twice I found a magazine recipe I thought of asking him to try. But somehow the gulf yawned too vast to bridge between the glossy illustration and my own kitchen scene—no cooking editor, however imaginative, could have thought up *that*! Anyway, I knew his opinion on printed recipes. At the end of one dismal experiment, he had remarked, 'Memsahib, your book and my cooking very different,' in tones which left no doubt as to which he thought the more reliable.

Every now and then he would think up a little surprise of his own. On one occasion it was a pie for pudding. When Ronald said he didn't think he would have any pastry afterwards 'So-help-me' exclaimed in the most indignant tones, 'Him no pastry, sahib! Him lemon tart!' He also developed the habit in our morning conferences of demonstrating the joint of meat he was cooking by pointing to parts of his own anatomy. 'Da good chops,' he would announce gesticulating to his own ancient ribs—which somehow rather blunted one's appetite when the dish eventually appeared that evening.

Everything that could happen in the way of domestic diversions seemed to happen to us within the space of a few months. After only a couple of weeks we were treated to our first sand-storm which came up to every expectation. First came a faint warning whistle while the sky turned an uncanny sulphur colour, and Aboker and his brigade rushed on to the scene fastening doors and windows at top speed. Then with Wagnerian relentlessness a dark cloud, ten times as thick as the legendary Baker Street fog and nothing like as cosy, rolled up over the horizon. Suddenly, before we could say so, it was on us and the house was surrounded by a sheet of whirling sand. On the other side of the glass a shutter leaped off its hinges with soundless violence and shuttled away into the dark torrent of air. The verandah heaped slowly up like a miniature Sahara. Along the road, cars, like shadows glided to a standstill with headlights flickering faintly. Inside the house there was a delicious sense of drama without, and barred security within. The musty smell of desert sand seeped in everywhere, prickling the eyes and nose and the inside of one's throat. After only a few minutes there was a fine film of dust over cushions and tables and in the air itself. It had a strangely sinister passage-of-time effect, as though we had awoken Rip-Van-Winkle fashion and the few minutes had mysteriously been centuries. And then as suddenly, the darkness dissolved, a pale sky came into view again, and it was all over—apart from the sweeping-up.

Only a week later a swarm of locusts descended on the locality, just at a point when I was exclaiming joyfully over Aden's dearth of unpleasant insects and animals, apart from the wall-lizards. These I was training myself to become quite fond of, in a detached sort of way. But locusts! The vaguely pleasant biblical associations of milk and honey and so on were rudely dissolved at the sight of the first visitors which flopped in through the open windows that evening and fastened their nasty pink armoured bodies—like large winged prawns—on to every available piece of furniture or body. Against the glass of the french windows, a second detachment clung and followed our every movement with unpleasantly human turns of their heads and beady black eyes. The more adventurous specimens toured the floor space, leaping and whirring upwards at any movement towards them. In vain was I assured that, apart from their immense damage to crops, they were quite harmless. All I knew was that they were the most horribly hardy creatures. Even Halsbury's *Laws of England* dropped from a height failed to finish them off. Apart from sweeping them out of the bedroom all one could do was to wait until they flew away next morning.

When they did we thought peace had finally settled. But the following evening just before dinner all the lights in the house suddenly snapped out, the overhead fan gave a last despairing flutter and within a few minutes sinister dripping sounds came from the 'fridge. 'Just a cut in the area—we don't know how long, sorry,' I was told over the telephone, while our last match died away between my fingers. But we need not have worried. Implacable as ever, Aboker appeared in the doorway, Rembrandt-esque in the glow of a huge paraffin lamp. He had brought it from his own quarters. So we spent the rest of the evening out on the verandah wall, bloated with lemonade shandy, perspiring but happy in a butter-yellow pool of light, with the magnificent Arabian night sky overhead. The suburban houses were forgotten in the darkness and, listening to the steady, drowsy pulse of the Levies band rehearsing nearby, we told ourselves it must have been just like this in the old days.

More serious was the butchers' strike in the bazaar when Government decided to reduce the price of meat from 2 shillings 50 cents a pound to 1 shilling 75 cents. Gloomily we reviewed a muttonless prospect and pondered on how many tins of corned beef would see us through the crisis. It was at this point that Aboker informed us, for the first time, that his 'bearer work' was only one side of his many-faceted personality, a sort of hobby which he carried on at the same time as his real life's interest, sheep-trading. Feeling nothing could surprise us any more, we merely nodded dumbly and went on listening. 'I have sheep coming from Somaliland day after tomorrow,' explained the amazing man, 'so I kill him and you have my mutton.'

Congratulating ourselves on the resourcefulness of our wonder bearer we went to bed. Even so it was something of a shock on awaking three mornings later to look out of the bedroom window and discover the back garden transformed into a miniature Somali village. All around the house a good-sized flock of sheep roamed and baa'ed and plucked in leisurely fashion at the newly-sprung shoots of purple creeper or basked in pairs along the walls in the early morning sunshine. Just outside the servants' quarters arose the smell of cooking, the clatter of pots and chatter and the smoke of a communal fire, around which were happily gathered about a dozen sheep-drovers plus friends and relations. In the background the womenfolk were already hard at work at the day's washing. Whenever a stray sheep wandered in the direction of the gate two or three Somalis would spring to their feet and pursue it back again, waving their sticks with traditional tribal cries of round-up. Dazed, we watched the scene for some moments. Then silently Ronald pointed across the road to where the startled faces of neighbours were beginning to appear at verandah shutters and bedroom windows. The reality of the situation began to dawn on us. How long were these people staying? Were all these animals destined for Knox-Mawer consumption? And with the butchers on strike where and how were they to be slaughtered, skinned and dismembered?

But we were never to know the answers to these questions. Fate was kind to us. The strike ended that very morning. With expressions of gratitude on all sides the Somali village evaporated like a mirage. Neatly parcelled joints in the shopping-basket took the place once more of our vision of succulent whole sheep roasting at a barbecue surrounded by several hundred admiring guests. But Aboker never ceased to remind us how much better his meat would have been than the variety offered by the butcher.

And then, most outstanding event of all, it rained. As this only happened three or four times a year we were thrilled to the marrow, even though it descended through a flat unwaterproofed roof on to a surprised household in the middle of the night. In no time, Aboker and helpers arose from their sleep with cries of astonishment and exclamation, and pattered excitedly around the house putting pots, pans and buckets at vantage points to catch the heaviest torrents. Meanwhile we stood out on the doorstep in our pyjamas letting the rain, now an English-type drizzle, fall on us in an ecstasy of nostalgia. The next morning, the house was very wet, it was still raining, and our enthusiasm had flagged a little. For a moment or two it stopped but there was still a strange chilly greyness everywhere, monochrome colours instead of the usual blues and whites and yellows, as though one had suddenly put on a pair of cheap, too-dark sunglasses. Overhead the sky looked cold and colourless, with Victorian photographers' swathes of grey chiffon around the highest peaks of rock. The sea in the distance had taken on a dull, speckled appearance like the face on an old looking-glass and the sand was sawdust under the grey sagging folds of the Big Top. The European houses usually bright and white and slick seemed to cluster together forlornly, bleak and clinical without the arc-light dazzle of the tropical sun.

I was standing in the garden thinking, English-style, 'looks like rain again', when a gust of wind and the first drops of the second instalment drove me in to the verandah again. Fascinated by the novelty, I watched the view of the houses, the sand and the sea and the mountains merge and dissolve like a water-colour touched by damp. In a single spasm the veil became a curtain, a dense curtain of fine steel rods drilling into the ground, swinging violently down between us and the outside world, and the shower was a storm. Mysteriously the traffic disappeared from the main road. The excited shouting coolies going to work crammed together on open lorries had vanished and the servants discussing the rain outside the nearby houses went in again. Those who were caught between houses ran bent for shelter, their jackets pulled over their heads. From the direction of the bedrooms I could hear the sound of water bursting jubilantly through the ceilings again with all the enthusiasm of a fresh spring in desert country. Then after ten minutes everything stopped with the same suddenness as its start and I decided to drive into Crater to shop as I had planned.

In the town the colour of things was washed away completely. The old carved white-stone fronts of buildings seemed to sag like wet cardboard, the gutters were sticky with mud and the pavements greasy to bare feet. Kaleidoscopic turbans and shawls and *futahs* had become so much wet cotton flapping against shivering bodies. But half an hour later the infallible sun had burned its way through the grey cottonwool again. The familiar blue-black shadow and yellow-white glare returned as the streets dried before our eyes, the mud began to be dry baked earth again and the brilliant rinsed light brought back the colour everywhere as dramatically as a dye-bath.

I arrived home just before the dripping in the garden stopped and everything began to dehydrate again. For one marvellous moment there was a varnish on the stones and shells underfoot, a damp shine on the soil and a crystallised beading on the fringes of shrubs and bushes. A fine sweat still hung on the mauve petals of the creeper and there was a rich vegetating smell everywhere.

Stirring the sand idly with my foot I suddenly noticed a glint of blue showing through. From just beneath the surface I picked out two fragments of a strange antique-looking turquoise mosaic, obviously pieces of a curved vessel of some kind. What exactly they were, how old and of what origin, I never found out. The next time it rained and the next, I came across other rougher pieces, equally mysterious, but nothing gave me quite the same feeling of delight as this first discovery, a tiny new splinter in my own growing mosaic of love for Arabia.

The rain certainly gave a dramatic, if short-lived, impetus to our lethargic garden. For some weeks now Ali-sweeper had been toiling over a complex irrigation scheme whereby innumerable small cross-channels carried our morning bath-water away from the drains in the direction of the shrubs and 'flowers' he had so hopefully planted. Now, as a result of this extra gift of water from Allah, he could spend happy hours admiring the effects of his labours—one circular bed of white oleander, a cluster of budding lilies, two clumps of adolescent marigolds and a trail of bougainvillaea. That is, until the charming little ibex who was the pet of the family next door consumed the lot at one early morning sitting, leaving only the forlorn oleander as survivor. Obviously oleander leaves were poisonous to ibex, and I handed this on to a disconsolate Ali-sweeper as a useful gardening hint for the future. A collection of barren window-boxes I had carefully sown with unknown seeds were infected too by the general air of vitality and began showing green shoots. I pointed these out excitedly to Aboker whose reply was brief and to the point— 'Da spinach, memsahib.'

Aden's heat reached its annual peak about the same time as the beginning of the Moslem fast of Ramadan. During this time, for roughly thirty days, no good Mohammaden was permitted either to eat or drink during daylight hours. The traditional way of deciding on the exact moment of transition was when a black thread became indistinguishable from a white one, but the sounding of a gun in the morning and in the evening formally marked the beginning and end of each day's fast.

Although we had now been in the Colony for some months, like almost every European wife I met, my knowledge of the Moslem life around me was scant. It was restricted to daily contacts with the servants and a few polite handshakes and words of greeting with the very small band of leading Arab worthies to be found at official parties. Even so one was intensely aware of the tremendous change of atmosphere which the month of Ramadan brought—the emotionally-charged lassitude of the days with their interminable prayers, the sense of relief and jubilation at early evening and the social comings and goings, and feastings of the nights.

Aboker, So-help-me and Ali-sweeper all fasted with great strictness throughout Ramadan, without a single lapse, apart from one occasion when the eldest of the trio submitted with much protest to a dose of aspirin for a very bad headache. This was particularly hard for Aboker, constantly serving out cold drinks from the 'fridge, but he never complained and even added a new trick to his repertoire by serving gin and water in a pink glass to a guest demanding pink gin when there was no angostura bitters in the house. The guest said it was a splendid pink gin.

Ronald was finding his court work fascinating, with the prospect of acting as Chief Justice at regular intervals and playing a part in legal situations and cases involving complex religious and domestic customs all covering a scope unimaginable to the average young barrister practising in England. His surroundings were as unconventional as the litigation which came before him. When I was taken to view the Supreme Court for the first time I refused to believe that the sprawling ramshackle building which met my eyes was not an extension of the local market. In front of the main porchway were proudly parked three bedizened go-carts dispensing highly-coloured soft drinks. On every available step along the front squatted sellers of peanuts, roasted corn and sweetmeats with their wares spread out temptingly alongside. Just around the corner in a patch of shade a party of fishermen were doing a brisk trade with catches fresh from the sea which lapped at the back of the courthouse. At that moment the Chief

Justice himself was seen to emerge through the front entrance on his way home, briefcase in one hand and string of plump herrings for tomorrow's breakfast in the other, and it was only this that convinced me.

Apparently the building was fairly historical, being once an old army barracks. A brand new Supreme Court was promised any year now. As most of the staff, lawyers and regular clients had by now memorised the exact spot of the two gaping floorboards, the ceiling fan which tended to shed one of its wings at high speed, the filing cupboards where the rats were most voracious, and the balcony railing with the two-foot gap, it could not be termed exactly dangerous. Indeed the term applied to it by a leading member of the English bar on a professional visit was nothing less than 'picturesque, most picturesque'.

It was a double-storey building with a shaky verandah half-way up, over which impatient litigators could lean to spit (thus obeying the notice 'No spitting on the Court Premises') in moments of exasperation. Here, too, knots of shy ladies involved in matrimonial cases could gather and peer at the passing scene from beneath their *purdah* veils. It was from this very verandah that one of the first men to appear in court before my husband had leaped into the sea below, wrenching himself away from the police in the middle of the trial and rushing out to freedom in a frenzy. He obviously preferred to brave the sharks rather than the *Chief* Magistrate. This may have been due to my husband's somewhat sinister appearance at the time in an all-black tropical court suit run up to weird-looking proportions by an Indian tailor and needing, as I said at the time, only a black eye-patch, an ebony cane and a Boris Karloff limp to complete the effect. The tailor had assured us too that he had made identical outfits for 'every British worship come to Aden'. How disillusioned he would have been to see So-help-me soon proudly sporting the combination for Sunday (or rather Friday) best.

Ronald's departure for the ex-army barracks every morning was less dignified than his appearance. On our arrival in Aden we had bought a very decrepit Vauxhall. The performance of this noble vehicle was summed up by Aboker as we departed in it to our first dinner party—'One light on, one light off and him shout!' Occasionally she would spurt into action with the desperate passion of all fading performers, but more often than not a party of half a dozen cooks, bearers and sweepers gathered to push her boisterously on her way. Once this was accomplished my mornings stretched before me empty and uncomplicated. 'What do you women do with yourselves with so much spare time?' queried the harassed letters from hard-worked friends at home, with a slight note of irascibility in their voices. 'Good works' was the traditional outlet for the Colonial memsahib, and a number of women without young families spent their free hours in social work, most of it very valuable. This involved blind and hospital visiting, sewing baby-clothes for the clinics, running free milk centres for expectant mothers and small children and organising clubs to encourage Arab and English women to meet socially. In the new-style Colonial living, many wives without children took up morning jobs in banks and offices that perhaps encroached on their dignity as memsahibs but certainly enlarged their bank balances. Some, lucky enough to have cool modern kitchens, preferred to do their own cooking, run the house with one boy only and cut down the rising cost of living. Others took up hobbies, either new babies, or embroidery, dressmaking, painting and so on, according to age and taste. All of them in their less organised moments swore at the heat, ate too many chocolates, smoked too many cigarettes, indulged in inaccurate but fascinating gossip, nagged the servants, snapped at their husbands and wondered if it was all worth it anyway.

Opposite us lived a romantic survivor of the T. E. Lawrence tradition. I first glimpsed the famous Major at his own party, a tall bearded figure standing quite apart from the crowd, gazing out at the darkness through the window, lost in thought, smoking a black cigarette in a long bamboo holder. His evening trousers were tucked into a pair of very long highly-polished mosquito boots—a rarity in Aden where there were no mosquitoes—and, in place of the usual black cummerbund, he had swathed an Arab sash in striped silk around his waist. The beard concealed a scar inflicted by the dagger of an Arab tribesman who, with two or three others, had made an attack on him on one of his up-country expeditions. The assailant nearly killed him before being beaten off by the Major's bodyguard and his wife. As a result of his survival his name had assumed an almost superhuman aura with the Arabs in that part of the country.

The Major was now in charge of the administration of the Western Aden Protectorate and the ideal exponent of the British 'cloak-and-dagger' type of policy. All day long and sometimes through the night a procession of jeeps and Land-Rovers, grey with desert dust, would rattle past the black-turbaned Levy guards at the gates. I suppose they were bringing in the usual news items from isolated young political officers, and parties of tribal sheikhs and naibs all ready and eager for one of those interminable, round-about, highly-stylised conferences so dear to the Arab heart. For me, they brought with them, too, a breath of urgency and rumour, intrigue and counter-plot, and I cherished them as symbols of the outside world, that Arabian Aden to which I felt so drawn and so little a stranger.

The pattern of European life in the Colony was already as familiar to us as if we had never lived anywhere else. Unaffected by climate or surroundings the social merry-go-round churned blithely on and I was enjoying the ride. For someone of my generation, brought up in the austere sobriety of war-time and post-war Britain, there was a deliciously Edwardian flavour of frivolity and second-hand opulence about the Colonial pleasure-hunt with its gilt-edged invitation cards, candle-lit dinner-tables, long frocks and stiff-fronted shirts. There were the televisionless entertainments of cards, photograph albums, amateur dramatics, fancy dress and gossip. The compactness of the Colony made it impossible for everyone not to know everyone else at least by sight. Social strata had acquired almost nineteenth-century rigidity, and the various inter-groupings and relationships were discussed with the feverish intensity of all claustrophobic communities. There were weekly dances on the rooftop of the main hotel; there were formal balls with Scottish reels performed at roaring temperatures; there were parties on board visiting naval ships in the harbour which always reminded me of a Tissot painting with the women's fans a-flutter under the striped awnings on the promenade deck, polished brass, white paint and gold braid everywhere, and the ship's band pumping steadily away at the *Blue Danube* in the background. There were also the un-Edwardian cinema evenings, the telephone calls to 'come round for a drink', the steak barbecues at the swimming-beach, with moonlight bathing on the safe side of the net which kept out the sharks and poisonous fish.

Inside the little world of Aden were many other smaller spheres, each with a distinct self-contained atmosphere of its own. In one long evening one could watch Indian dancing, eating chipatties and curry at a reception at the Indian Commissioner's, go on to iced martinis and hamburgers off an eagle-stamped dinner-service in the air-conditioned hush of the American Consulate, and finish up with caviare and champagne in film-set surroundings where the leading French business tycoon was celebrating the completion of his new swimming-pool.

Less pleasant were the large-scale cocktail parties, given at regular intervals by the commercial firms, the R.A.F. and others. Here one was likely to find oneself breathlessly pressed in the centre of a steaming, milling crowd, wet glass in one hand, bag, cigarette, fan, savoury or all four in the other, wearing the same dress and saying the same thing to the same person as on the previous evening. Damaging to the morale, to say the least of it. Indian and Arab dignitaries were usually present at these functions, but in small numbers and almost always in an atmosphere of unease and social strain reminiscent of the brilliant garden party scene in E. M. Forster's *A Passage to India*. Arab wives were, of course, never to be seen. The Indian ladies, fluttering in butterfly-coloured saris and jewellery, always gathered in shy graceful clusters on their own, and were very rarely seen talking in mixed groups. I soon came to the conclusion that a European-style cocktail party was the worst possible setting for meeting a people whose social pattern was of an incredibly different convention.

It was all quite unreal, and the general mood of the place so artificial that even the idea of getting dressed at 5 a.m. to attend an official parade failed to surprise us. Our first was for the Queen's Birthday Parade, for instance—that hardy final fragment of imperial pomp and ceremony. But however *blasé*, one's first glimpse of a Colonial Governor in full-dress uniform, state-plumed helmet, sword, gold braid and all, could never fail to thrill. The air was cool and the sun just up, glittering across the parade ground on to the trappings of the Camel Corps and their riders in emerald and white jackets and turbans, each carrying a fluttering pennant in his hand. Immaculately uniformed, dressed and hatted, the British rose to attention and sank to repose in their seats at the correct points in the procedure enumerated on the invitation cards, while the sun stealthily warmed the iron backs of the chairs and the guns crashed out in salute. The surrounding population accorded polite, impassive applause to the tanks, the kilted Scots Highlanders and the bagpipes, the blue and white naval reserve, the grey-uniformed, bereted R.A.F. detachment and the scarlet-turbaned police as they swung past the saluting dais. Just as we were leaving a luxurious green-and-white American limousine, later to become so familiar, pulled away from the pavement in front of us. A red-and-white flag flew from the bonnet, and behind the chauffeur I had a glimpse of a grave-faced, handsome young man in a white turban. 'The Sultan of Lahej,' someone told us. Somehow, the ring of the name, the quick mental snapshot in profile of this leading Protectorate ruler, whose family had once owned Aden, remained in my mind more vividly than any memories of the parade.

On the evening of the Queen's birthday we were to go to dinner at Government House, where one of the many visiting V.I.P.s, who in these days hardly ever seemed to be on the ground, was flying in to be the guest of honour. The batch including our name had been reached in the visitors' book where we had signed in on arrival, and the crested card bearing the summons had been delivered by hand on the appropriate day. It was our turn for the big dip on the social roundabout.

To imagine, as I originally did, that dinner at Government House is nowadays merely a meal out on the grand scale is to miss the whole point of the function. The actual business of eating is its least concern. Dinner at Government House is a solemn ritual of initiation, an esoteric ceremony with its own high priests and acolytes, its inflexible rules and commandments, a unique and rapidly-disappearing relic of pre-twentieth-century aristocratic living, carefully fossilised for future generations to partake in with awe and reverence.

Well primed beforehand we managed to arrive within the requisite three minutes after the hour, parking the unsightly Vauxhall a discreet distance away from the shining string of cars already lining the driveway. Like a still shot from a musical comedy of the 1930's, a cluster of figures in full evening dress has gathered under the chandeliers in the be-flowered entrance hall. Coming up behind them we exchange murmured greetings and wait our turn to inspect the table plan, extended stiffly in space in the white-gloved hands of an enormous, motionless Somali bearer. The young fair-haired A.D.C. hovers around the guests like a ring-master among the performers in the wings of the Big Top, shepherding, soothing, leading them in pair by pair into the arena beyond. Some treat The Plan with a kind of jocular dis-respect, evidencing to less *blasé* visitors a long familiarity with this sort of thing.

'Now let's have a look at this nonsense. Where am I tonight, David, eh?'

Others approach it in an earnest, methodical manner, like a campaign of battle—'I see—third to the right on the left-hand side of the table opposite H. E. That's just about where the second french window is, isn't that correct?'

New initiates, like myself, reveal an unmistakable nervousness, horribly put out already by a host of minor details. The G. H. clock is a distinct five minutes in front of the church one, and why on earth is the Chief Justice's wife wearing a shoulder wrap on such a hot evening—were Arab guests expected? And why ever hadn't Harry told her the second button was missing on his shirt front? The ladies seem particularly careful to preserve a mask of indifference as they make a number of rapid mental calculations as to the correctness or otherwise of their placing, according to protocol—not a quiver touches their features as they scrutinise the chart, whatever the seethings in their souls may be. No one has ever been known to protest formally against an injustice anyway.

The two circles of wicker armchairs on the terrace beyond fill up with lightning rapidity. We are introduced to our V.I.P., a tall, slim, young-looking man with a lot of wavy reddish hair, strong regular features and an air of having a number of top security matters exerting their pressure on his mind at that very moment. If he had a moustache he would look the perfect major in a Scots regiment, except for that intangible aura of sealed documents and gold-embossed brief-cases. Standing with him is a grave-faced young Arab in a dinner-suit which looks better cut and more expensive than those worn by the Englishmen. This time the turban is black, but I recognise the owner of the green and white American car. We are formally introduced to the Sultan of Lahej. There is time for him to remark with surprising accuracy that he remembers me wearing a red hat that morning and for me to notice the unusual slanting lines of his eyes and the monogram 'A' on his pocket handkerchief. Then we move on to shake hands, and smile to the people we know.

The bearers go round with trays of tomato juice and whisky-sodas. Their uniforms crackle with a monumental stiffness and their brown faces have the blank impassivity of sleep-walkers. As the second glasses are emptied the ritual moves into its second phase. The Governor rises from his chair, walks over towards the first lady, the Air Vice-Marshal's wife, and they move away chatting together. One might imagine that the only significance of this was that they felt like getting to know each other better at that particular moment. In fact it means we are going to eat. Without comment, or even a glance of confirmation, the robots rise from their wicker chairs, form roughly into crocodile pattern, and as though drawn by an invisible magnet, move off in the wake of the Governor.

This is a sort of charade we are acting out, an Edwardian country-house charade. Or a game where we can thankfully say we have all learned the rules and no one will let down the side. Across the terrace, through the french windows, and we find ourselves in the dining-room where the glow of a dozen clusters of candles reflected in the auburn sheen of a long mahogany table intensifies the mellow dreamlike quality of the scene. Even the shades have real Edwardian gilt tassels on them. We move to our correct places with the ease of a well-rehearsed play, but do not sit until H. E. has done so. Then, in a body, a dozen bearers step forward from the shadows and put the soup before us. We smile politely at our neighbours and pretend it isn't there until we are quite sure our host has taken his first sip.

Somewhere an invisible agency turns a handle, and slowly, wheezily, jerkily at first, the familiar record starts up. Weather with the soup on the right hand, home leave (when due, where spent last time) with the fish on the left. By the time the main course has arrived—good plain Anglo-Saxon cooking—the pre-dinner whiskies, the sherry and the white wine have accomplished their appointed task—that of enabling the English to achieve social intercourse without pain. Perhaps even with pleasure.

Gradually, imperceptibly, like those Japanese paper flowers in a glass of water, we relax and expand. Now we bask in a pleasant glow, combined with a faint humming in the head. We are the privileged ones, part of the world of affairs, dining with the visiting members of the Establishment at Government House, and comradeship vibrates in the air. Our neighbours seem to like us, positively to enjoy our company. So we enjoy theirs. We are full of an overwhelming desire to sparkle, to shine, to devastate the table with comet-like flashes of wit and brilliance. By the time the dessert-plates are removed, the scene is positively animated. Even the V.I.P., sitting on my left, has dropped the usual gambits and delivers himself of opinions on the English

Press, the London theatre, surrealist painting ('I could do it so much better myself'), radiating the same sense of power, drive and an almost irascible impatience, whatever the subject. As he talks he drums his fingers on the table, darts quick blue gazes at his audience from beneath a formidable pair of eyebrows, reveals an engagingly gap-toothed schoolboy grin.

Occasionally our V.I.P. strikes an ever-so-slightly false note with references to 'subject peoples' and 'holding back self-government', and other phrases all labelled 'Not in Current Usage' in present-day Colonial society. His particular benevolent-patriarch brand of Tory Colonialism, and the outspokenness of it, obviously disturbs the more liberal-minded administrators present, well schooled in the art of tactful evasion. But when it reached the point of the 'folly of education' and 'the failure of the democratic system' the young Sultan sitting on his other side, obviously with more hopeful ideals in view for his Protectorate peoples, had to express himself horrified at such cynicism and protested vigorously. Not so the Administrators who will suppress their disagreement until a beer-drinking session at home afterwards. The Sultan turns to the pretty secretary on his other side for light relief and, with the charming Air Vice-Marshal opposite, gets on to the unlikely topic of French perfume. H. E. seems a little alarmed at this worldly sophistication on the part of a 'local-colour' exhibit, a tribal ruler, and leans across to comment, 'So you are an expert on French perfume, Your Highness?'

But an Arab can be as tactfully evasive as an administrator. 'The Arabs are experts on all perfumes, Your Excellency.' Laughter and good humour all round, and then a sudden lull for the loyal toast. H. E. and guests stand and raise their port to 'Her Majesty the Queen'. This is performed—there is another pre-ritual silence and then the withdrawal of the ladies. Out we sweep and on upstairs to the powder-room where there is much hazy chatter as in the bonhomie atmosphere of the school dorm after a midnight feast. News is exchanged, a friend is very ill—and receives the traditional English response—'What rotten luck'. Even the secretary grows confidential and refers vaguely to ministerial affairs and the London world. After the powdering of noses, the mutual pinnings-up, discreet flushings of lavatories and well-bred washings of hands, we go down the marble stairs again to *purdah* coffee on the terrace. Slowly, condescendingly, the men stroll out again to bestow their company on us. Conversation is easy but has lost its sparkle. We are all exhausted by so much concentrated social effort and sigh with silent relief when at 10.45 p.m. precisely, Mrs Air Vice-Marshal rises and makes her departure and we can all follow—in order of precedence of course.

On the way home we decide we like the mysterious young Arab in the black turban and immaculate dinner-suit and wonder if we shall have the opportunity of getting to know him better.

In the middle of the night I wake up hungry. Devouring bread and cheese in the kitchen, it is sobering to try and remember what I had been talking so much about while everyone else was busy eating.

3

Roses from Lahej

'Can we have lunch with a Sheikh tomorrow?' my husband had queried over the 'phone one morning soon afterwards.

As a result of which we were now lost in the back streets of Crater while the midday sun oven-cooked us in our Vauxhall at a steady temperature and a trail of small urchins, disappointed of *baksheesh*, tattooed rude marks in the dust of our bumpers. We were trying to find the premises of Sheikh Mohamed Omar. I had prepared myself for the function in the ordained full-skirted dress with covered shoulders, even removed the nail-varnish from my toes (Mrs Cunningham's last words), and had now missed the turning four times on the street map which Ronald insisted on using.

'We'll never find our way around by asking people.'

Any visions I had cherished of being ushered into a black goats-hair tent by a bearded Valentino, hawk-like in burnous and cloak, amid scenes of Technicolor brilliance, had already been firmly suppressed—'He's a travelled and prosperous business man, not a Bedouin chief,' my husband kept repeating.

When we eventually reached our destination, accompanied by a helpful policeman, we were only fifteen minutes late, a mere nothing in Arab eyes we learned afterwards. A young Arab welcomed us and led us through a Dickensian counting house full of clerks on tall stools and a warehouse full of bales of cotton, then upstairs into a small drawing-room. Here the Sheikh awaited us. He was a small spectacled man of about sixty in a robe like a nightgown of brilliant whiteness and an embroidered linen fez cap. His opening gambit was a startling one. 'How is Manchester?' he greeted us. 'Still raining?' I said probably it was, and the three of us laughed and sat down in a row on an immense stuffed sofa with Sheikh Mohamed in the middle. He handed me a fan from the table in front of us. Did I find Aden so very hot? I said that I did. He said it was not like Manchester weather. He added that he had installed air-conditioning in his house, of course, but they very rarely used it. His wife did not care for it and it gave them all colds. He enquired whether I liked his drawing-room; I replied, trying to take in at one glance the china cabinets, the veneered tables, the embroidered Koran texts and the calendar of Buckingham Palace, that it was most modern; he said not as modern as Manchester. I was at that moment hotter than I had ever been before in my life, as the windows were closed and the overhead fan motionless. I said the scenery was much more pic-turesque than Manchester. He said that soon they would have television and modern shops with neon lights and plate-glass windows. Then we drank some fizzy squash, served to us by his eldest son, and left for the Sheikh's domestic establishment where the luncheon party was to be held. The squash was a new local product, turned out in bottles bearing the trade legend '*al-Kawthir*'—literal translation, 'River of Paradise'.

We followed his Chevrolet in our Vauxhall for about a mile outside the town. This was obviously the fashionable suburban retreat of Arab merchants of wealth, and large, square houses of mixed Arab and British-Indian design flanked the roadside behind high walls of mud surmounted with broken bottles. We turned in at the entrance to one of these country villas. A huge pair of fortress-style gates was opened from within and we drew up outside the front door. Inside in a small reception-room a number of guests, mostly European, were already sitting in silence with glasses of lime juice in their hands. The chairs were not grouped together in the European way, but lined the walls Arab-style in a rectangle so that any remark, however trivial, was general pro-perty and received the grave attention of all present. This arrange-ment may work with a traditional Arab 'divan', all cosy cushions and floor couches, but translated into terms of small straight-backed chairs equals a dentist's waiting-room. Hence the silence.

Our host seemed not the least perturbed on finding most of the company there before him. Meticulously he shook hands all round then disappeared in the direction of the doorway again. Obviously someone of importance was still to arrive.

A few minutes later there was a flurry outside, and through the doorway swept the Sultan of the parade and the dinner party, looking remarkably like my original Valentino vision except that he was clean-shaven and a little too well-fed to be called hawk-like. Around him fluttered a long black gown of some coarse material with wide sleeves edged with rich gold embroidery. His turban this time was black and gold, and an antique dagger was tucked in the scarlet sash he wore outside his white Indian-style tunic and narrow trousers. With a slight smile he bowed to the room in general, then went over to where two Arab guests, also in gala dress, were standing. Their style of greeting was fascinating. Taking his right hand each one in turn bowed his head low over it but did not kiss it, merely sniffed it appreciatively, as though savouring the very odour of sanctity.

A small pet kid wandered in from a side entrance wearing a festive red bow round its neck and ensconced itself at my feet. Sheikh Mohamed sat in the chair next to mine and talked to me about the guest of honour.

'He is progressive,' he said solemnly. 'He was educated abroad.'

'How old is he?'

'But a little hasty perhaps. Not so clever as his father.'

'Over thirty, would you say?'

'Now his father had the people in the palm of his hand.' Sheikh Mohamed continued inflexibly. 'He was like a brother to me, that man.'

I tried another tack. 'How many wives has he?' But Sheikh Mohamed embarked on a lengthy description of his friendship with the old Sultan, and I had learned the valuable lesson that for an Arab, talking is pleasure, not business. He disdains to regard himself as an information bureau for the curious. Arab conversation is all intricate recollection, vague surmise and veiled allusion. And there is all the time in the world for it. Nothing could be further from the clipped, fact-finding, money-in-the-slot exchanges of Europeans and Americans.

On my other side was my friend, the wife of the United States Consul. In just under five minutes I was told that the Sultan was aged thirty-four; that his name was Ali; that he had one wife only; that he was shy of European women; that he admired Colonel Nasser, the French Riviera and fast sports cars. Apparently this party was to celebrate his return from his latest visit to Europe. He had been Sultan for only a few years, succeeding, amid scenes of incredible feuding, intrigue and bloodshed, a step-brother whose goings-on had caused the British Government to intervene to have him removed elsewhere.

A servant came in and murmured something in the ear of our host who rose to his feet and gestured us all into another room at the back. Mrs U. S. Consul was an experienced Arabist and I followed her every movement slavishly, standing back for the Sultan to walk in first, removing our shoes in the doorway, receiving with outstretched palms the incense smoke wafted around us in small brass burners by the two attendants at the entrance.

'Cover your feet,' she hissed as we flopped on to the floor-cushions in the dining-room. Mrs C. had omitted to tell me that to extend one's feet in the direction of the person opposite is almost the worst form of Arab insult. I noticed that the Arab guests seemed able to fold themselves up into a cross-legged tailor position in the easiest way imaginable, even the fattest of them. Most of the English sat sideways, leaning first on one hand then on the other as the meal progressed. This complicated the strict necessity of eating with the right hand only—knives and forks were provided but, in deference to our host, left unused. The rice was the most difficult problem until a helpful Arab opposite showed me that the art lay in spooning up in the fingers, not pinching it together as with peanuts. The only off-putting thing was a whole sheep's head which was the centre-piece of the sea of food—rice, lamb, kebab, pilaff, pancake bread, chutneys, chicken legs, sour cream—which stretched out around us on white strips of cloth. I was the nearest to it, and everything I had ever read or heard about sheep's eyes and 'honoured delicacies' and so on haunted me for the whole of the meal. But I need not have worried. The head was purely ornamental and both eyes stayed firmly in place, gazing into mine with an expression of almost unbearable sadness and accusation.

Already replete, no one showed much interest in the tinned fruit salad which followed. So back we went to the other room for excellent Mocha coffee. This time the attendants were ready in the doorway to minister rosewater to us as we passed. This was sprinkled over our cupped hands from a tall silver jug as we passed through—the large bar of washing soap and bath-towel proffered by the last servant rather unnerved me and I decided merely to shake my head politely and pass on. (My American friend was out of sight at this point.)

There was none of the usual English humming and hawing about leave-taking.

'Well!' exclaimed the Sultan, getting to his feet, 'Now we sleep!' Everyone else seemed to agree and the scene was transformed into a confusion of handshakes, thanks and farewells, and the guests were gone.

When we walked out a few minutes later, talking to Sheikh Mohamed, the long green-and-white car was still there, parked to one side of the drive. The lid of the bonnet was up and the white-uniformed chauffeur invisible save for a pair of brown legs extending beneath the chassis. In the shade of a tree alongside stood His Highness looking like an undergraduate, with his turban removed and the ancestral black gown flung across one shoulder.

'This stupid car!' He gave the back mudguard an irascible kick, as we walked over. 'Won't start for the second time today. If only I had my beautiful American Thunderbird here——'

Expressions of concern streamed from our host who summoned servants from all sides. Vastly interested, they stood in a second outer circle around our group discussing the incident with vivacity.

Moodily the Sultan watched the chauffeur's efforts. 'I'm so

tired!' he added suddenly, stretching his arms. 'And before I can sleep I have a conference at the palace at three.'—Thus was the Vauxhall dignified with her first, and undoubtedly her last, royal passenger. His Highness shared the front seat with Ronald while I took my proper woman's place in the back, from where I watched fascinated as he clapped his turban back all in one piece on his head like a schoolboy's cap. 'Sorry,' he murmured, 'but I have to wear this thing driving through the town.'

I had just decided he had a most paintable profile, Ronald was apologising about the deafening rattle for the third time and H. H. was in the midst of explaining how his family disapproved of his Thunderbird sports car, when we overtook a large and elegant green Land-Rover. The Sultan gave an exclamation, leaned out of the window and signalled it to stop.

'My cousin coming in from Lahej,' he said. 'He can take me on to the Palace—it's a long way from your house.' (How did he know where we lived?)

'By the way,' he said as he jumped out, 'I would like you to come to see Lahej—are you free on Saturday?' Yes, we were. Then his car would pick us up at 10 a.m.

When we turned to wave, driving away, the driver was hastily fixing another edition of the Sultan's personal red-and-white standard on to the bonnet—obviously a spare one was always on hand in every royal vehicle in case of emergency.

We were surprised to see the green-and-white car and not the Land-Rover draw up at the door on Saturday morning. 'Won't it get stuck in the sand?' we asked Aboker, who was hovering around to see us off with the anxious pride of a parent whose offspring cannot be altogether trusted to behave themselves at the Sunday school treat. At this Aboker threw back his head and laughed. Then he translated our fears to the chauffeur, a stocky beetle-browed Arab in a red-and-white uniform, who merely bared his teeth in a jagged smile and ushered us into the back. Later on he made us feel rather foolish by remarking that this was the car in which he drove the Sultan out to Lahej every day.

We took the old road out towards the Colony border, past the neat white and pastel ranks of suburban housing estates, past the R.A.F. airfields and the civil airport. Out of the dusty landscape loomed a number of surprises. First, people playing golf, files of indomitable figures armoured with dark glasses, large peaked caps and canvas umbrellas, fiercely stalking the small white ball across the sandy, sun-baked acres of the Union-Khormaksar Club. And then, windmills—genuine Dutch-calendar windmills, standing in what appeared to be fields of half-thawed snow. Mercifully, this mirage had a scientific explanation. These were the famous salt-pans. The latticed sails spinning on squat whitewashed turrets provided the power for drawing off the sea water into the pans— or so the guidebooks had said. And the polar molehills were just so much evaporating salt. I remembered then that I had seen it all before, set down in dainty water-colours and framed on the walls of most Aden living-rooms. It was the first and favourite subject of any amateur female artist who could be relied upon to point out the weirdly Christmas-card scene as 'my little bit of local colour'.

We drove on towards the border town of Sheikh Othman. 'To the Zoo' announced a zany-looking signboard on a sand-dune on our left, but we hadn't the time to obey this unexpected direction. At the end of the winding back lane into the town we saw a beautiful thing—a small and ancient mosque standing on a sand-hill under a spray of palm trees. The bleach-white outline of its domes and turrets against the blue sky gave the scene the compact perfection of a cameo. Our driver, who spoke no English, was unable to tell us what it was, but he pulled up and beckoned to some Indian boys coming towards us. They were walking from the direction of the Sheikh Othman gardens, wore European clothes, and looked like students. One of them carried a battered gramophone, another a pile of records, equally battered, a third had a few textbooks in his hand and the last one was absorbed in one of the highly-coloured magazines that were his particular burden. While the driver spoke to them in Arabic I studied the cover with interest—it depicted an Indian pin-up girl being delicately dangled from the talons of a Boris Karloff monster with strictly European-type features and colouring.

The leader of the group, an intensely thin, spectacled youth, sprang to attention and declaimed all in one breath, 'I would like to tell you sir that this building here is the extremely interesting shrine of the namesake of this town the famous Sheikh Othman a pious saint who lived many centuries ago and worked many miracles.' He then relaxed a little and added, 'Excuse me but the Taj Mahal sir is a very much more bigger and noble edifice. Perhaps you yourself have witnessed it sir?'

We said no, we hadn't, but certainly hoped to do so some day, and drove on so much the better informed. Other parties of students and small children of all nationalities in best clothes, families with picnic bags and reckless boys on bicycles were streaming through the gates of the gardens. Inside we glimpsed vistas of bright flowers, tree-shadowed paths and real grass, and vowed to pay a visit the following afternoon.

The town itself was crowded with people. Any empty space there was took on a patchwork quilt effect where the squares of scarlet and black cotton material from the local dye-works were spread out on the ground to dry. Tall clay jars in traditional Ali-Baba shapes and sizes were stacked up in every other shop doorway. There were mounds of fruit and vegetables on the street stalls and lurid-coloured globes of squash drinks sheltering under elderly black umbrellas. Overhead hung a fascinating medley of street signs. The 'New Eara (sic!) Restaurant' seemed to be the most popular coffee house. Here clients were leaning on iron chairs against the shade of the wall in a gentle stupor, though others, more sprightly, read the newspapers and leaned forward on the lino-topped tables to argue. The women were heavily veiled as in Aden itself and moved like black shadows among the brightly-dressed men to do their marketing. There were open-air food kitchens with steam and cooking smells rising up under awnings of sack-cloth.

Away from the main street we passed herds of goats and camels being brought into the town by long-haired Bedouins stained with indigo. Sometimes they had clustered to rest around a thorn tree's ragged disc of shade. More often they walked steadily on in the hot roadside dust, looking neither behind nor ahead but with heads bent against the glare of the sun.

The frontier between the Colony and the Protectorate was a ten-foot wooden bar, striped like a barber's pole in red and white. Alongside was a small wooden building labelled 'Police Station'. As we approached, half a dozen policemen, recognising the Sultan's car, emerged and raised the barrier for us to pass through. The presence of a European woman in the car seemed to cause a certain amount of interest I thought, exhilarated, and added to it by bestowing on them a regal flutter of the hand as we passed through. They saluted back anyway.

Our silent driver rose to the occasion with a word 'Lahej' which he announced with an effective gesture from horizon to horizon of the surrounding desert. Then he concentrated again on his driving. The road to Lahej was in fact no road at all—just a jeep-ribboned, camel-trampled track through wind-blown shelves of sand. But our friend in front obviously knew his way as a blind man knows his braille, guiding the long plump saloon-car over the bumps and curves of treacherous dust. Whenever we were thrown together in the back over a particularly nasty mound in the path, his massive frame remained immobile in front and he merely shifted from one cheek to another the wad of *qat* he was chewing. Occasionally we passed a camel train laden with crates of foodstuffs on its way to the Yemen. Sometimes the broken mud walls of a forgotten village rose out of the distance like cardboard cut-outs, and once we saw perched on a disused well-head a raven who was only too obviously crying 'Nevermore'.

A few miles out of the town the dust from our wheels flew up against the foundations of an old army camp, the shattered concrete lines heaped up on either side like driftwood. For quite a lot of the way our car followed the last remains of a half-completed road which must have been the pride and joy of some British administrator, and a past ruler of Lahej.

Gradually the harshness dissolved. Tough scrubby bushes started to tassle the edges of the dunes. In the distance lay bright green meadows and groves of coconut and date-palm, and beyond them the capital of Lahej, a skyline of mud and brick rooftops, scalloped at the edges like medieval castles and bathed in the bright steady light of the afternoon sun.

The Palace itself stood on the edge of the town. Painted off-white and with the odd turrets and gables of a number of European schools of design, it had the shabby impressiveness of a very large south-coast resort hotel. From the topmost pinnacle flew an enlargement of the car standard, the crimson *jambias* clearly crossed on a white background. The Sultan was at home.

Guards in vaguely assorted uniforms stood outside the tall columned gateway, rifles poised stiffly before them. As we drew up we saw someone waiting on the top step to greet us. A plump and genial-looking man of about forty, he was the personification of the oriental *bon vivant* as pictured by the West with his luxuriant black moustaches, rich silk turban and general air of Omar Khayyamish ease and indulgence. Arab-fashion he modestly refrained from introducing himself, but we were later to know him well as one of the Sultan's closest friends and a member of perhaps the most powerful family of the Protectorate. By him we were conducted through courtyards designed in a pattern of flower-beds but, as yet, flowerless.

'The water shortage,' he hastened to explain. Then up more steps and into the main reception-rooms of the Palace itself, large, lofty rooms, furnished in an elaborate combination of oriental brass and brocade and European plush and fumed oak. Long opulent couches flanked the walls of the main room where an immense polished hookah, coiled about with its multi-coloured length of pipe, held a position of honour in the centre. Here we stood and awaited the Sultan. Unable to resist the temptation, I bent down to touch the wonderful velvety patina of the superb Persian carpets which covered the entire floor. It was in this suitably respectful posture that His Highness discovered me when he came in a few minutes later. Perhaps it was on such minor embarrassments that our friendship was founded.

In that room he looked almost incongruously unimpressive,

bareheaded and wearing an ordinary cotton *futah*, sandals, and a dashing khaki wind-cheater jacket, obviously a trophy from Italy. At close quarters I noticed that there were surprising flecks of grey in his hair, which was too close-cropped to be called curly; that the slanting planes of his face with its high prominent cheekbones and square jawline, smoothed his features into a permanent shadow smile; that when he grinned, as he often did, he looked like a schoolboy, his teeth startlingly white and ever so slightly prominent against the coffee-coloured skin. It was a face to delight a sculptor, with something about it of a polished woodcarving of some eastern idol. The most striking feature was the oblique line of the eyes, long and narrow under the tightly drawn lids. It was very different from any other pure Arab face I had seen and seemed to have definite traces of African and Malayan blood about it.

Suddenly he clapped his hands together once and with theatrical promptness a servant brought in a tray of black coffee. Behind him came another servant with cold water in crystal tumblers. 'Coffee and water always go together in Arabia, didn't you know?' A few minutes later, he asked us diffidently, 'Would you like to see some family portraits?'

In an adjoining room the walls were hung with massively enlarged and elaborated photographs, heavy in their gilt frames. One by one the Sultan introduced them, these potentates, larger than lifesize, in sepia and white, posed in stylised Byzantine attitudes of power and splendour. Each one wore an elaborate version of the black-and-gold gown of the lunch party, the stern impassive faces heavily bearded and framed in the folds of ceremonial turbans, the traditional scimitars of office at their sides.

'My father, my grandfather, my great-uncle—the Sultan is always known here as the Father of the People—a heavy title don't you think?' commented the young clean-shaven man at our side. There was a pause and then he went on, 'I suppose you imagine me the Playboy of the Western World like all the other Europeans here?' It was difficult to know what to say to this but he went on in his clipped English, smooth but oddly formalised in patches, 'I think, when you come to know me better, you will realise what a very unimportant side of me that is.' As he spoke, his eyes flashed and his whole face and attitude hardened with purpose. He pointed through the window to the dusty streets and desert landscape beyond. 'I am an Arab. This is my world. These people are my responsibility, each one of them. There are things in it I want to preserve, and many more things I wish to alter, and no one can say my way will be easy. But I have certain ideals. I have plans . . .'

And then, as swiftly, he became the social host again, the polite guide to European visitors. Except that as he closed the door of the portrait gallery he added with a grin, 'Who knows—we may see the day yet when we have some portraits of the ladies of the family to hang up alongside.'

Our friend of the long moustaches was waiting for us in the next room. 'Hassan will take you to look at the town and then you will come back for lunch—good?' said our host.

Incongruous as a space-ship, the big American car nosed its way through the crowded mud-walled streets of the *suk* noisy with colour and smells and the raised babble of voices. But this particular space-ship was familiar to everyone and interested faces peered in whenever we stopped to have a look at the Sultan's *Ingleesi* friends. Two or three times we got out and bent our heads to enter a dim little cave of a room under a thatch of dried branches where the local *futahs* and turbans and shawls were being woven. Each man sat at the edge of a small pit in the ground, his legs inside the hole, an ancient frail-looking apparatus of strings and shuttles and wooden handles across his lap. 'It's easier that way,' Hassan explained. 'No village Arab ever sits on a chair.' The thin fingers picking and threading the jewel-coloured strands into a compact web of material had a hypnotic effect as we stood and watched. I admired their skill and patience. They told us proudly it took only two days to complete two yards of cloth.

In another place they were making the sharp curved knives which all Protectorate Arabs wear in their belts as soon as they are old enough to afford one. Prospective buyers squatted around, turning over the shining blades of the finished *jambias* lovingly in rough hands, evaluating the patterns inlaid in silver along the thick wooden handles.

At the corner of the main street we passed the leading local cinema, just another mud-walled house to the stranger, but garish posters announced unbelievable interior attractions. 'Only men visit the cinema, of course.'

Driving back we saw through an open doorway a blindfold camel walking in an unending circle, small chickens jumping around its feet, to pull a wheel that was grinding the oil out of sesame seed. We saw a procession of pilgrim families, half-way between India and Mecca, unloading the children and provisions from their backs to camp for a while by the roadside—and to give the grandparents a couple of hundred yards behind a chance to catch up. We saw the local madman walking placidly unconcerned and unremarked stark naked down the main streetway. We saw iron kettles, tinned peaches, alarm clocks, gold necklaces and pictures of Colonel Nasser in the tiny one-room shops. We saw the Aden 'bus start off on its return trip, be-ribboned and plumed like a medieval war-horse, a saddle of flowered silk across its bonnet, handclaps and wireless music cascading through its crowded windows as it bounced off across the desert once more —— We saw Lahej.

We were to have lunch in the Husseini Gardens. These proved to be the grounds of a rustic-style guest-house on the outskirts of the town. The guest-house, half gazebo or 'Sultan's Folly' and half sports pavilion, had a shabby grace and all around it sprang a profusion of rambler roses, crimson bougainvillaea, jasmine and magnolia and overhanging trees of quince and mango, wild and luxuriant as the gardens of the Sleeping Beauty's palace. Nearby lay a disused tennis-court, the asphalt cracked and dusty in the glare of hot sunlight. There was moss growing underfoot and pigeons fluttered up in front of us as we walked across. The last remnant of a tennis-net hung like a cobweb over a rusty roller in the corner.

'It is a picnic lunch,' remarked Hassan, leading the way through the trees and the long grass beyond. He gestured to where two figures reclined on an oasis of thickly piled cushions and carpets in the densest patch of shade. One of them was Sultan Ali. He jumped to his feet as he saw us and waved a welcome. His companion was a shy little man with great charm of expression who was introduced to us as Sheikh Ali, the Minister for Tribal Affairs. He spoke very little English but smiled frequently and courteously, following the conversation with quick darting glances from speaker to speaker. 'He looks quiet, but do you know, this man is a power in the land. He has a quick temper too. Everyone is terrified of him,' said the Sultan in English. Everyone laughed and, with a characteristic gesture, the little Sheikh's hand flew to his *jambia* as a sort of mock threat—then he relaxed and joined in the laughter.

'Show them your belt, Sheikh Ali,' commanded the Sultan. The belt in question appeared to be the usual leather band around the waist of the *futah* but on closer inspection it proved to be nothing less than a rack to carry the most complex variety of equipment. Apart from the usual *jambia* and revolver, the proud possessor took out one by one and with impressive slowness a fountain-pen, a table-knife, a fork, a screwdriver, a pair of scissors, a revolving pencil, a thorn-extractor, and a stick of solid iodine!

White-uniformed servants appeared out of the undergrowth carrying glasses of iced mango juice and fresh lime on heavy silver trays. 'Everything is a bit informal out here—I hope you don't mind,' said the Sultan. 'They are cooking the food over there,'—he pointed behind a screen of banana trees to where a mobile camp kitchen was in operation complete with paraffin stoves, steaming pots, and a small army of cooks. A few minutes later we were sitting demurely on leather-backed chairs around a damask-covered table eating roast chicken, European style, under the shade of date-palm. During lunch Sultan Ali reminisced about the Coronation.

'I was in the first coach behind the Prime Minister, but the Queen of Tonga was sitting next to me so fortunately nobody noticed me. It rained all the time, but it was a wonderful sight—

you should have seen all the purples and reds from the peers' robes running down the gutters as they waited for their carriages!'

'Did you go to the races in England?' Ronald asked.

'Yes, I went to the Derby.'

'What did you think of the horses?'

'Horses? I didn't see any horses, lots and lots of people but no horses.' He started to laugh. 'I think I got lost, you see. Well, nobody had ever heard of Lahej and it's a queer name to remember, I suppose, and I was always finding myself somehow separated from the main party. I didn't know many people—Clarendon came up, I remember, and Lennox-Boyd—it was certainly an experience.'

Cocktail parties were particularly trying, he told us, for a non-drinking Moslem. Invitations had been accepted for him beforehand by the Colonial Office but the hostesses on the whole seemed a bit vague about the unknown personage they were to entertain, and in what fashion is one expected to entertain an oriental prince in a Mayfair flat? 'I usually only stayed fifteen minutes. I must say I think your cocktails an extremely exhausting custom, you know. Does it show any signs of dying out yet?'

We said unfortunately no, not that we knew of.

After lunch came a wonderful interlude of indolence, while the whole party lay down and rested on the Persian carpets under the trees. There was Turkish coffee, desultory conversation curling upwards with the cigarette smoke, and the murmur of wood-doves. A few feet away, Sultan Ali said dreamily, his eyes closed, 'My father used to entertain tennis parties here in the old days.' Seated on the same carpets the Edwardian ghosts sipped China tea between sets, discussing polo and the need for rain. Overhead the afternoon sky seemed to enclose us in a glistening, tree-veined bubble that rose, floated . . . until I woke to hear our host refreshed and commanding, 'Now we must walk or else we shall become fat like Hassan.'

By now the sun was lower and it was quite cool. We crossed a network of miniature canals running through groves of banana trees with long drooping leathery leaves like shabby gloves hung out to dry, and took the path alongside a running stream. Orange butterflies flickered in the long grass. There was a flash of yellow in the bushes where some bird perched and swung from a hanging nest. With a sinister squeaking chorus a cluster of fruit bats flew out from the date trees high overhead, wide umbrella-veined wings transparent in the bright light.

In front of us a biblical picture moved forward to meet us—a nudging, tumbling, trotting flock of sheep, the dust rising behind them against the glow of the sky. In silhouette on either side walked the two shepherdesses, trailing black robes, black shawls over their heads. As they came closer we could admire their unveiled faces, the heavy silver rings in their ears and around their arms. The older one with proud, heavily-lined features was carrying a lamb like a baby; the younger of the two had the same sharp, beautiful, aristocratic face and glittering eyes. Drawing level they still ignored us, and strode past, heads erect, draperies fluttering, guiding the sheep with long crooked sticks and calling to them with a strange trilling sound like the noise of a cricket. As they passed the Sultan stepped quickly back to one side. Then, with an exaggerated sigh of relief, he grinned and mopped his brow with a silk handkerchief. 'They are fierce women, the women of that tribe. They beat their husbands with those sticks too! . . .'

Suddenly he turned and took a loaded rifle from his bodyguard, an armed soldier who had followed us like a shadow all the way. 'Now I will shoot for you.' He took aim at a coconut tree on the other side of the stream, standing quite still, a slight but compact figure, the fringe of his turban fluttering over one shoulder, the polished profile pressed to the grained wood of the barrel. The shot splintered the silence. On the opposite bank a coconut dropped into the ferns and the marksman swung round triumphantly, pleased as a small boy.

'But I wanted to keep it and now we can't get it,' I protested.

'You shall have another—riper than that one—see? *Ya Abdul!*' He pointed to a tall coconut tree just in front. The next minute an Arab stripped to the waist was climbing up the smooth shining stick of a trunk with the ease of someone running upstairs.

Moving hand over hand, feet curved to the bark, his body swinging out in an arc away from the tree, the climber eventually reached a branch full of fruit, drew out a knife and hacked it off. It thudded to the ground and quickly he slid down again to retrieve it and hand it to the Sultan in person. But first he knelt down and kissed his ruler's right knee, flashing a shy smile upwards when he was thanked. The coconut was cut open with the soldier's bayonet and we took it in turn to drink the sweet colourless liquid inside.

There was a moment of horrid shock walking back to the car. Just in front of the guest-house there was the sound of a shot and we came upon Sheikh Ali, who had stayed behind brandishing a pistol in his hand, while a few yards away the portly chauffeur was scrambling off the ground. Had the Sheikh's famous temper at last betrayed him? And what was the insult? . . . A torrent of Arabic, then gusts of laughter all round. . . . Gasping for breath, the Sultan explained. 'You see my driver tripped and fell on the step and of course my Minister for Tribal Affairs had to shoot away the devils who had caused him to fall!' With a sheepish giggle, Sheikh Ali replaced the revolver in the famous belt, and we walked on to the car, with me being particularly careful about talking a false step on a loose stone. Sheikh Ali might be a prize shot, but even so!——

Just as we were getting into the car the Sultan stopped and struck his forehead with his hand. 'I am a fool! I forgot to tell them to get you some flowers to take back.'

'Never mind—another time.'

'No—I will cut you some myself now, just a few. Come on. . . .' In the rose garden next to the guest-house he took out a pocket knife, sliced off half a dozen pink roses—Arabian roses, small and tightly curled like sea-shells, and handed them to me with a flourish. Passing along the verandah, he suddenly took a run forward and swung himself over the rail in an exuberant long jump. He picked himself up laughing, threw back his head and shouted to Hassan 'Try and beat that . . .' Two servants in the doorway looked on with indulgent smiles.

Hassan turned to me and asked, 'Do you know His Highness well?' When I replied we had only met him once or twice before, he said, 'Today he is happy. This is a rare thing and I am glad. He is my friend. Many Europeans in Aden will tell you he is an arrogant and dangerous man. I hope you will never come to believe this. . . .' He paused then added slowly as we walked ahead, 'I think the friendship of people like yourselves could mean a great deal to him.'

At that time I was ignorant of so many things and merely sniffed my roses and felt flattered. But later I was to remember these words and understand them better.

4

Farid

Memories fade quickly in a hot climate but it would be impossible for anyone to forget a first meeting with Farid. It was late afternoon and we were sitting drinking Coca-Cola on the terrace of one of the Moslem tennis clubs, when there came a roar from behind us as of a rhinoceros in pain.

'Riff-raff!' rang out an enraged voice, with a terrifying roll of r's. 'Riff-raff!'

I turned round nervously. We were guests of the club and apparently some foundation member failed to approve of us. But the figure in the doorway behind us didn't even know we were there. He was an impressively large and handsome Arab of about fifty, in tennis-shorts and shirt, his portly frame quivering with indignation, his eyes flashing fury in the direction of the four Arab youths on the court in front of us. Tables and chairs vibrated as he strode past us, his racquet swinging like an axe. In a gale of Arabic, interspersed with such phrases as 'no-good sons of dogs', the offenders were swept off the court protesting feebly. Then a party of three seasoned players, two Indians and one Arab, joined the irate gentleman and play commenced.

'Who is he?' we asked. The Club Secretary who was sitting with us, smiling and shaking his head at such goings-on, was incredulous. 'What is that?' he said. 'You mean you don't know Farid?' We said no. 'But everyone knows Farid. Dear me—Farid—what a fellow! Every Monday, he thinks the best court is reserved for him. Every Monday we tell him according to the rules no court can be reserved. But he never listens. It's been going on for years.' He smiled again, shrugged his shoulders and settled back again with his coke.

'And what does he do?'

'Do? Farid? That is a good joke. He does nothing. He has money from his father. You know his family—they are wealthy, one of the leading families here. But Farid is—what do you English say—the dirty sheep, eh?' He added, 'The Sultan looks after him too, of course—the Sultan of Lahej. I suppose if you called him anything you could call him A.D.C. to His Highness.' He laughed and pointed to the court—'He still plays a good game, you know.'

Farid certainly did, in his own way. Fascinated, we watched him through two sets. He lost the first and won the second. When he was losing he scowled, bit his lip and examined his expensive racquet with suspicion. When he was winning he laughed a lot, flexed his muscles and shouted cheerful insults at his opponents. He played most of the time standing still, unhampered by the exceptional rotundity of his stomach. To Farid the score was an elastic affair, depending on the state of the game. He also foot-faulted, placed his opponents to face the sun, and criticised his partner's play freely. At critical points in the match he would hold up his hand to stop play and call out to his servant, squatting nearby, for a glass of water, or a change of racquet, or a pair of sun-glasses or a clean handkerchief. Whenever he delivered himself of a particularly flamboyant shot his enthusiasm was infectious. 'Just like the one when I beat the Prince of Wales!' he cried out once.

Eventually the game finished and Farid led the way off, apparently untired, slapping his exhausted companions across the shoulders and urging them to do better next time. The Secretary called him across and performed the introductions. When he heard the name he let out a great cry of gladness and shook us by the hand for about five minutes. The Sultan had told him all about us. Was it possible that we had been in Aden so long without our meeting before. What could we have been doing with ourselves?

He sat down between us and drained off three bottles of Coca-Cola in quick succession, belching appreciatively at the end of each draught. Then he wiped his mouth on a large silk handkerchief and outlined to us briefly the salient points of his career, the various follies of Government despite the advice he gave them and the newest items of current gossip about local personalities and mutual friends. 'Ah, but Aden's not what it used to be,' he sighed. Apparently one of the great spectacles we had missed was Farid in his youth. 'I was handsome then, not fat like this,' he said, proudly massaging his heavy Persian-type features and his grey hair, still thick and wavy. 'Oh, the girls! the parties!'

We couldn't resist asking him about the Prince of Wales. 'A very nice fellow. He was here on a visit at the time and they asked me to give him a game at Government House. And it was very interesting, you know. Afterwards we had long talk and he put his confidence in me. "Look here, Farid," he said to me, "this other job I'm due for next—I don't think I shall be keeping it for long. Doesn't appeal to me, you see." So I told him, I said, "Quite right, Your Highness. You're quite right." ' Farid shook his head reflectively, 'Poor fellow . . . who knows? . . . I was probably the first to hear of it . . .'

He went on to tell us of his various travels around the world. 'I was in London with His Highness. Sometimes we have a trip to Cairo. Now I have just come back from India—magnificent trip, wonderful food, beautiful air hostess—all free of course. I do a little business for the airlines here. I'm so busy these days—always running around about something or other. His Highness wants this, His Highness wants that . . . .' He gave the weary sigh of an overburdened man of affairs.

As we got up to leave, he repeated that he couldn't understand how we had been getting on in Aden without him. However, all was not yet lost. Solemnly he laid his hand on his heart and pledged, 'From now onwards Farid takes care of everything.' And to a certain extent this turned out to be true, sometimes only too true.

The next morning Aboker aroused us five minutes earlier than usual and informed us with a broad grin, 'The Farid on the telephone for you, memsahib.'

Farid's telephone manner was as individual as his flesh-and-blood presence. When I picked it up there was dead silence from the other end, then a scrambling sort of noise and a voice, off-stage as it were, exclaiming non-stop in Arabic for quite some time. Eventually the voice applied itself to the telephone again and told me it was Farid and could we come up to his house for a party that night. Then followed a stream of directions. These were quite impossible to follow owing to the fact that he was alternately mouthing into the receiver trumpet-fashion, full blast and close range, or waving it some feet away from him with an excited gesture. Also the rate of his speech had the effect of an old-fashioned operatic record played at high speed.

I said anyway we would see him that evening, which in fact we did with the assistance of the usual helpful policeman. The house was on the Marshag peninsula behind Crater, a sprawling, wind-blown shanty perched on the edge of the cliff face at the very top of a corkscrew road which rose out of the rocks at a semi-vertical angle. The view was breathtakingly romantic. On one side winked the tall hooded lighthouse, on the other stretched the scalloped bays of Aden, the humpback outline of Whale Island below and beyond the lights of Khormaksar and the ships in the harbour. Behind us a full moon was rising over a battlement of jagged roads, like the illustration to some Gothic tale of the nineteenth century. We got out of the car and stood peering over the edge at the faint line of white foam breaking far beneath. 'And you can see the big fish in the daytime as clear as anything,' cried a familiar voice. 'Come on up—we are waiting you every minute.' Our host was standing outside the house at the top of a flight of steps. Clinging warily to the hand-rail—there was a stiff breeze whipping round us—we climbed up to meet our host. 'Forgive my informality,' he said, waving a hand at his white tee-shirt and green cotton *futah* swathed sarong-style and bare feet. 'Tonight I am relaxed. I have just had a wonderful massage with oil and I was too lazy to get dressed properly.' His beaming face and fat prosperous figure exuded geniality and goodwill.

Crowded on to the little terrace was a collection of people that any English hostess, however spirited, would have dismissed as an impossible mixture. Under Farid's magic influence however the scene was one of cheerful animation—next to us an Indian airlines agent, an Italian count, a French businessman and a pretty R.A.F. wife, to our right the American Consul, an Arab hotelkeeper, a Somali politician and a voluptuous-looking Lebanese dressmaker, in the far corner a senior Government official in earnest conversation with the local representative of a new bottling firm, and a number of other equally incongruous groups.

'And now, a long *ice*-cold beer,' Farid said to me. He crooked his fingers in a gesture of perfection and rolled the words lovingly around his mouth like a good taste, in a way which made every other beer I had ever drunk seem like so much warm water. While he was getting it the elderly Government wife next to me asked me if this was our first evening at Farid's. I said yes it was. 'Oh, it's always like this,' she told me. 'By all the rules it should be ghastly—no organisation, no grouping, no introductions. But somehow it just goes. It's a change, I suppose—and it's got atmosphere,' she added to quell a hostess's slight envy at such inexplicable success. 'I sometimes think,' she said sentimentally draining her gin and tonic and gesturing with her glass, 'that this must be the heart of Aden.'

We leaned over the railings feeling irresponsible and detached from the everyday world like a shipboard party on the top deck, admiring the sea in the moonlight, inspecting the heads of new passengers mounting the gangway. The next minute the tiled floor would start to throb under our feet, the landscape in front glide slowly away. I accepted my ice-cold beer from the Captain's hands and asked him what this party was to celebrate. 'To celebrate?' Farid echoed, slightly wounded. 'Celebrate nothing. Except my friends. It's just a party—for enjoying ourselves. You English, you have to have a reason for everything, don't you?' He excused me and the English with a bellow of laughter and a jolly clap on the shoulder, then added, 'though there is someone here tonight I would specially want you to meet.'

He drew me to one side and pointed discreetly through a gap in the gathering. Sitting in an armchair in a corner of the terrace a few feet away was a handsome solidly-built Arab of about thirty wearing an unusual turban, neat and flat and shaped like a toque in grey silk. His profile was reminiscent of the side-turned faces of young men in an Egyptian frieze, the nose small and fine, a narrow fringe of beard outlining the square jaw, dark eyes and brows slanted and drawn-out at the corners with a symmetry that looked almost like artifice. His skin and colouring were pale and there was an indefinable air of distinction about him, in the controlled immobility of his pose, in the respectful attitudes of his listeners on either side. He was speaking in Arabic, quietly but forcefully, in a soft modulated tone, strangely different from the harshness of the typical South Arabian voice. 'That is the famous Sultan of Audhali,' said Farid. 'This is the second Sultan you are meeting and, remember, he is very different from our friend of Lahej.' I tried to recall what else I knew about the Sultan except that he had a reputation for bravery and ruled the Protectorate state most constantly under attack by the Yemen.

As we went up to him he leaned back in his chair and viewed our arrival with a detached interest. Farid's manner became equally formal as he presented me to His Highness, Sultan Saleh bin Hussein. The Sultan remained seated to shake hands but exchanged his almost insolently proud expression for a flashing smile of tremendous charm and sincerity. His two companions got up and we sat down on either side. *Takalan Arabi?* he asked eagerly. I knew just enough to reply that I couldn't speak the language, at which he grinned ruefully and indicated Farid. 'He will . . . interpret,' he said with a hesitant precision. 'My English . . . not good.' He shook his head as though it was a matter of concern to him. 'Not good at all.'

With Farid as a somewhat erratic interpreter he told me that his country was far superior to Aden. The air was cool and clear as crystal ('like glass' as Farid put it) up on top of the hills. There were vegetables, flowers and fruit, grape-vines and fields of corn. I would have to see it to believe it. In fact, I must see it. My husband and I must go up for a holiday sometime, away from the dust and glare of this place. 'Sometime when my Yemeni friends are not so busy,' quoted Farid. It was just a short air trip away. Such a fresh free atmosphere. The women worked unveiled side by side with the men in the fields. 'They wear this—what you have,' he said laboriously in English, with a grin, pointing to my cummerbund sash. 'But the dress . . .' he gestured groundwards beyond my immodest mid-calf hemline, and grinned again. In between questions and answers he sat with his hands on his knees looking on with a countryman's suspicion at the scene around him. Apart from a magnificent gold *jambia* at his waist his clothes were oddly in contrast with the natural elegance of his features—a khaki bush-jacket, cotton *futah* of the same material, thick woollen socks and heavy walking shoes which gave a schoolboy appearance to his short sturdy legs. He must have noticed me inspecting the details of his dress so rudely for he raised a quizzical eyebrow and explained, 'You see . . . I am a Bedouin.' He nodded towards the crowd of guests, producing his words one by one then repeating each finished phrase with a kind of surprised delight. 'So many people . . . I am shy . . .' He sighed, then with a fifth-form grimace, removed his turban and threw it under his chair. The shape of his head was as classical as his profile, the black close-cropped hair with a fine bloom of desert dust on it from the day's travelling. I thought he was delightful. As Farid had deserted us to welcome some newcomers, however, our conversation consisted mainly of smiles and misunderstandings and I was quite relieved when another friend came up to greet His Highness and I could give up my seat to him. I stood up and Sultan Saleh said, 'Remember . . . you teach me English . . . I teach you Arabic . . . then our talk will be bigger.' 'But you are modest, Your Highness, I think you know much English already.' He laid a forefinger against the side of his nose and grinned. 'Sometimes . . . is useful . . . I am thought not to hear . . . then I find truth!'

During supper, which was served buffet-style from a table inside, my crocodile-owning neighbour sat next to me and talked to me about the Audhali Sultan. I was glad to see His Highness take a seat on the opposite side of the terrace. All the advantages of T.V. over radio are experienced when hearing the details of a new acquaintance and being able to watch him at the same time. From Mr S. I learned that Sultan Saleh was one of the staunchest and most loyal of the Rulers of the Protectorate. His state lay alongside the borders of the Yemen, that mysterious and medieval Arab kingdom about which the outside world still knows so little. He was immensely popular with Government, partly because of his loyalty, and partly because the British have a fundamental admiration for the natural Bedouin, with all his picturesque attributes, as opposed to the innate distrust they usually felt for an educated and westernised Arab like Sultan Ali of Lahej. Sultan Saleh's life, he said, was centred around his struggle to defend his state against the Yemenis, a struggle that had moulded the existence of the people of that area for centuries. To understand the unrelenting intensity of his stand, one had to realise that up to 1934 the Yemenis were in occupation of at least half his territory and members of his own family were among the boys and men imprisoned as hostages to ensure the good behaviour of the Audhalis. Border fighting was still an everyday occurrence—for some periods it was worse than usual, other times the struggle was reduced to raids and counter-raids on crops and herds. The British Government did what they could, dogged by the bugbear of 'world opinion' and additionally hampered by what was to the Arabs an unbelievably stupid adherence to something called 'the rules of the game'.

Mr S. interrupted himself. 'Oh dear,' he said, nodding in the direction of the Sultan, 'I do hope he's not taking offence.' A Government official, new to Aden, had advanced to examine the famous gold dagger at closer quarters. As he swooped over to touch it with his fingers, exclaiming volubly on the beautiful workmanship, the Sultan sat rigid and withdrawn, not speaking, his eyes lowered. The look on his face was almost one of contempt. 'It's not considered the thing at all you see,' Mr S. explained nervously. The moment of tension passed however. The brash newcomer moved on and His Highness returned to his peaches and cream, spooning up the last spoonful of juice with the economical appreciation that comes from experience of hardship.

Somehow it was not altogether surprising to learn too that, unlike Sultan Ali, Sultan Saleh had provided himself with the maximum four wives permitted by Moslem law.

Our conversation throughout was punctuated by incessant shrillings from the telephone inside, sometimes stemmed with floods of exclamatory Arabic conversation from our host, sometimes just ignored and left to ring. We happened to be inside the room during one of these calls and saw a stricken expression appear on Farid's face as he replaced the receiver. 'What is it this time?' enquired Mr S. Farid moaned weakly and thrust his hand through his hair. 'Allah is doing this to punish me. Here on the 'phone is the young brother of the King of Yemen, the Imam, on a visit to Aden and saying he will be up here in five minutes. And here on my terrace is the Audhali Sultan, the Imam's worst enemy, and here am I, Farid, the host—all I do is entertain my friends. I like everyone to enjoy himself. I don't want any politics, no bad feelings—that is the one thing I will not have—and now what will happen?' He groaned again.

Mr S. suggested that he should explain the situation to the Sultan who would understand and leave. Farid only threw his hands in the air, 'And give him the worst insult you can give an Arab, let alone a Sultan? Tell him to leave my house?'

There was then a feverish consultation in the corner of the room between Farid and two of the older Arabs present, as a result of which our host returned with a beaming face and seized the telephone again. 'My cousin,' he explained to us in a highly audible hiss of conspiracy. 'This is him ringing up His Highness to ask him to his house on an urgent matter of business.' In no time Sultan Saleh was called to the telephone, accepted the invitation, and made a courteous departure. 'This is the trouble of having a good heart and an open house,' was the summing-up in martyred tones of our host. He then mopped his brow and composed himself to welcome his next distinguished visitor who arrived a few minutes later. He turned out to be a short, slightly-built young man who looked more like an Italian student than the 'Prince Abdulrahmen' of his introduction. When he told us later that he was studying at the university in Rome, it explained the flashy pinstripe suit, cut in the taper-leg Italian style, the continental hair-cut, the iced whisky in his hand, the subdued but sophisticated manner. Someone asked him what he was studying. 'Politics,' replied the Prince, with a sheepish embarrassed smile, and for an instant one saw the whole schizophrenic gap between the European textbooks and the Arabian Nights' world to which he was returning. Only a few weeks ago gruesome photographs were circulating the *suk* of the public execution of two of the Imam's brothers who were plotting a coup against the present régime. 'And who knows? We may never see this poor fellow again outside Yemen,' murmured the Arab merchant next to me. 'Why do you think he was sent out of the country for so many years unless the King feared him as he fears all the men in his family?' He shook his head and relished the drama of the situation. 'Yes, he may well enjoy himself while he is still free.'

This was obviously the main intention of the handsome young man with the pale olive complexion and the extraordinary eyes—large, greenish-coloured and a perfect almond in shape—of his legendary brother. After shaking hands all round with a shy well-mannered charm, His Highness had taken an unobtrusive seat in the corner. Here he discussed in animated undertones the virtues of Fiat cars and Espresso coffee. Later on he discreetly brought out from an inner pocket a snapshot of some Italian film starlet to show Farid. I had the feeling though that this role of oriental playboy was being underlined for the benefit of the Europeans present. It was, after all, what was expected of him, and in the Arab world it is one of the first rules of politeness to behave in the way that is most gratifying to one's companions. But beneath the assumed banalities one was aware of a sharp intelligence and a quiet sense of purpose which promised well for the future of Yemeni relations with the outside world. It was not for nothing, I imagined, that he had selected politics as his subject at university rather than any other.

I already knew that Farid was an old friend of the Imam and his family, but it must have occurred to him that some of the guests did not—and should now hear about it.

'How is your brother's health these days?' he suddenly asked the Prince. Without waiting for a reply he went on, raising his voice, 'It is years since I saw him last. I went to him to buy some horses for the Sultan, and His Majesty said to me "Farid," he said, "there is nobody in the world who knows as much about horses as you—horses and women."' Farid was launched upon his favourite topic and it was not until an hour later that the guest of honour was permitted to go.

There was no question about when the other guests were expected to leave. With a mighty yawn and stretch of his arms Farid announced, 'Very good party, heh, don't you think? and now everyone goes home and has a beautiful sweet sleep.'

I learned later that this was his customary way of ending an evening. From then onwards we went often to Farid's, usually on the same night each week which became known to everyone as Farid's Night. These gatherings were much smaller, with only about half a dozen regular guests. Sultan Ali was usually there and it was at these meetings that we began to know him well. The ritual was always the same. First we would quench our enormous Aden thirsts with innumerable glasses of Coca-Cola—whisky for Wadia and any Englishmen. Then we would process into an inner room to see a film lent out by the R.A.F. for private viewing by the Sultan who was not expected to endanger his dignity by visiting the local cinemas. The inner room was actually a bedroom—at least there was a large brass bed adorned with embroidered pillows at one end of it—over which the screen was hung. The rest of the room was a murky conglomeration of assorted chairs (a cushioned one for H. H.), coloured texts of the Koran, a dressing-table strewn with Arab cosmetics and a large cut-glass chandelier, a gift from the Sultan, blazing with un-expected splendour just a foot above our heads. As the Sultan entered the room there was always a squeaking flurry from the back of the room where the ladies of the family and women servants hastily concealed themselves from masculine eyes until the lights were turned off and they could safely emerge again with much whispering and giggling to watch the film from behind us. The performance lasted anything from one to two hours, depending on Farid's manipulation of the projector. Sometimes one of the reels got lost and there was a prolonged interval while everyone searched for the missing excerpt, usually discovered tucked underneath a sleeping baby or replacing a saucepan lid in the kitchen; sometimes they appeared in the wrong order and everyone reviled Farid and explained his own version of the plot at the top of his voice; occasionally Farid would miss out a reel altogether whenever he thought the film was becoming boring or he was growing hungry. Most popular favourites were Westerns and slapstick. Ever-so-subtle English comedies won little enthusiasm from the Arabs. 'What is funny?' they kept demanding. Obviously there could be no reply to this. Sheikh Ali from Lahej was persuaded to come once, and displayed tremendous approval of *The Vagabond King*, humming a minor descant to himself during each chorus, and thumping his staff on the ground in his excitement over the duel scenes.

After two or three visits Farid took me behind the scenes to meet the rest of his relations. Here in one long room revolved the real life of the family. At the centre of affairs was his mother, an imposing stately woman in a long flowing robe with her son's handsome features and a thick plait of heavy hair dyed a brilliant red to show she had travelled to Mecca. She welcomed me with a grave, heavy-lidded dignity and showed me the dress she was working on at her new sewing-machine. Farid's wife was extremely pretty and vivacious, several years younger than her husband. She wore European dress and laughed protestingly and fluttered her eyelids when Farid tried to persuade her to speak a little English. She told me she had no children—the various sleeping offspring curled up on beds and mattresses in the far corners of the room were 'children of the family—nieces, cousins, you know'. Farid then murmured something in Arabic to the women and after some deliberations he went outside and brought Ronald in to be introduced, a ceremony in which they took part with modestly-lowered eyes and murmurs of welcome. This introduction was almost the highest compliment an Arab could bestow on a European friend. Even today it happens rarely, and hardly ever between two Arab men. Sultan Ali who had known Farid all his life had never of course set eyes on his wife and would be horrified at the suggestion of a meeting. I had learned that even to enquire after the health of a wife in the presence of others is considered the worst possible taste.

The one female of the household who always mingled with all the guests was the cook Fatima, an immense black-skinned woman of slave stock. Her parents and grandparents had been servants of Farid's family, and she herself was nothing less than an institution as she waddled to and fro between the kitchen and the guests with beaming assurance, even condescending to dance for us when she knew us better.

Farid's father, a wise and much-travelled old man with aristocratic Persian features and expansive gestures, had a corner of his own in the family room. He was now almost blind but always intensely eager to discuss the latest events in foreign affairs or lead an argument about local politics from his armchair next to his beloved wireless. He told me about his visit to London with Sultan Ali's father for the 1935 Coronation. 'Sultan Ali came too —a little boy, so high.' He showed me an enlarged photograph, brown and faded, hanging behind him of a small wide-eyed boy in a towering turban and Indian-style tunic and sash and fitted trousers. 'Oh, London was wonderful. But there was always too much going on. On my last day I couldn't decide whether to go to Ascot or Selfridges. In the end I went to Selfridges.' He held up his hand with tremulous gravity. 'It was magnificent, quite magnificent ... what a product of western civilisation!' Farid, he referred to, shaking his head slightly, as 'a naughty boy sometimes, I'm afraid, but he has a good heart!'

It was on this evening that on leaving Farid said to me, 'You like riding? Well, we'll take a couple of my horses out on the beach tomorrow. I'll call for you at four.'

As we drove up to the beach the following afternoon I saw that there were three horses waiting for us and someone already mounted on the grey, waiting with his back towards us. I was an inexperienced rider and I was nervous of any company. 'I thought you told me we were riding on our own,' I reproached Farid. 'But His Highness suggested it himself—what could I do?'

It was Sultan Ali, not Sultan Saleh, who turned and waved to us as we got out. 'Come on. It's a lovely afternoon for a ride—quite cool.'

The Khormaksar sands stretched for miles ahead of us, flat, burnished, and quite deserted in the sunshine, but for an occasional paddling party of children and ayahs and a laden lorry taking the beach road into the Protectorate. My horse, a beautiful chestnut mare by the name of Ayasha, twitched with excitement and strained at the reins. But I had already impressed on my companions that I was very out of practice and refused anything faster than a walk for the first day. So for about a mile we walked the horses, elevated and sedate and fanned by a delicious breeze blowing off the sea. Once we passed a group of the Sultan's tribesmen, idling along the edge of the sea arm-in-arm in fine new *futahs* and turbans for a visit to the town. He called out a greeting to them which they returned standing staring in delighted surprise. 'They will never get over this,' Sultan Ali said laughing but somewhat uneasily. 'Not only am I out riding in Aden, but riding with an English-woman.'

Both the Sultan and Farid were excellent horsemen in a nonchalant, long-experienced fashion and both showered me with contradictory advice on how to improve my riding. 'Why two hands on the reins?' asked His Highness. 'The Arab way is surely best, with one hand free for the sword—or any emergency that might happen!' So for the sake of diplomacy I rode from then onwards with one hand on the reins and a quaking sense of unbalance in every limb. On the way back neither of them could resist urging their horses first into a trot and then a canter. 'But what about the syces?' I cried as a final resort pointing to the grooms who had followed us on foot and were now panting alongside. The other two were unmoved. 'They don't have to keep up—they like running.' But Farid eventually took pity and slowed up with me. From the Sultan now some yards in the lead in front of us, a wild-sounding Arabic song floated back to us, and Farid joined in. '*Al-kheil wa'l-leil wa'l-faidhe, taerifuni, wa's-seif, wa'l-breim wa'l-qartas wa'l-qalamu.*' Farid translated—' "The horse, the night and the desert know me. The sword and the spear, the pen and the paper know me too." This is a very old poem—all Arabs know it.'

'Now one from the English,' His Highness shouted back. Some mysterious lines by Swift I could never forget suddenly found their rightful setting, and gesturing at the barren landscape around us I responded with

> 'Byzantians boast that on the clod
> Where once the Sultan's horse hath trod
> Grows neither grass, nor shrub, nor tree . . .'

'Now the Aulaki chant, Your Highness, the Aulaki chant,' called Farid, anxious to keep the entertainment up to its original level.

The Sultan turned round with a wave of his arm and responded, '*Sheddat kheil al Awaliq latini Aulaki,*' adding, for my benefit, 'The Aulaki horses are all saddled. How I wish I were in Aulaki.'

Then he turned his horse round and came back to join us at a gallop, raising his fist in a mock fury and shouting something that sounded like '*Bas el awl! Bas el awl!*' 'And what is that?' I asked him when he drew level and reined in to a trot with us. 'That?' he said, out of breath and laughing, 'why, that is the Sultan of Lahej's battle cry. "*Bas el awl!*" "I am the might of the young men", or something like that. Young men with something of the meaning of your medieval English chivalry, if you understand.'

But it was to the less dignified rhythm of *Mambo Rock* that we bounced back to our starting point. 'I like this thing, you know,' said His Highness with enthusiasm. 'Hey mambo, the mambo rock! I must learn this mambo next time I am in Europe.'

As we dismounted and walked to the car Farid said to me, 'He is in good spirit. It is essential for him to get out of that Palace as much as possible. He must try to lead a more normal life. He suffers too much from his nerves, works too hard—too much politics going round in his head all the time—we will ride again together often now.'

Sultan Ali's car was waiting for him and we drove behind him back along the beach road. Half-way we saw a jeep coming towards us with Sultan Saleh next to the driver. Sultan Ali stopped, signalled to Farid, and we all got out and joined Sultan Saleh at the side of the road. He told us in Arabic, Farid translating, that he had nothing to do and after calling at the Palace had come to look for Sultan Ali and Farid.

'But now I have to take our riding companion home,' said Farid. 'Her horse is just the other side of the beach.' Sultan Ali nodded. 'You know, I can't help thinking how extremely nice a cup of tea would be now—especially an English cup of tea.'

And so for the first time, but not the last, the Sultans came to tea—and, of course, Farid.

5

The Green Turban

Soon after, a letter stamped with the seal of the green Laheji turban arrived by hand asking us to dine with Sultan Ali in Aden the following week.

Having been with him at Lahej, and informally at our own house and the houses of friends, I was interested to see him in the more formal setting of his own palace at Crater. The letter was typed by a secretary in immaculate English. The only trace of its Arab origin was that, true to custom of their right to left script, the printing appeared on the back page of the double sheet.

I had passed the Palace in daylight before, a formidable Victorian-looking block of grey stone and tall arched windows with its back to the sea. Now, driving up at night-time it looked sinisterly quiet and half asleep, with the upstairs in darkness and a streak of light slanting through one of the half open side doors to the front entrance. A white-uniformed servant stood in the doorway and bowed as we passed through. Once inside, both the coconut fibre footmat and the mirrored hall stand was a slight let-down, startlingly reminiscent of any English seaside boarding-house. But inside the main rooms the carpets were as magnificent as ever, glowing in brilliant pools of colour amidst a forest of the type of furniture chosen by heavily well-to-do English families in the early 1930's. Coming forward to greet us, Sultan Ali explained apologetically, 'I'm afraid my father chose all this from Harrods when he was in London for the Coronation of King George the Sixth. Next year I plan to have everything altered, in quite what style I'm not too sure—you must help me. You will, won't you?' This evening he was immaculate in Red Sea kit, white

75

shirt and trousers, black cummerbund, which made him look more slight than usual. He pointed to his initials A.A. embroidered on his shirt pocket and made his standard joke, 'Automobile Association'.

He led us through the main reception-room, across a long chilly nineteenth-century corridor and out on to a terrace. Standard lamps threw a yellow sheen on to the grey marble of walls and pillars. There was a holidayish tang of salt in the air and the plash of waves breaking below the garden walls about twenty yards away where the sea glimmered faintly under a moonless sky. There were more Persian carpets underfoot, small polished tables immaculately set with silver cigarette boxes and ashtrays, and canvas armchairs arranged in a circle.

We leaned out and looked up at the unlit upper storey of the Palace. 'These are the ladies' quarters,' said Sultan Ali. 'My wife is sick today otherwise she would have invited you to go up to meet them, but she hopes you will come another time.'

'They have all gone to bed early.'

'No, no.' The Sultan laughed. 'They always put out the lights when I am having a party, then in the darkness they can have a better view of the guests and still remain unseen. Or so they tell me.'

Then they are watching us now?'

'Of course—especially the lady visitors to see what they are wearing, if they are pretty and so on. They are very critical, you know,' he said teasingly.

Somewhat unnerved at the thought of this invisible scrutiny, I smiled in the direction of the darkened shutters. The Sultan moved away to welcome the other guests, but, throughout the pre-dinner introductions and small talk, I was conscious of that hive of suppressed movement and gossip overhead, and of a strange feeling I could only define as a sense of guilt at the unfairness of the situation.

Most of the other guests were close friends of ours—the shrewd and charming French business magnate, the American Consul and his wife, the earnest young spectacled Vice-Consul, and the ebullient Italian count. There was also Abdullah, a middle-aged, heavy-jowled gentleman of leisure, youngest member of a wealthy upper-class family, lazy, good-humoured and worldly. Standing next to the Sultan was another Arab, plump and solemn-looking with thick glasses and intellectual features, who was introduced to us as the Emir Ali, Sultan Ali's brother-in-law. The last arrival was Sultan Saleh, wearing his usual khaki bush-jacket and *futah* and gold *jambia*. But a vital link in the chain was apparently still missing.

'Where is Farid?' fumed Sultan Ali at three-minute intervals. 'Out of all the list of preparations I gave him for this party, he has done about three things. Emir Mohsim, my other brother-in-law you remember, had to call in at the Cold Store himself to choose the salad. One cannot depend on the servants for that sort of shopping. And now he has disappeared completely. He grows more stupid every day, completely unreliable.'

Eventually the culprit burst into the room like a small elephant, drowning all rebukes in a torrent of passionate explanations. In no time he was waddling and bustling about the place as full of bounce as ever, ordering the wrong drinks for everyone, twitching the chairs out of position, blocking the way of the servants and turning on the electric fans to hurricane velocity. We were offered a choice of tomato juice, Coca-Cola, and pineapple juice, served in tall tumblers in silver holders. It was unheard of for alcohol ever to be served in the Palace nor, strictly speaking, should it appear in the house of any true believer. As a rule the Arab's reputation for hospitality is unsurpassed—no effort to please his guests is too much trouble—and the survival of this custom is an undoubted tribute to the strength of their convictions.

The believers seemed happy enough without it, but the Europeans only too obviously found it difficult to relax without alcoholic assistance. Conversation flagged and His Highness suggested dinner, which was just like any other formal dinner—roses on the table, printed place-cards in ebony stands, the glitter of crystal and heavy silver. We ate melons, fish mayonnaise, sand-grouse, papya cream, and fresh fruit—'All Lahej produce,' said Sultan Ali proudly.

From the walls another collection of royal family faces of the past gazed sternly down at us—frivolous, treacherous Europeans. Behind the Sultan hung the Fadli crest, crossed *jambias* surmounted by a turban and a drum. In those conversational silences so dear to the hearts of Arabs we could hear Egyptian gramophone records being played in the harem and from time to time a baby cried—the sounds of the real life going on behind the formal façade.

After dinner the plump Emir Ali came and sat next to me with a shy, rabbit-toothed smile and started talking about Arab music and poetry. He told me in smoothly ornate English that he was educated at Cairo and liked to travel abroad. 'But my great interest is music. I play the *ond* and the violin—but so do most of our family. We are famous for our poets, you know.' The best known, apparently, was a certain Emir Ahmed who had died only a few years ago. He would write a poem, usually a love poem, and then compose music to accompany it. 'Oh, many, many times, when the fever of inspiration was upon him, he would arise from his bed in the middle of the night, scribble down the lines that flowed into his head and rush out into the darkness to the big family house nearby. And there, whatever the hour, he would wake up the inhabitants from their slumbers and pour out his new composition for their approval.'

This was evidently the Emir Ahmed Fadl of whom Sultan Ali often spoke, the pious and scholarly man with exquisite manners also described by Evelyn Waugh in his book *When the Going was Good* as the 'complete counterpart of the enlightened landed gentleman of eighteenth-century England'.

Emir Ahmed also had a small orchestra of his own and was the author of several pamphlets on the ethics and traditions of South Arabian music and other learned topics. Some of his songs had been recorded but as the records were at Lahej we were not able to hear them that evening.

'And who carries on the tradition today?' I asked, and was

amused to hear that the poet of the 1950's was none other than the prosaic cold-store shopper, the young Emir Mohsim.

'These days his favourite subject is the beauty of his betrothed,' said Emir Ali in those tones of humorous despair used by all older brothers of poets everywhere. He added hastily, 'She is his cousin, that is why he knows she is beautiful—they were brought up together.'

One realised that there were advantages to inter-family marriages in a *purdah*-bound society, especially when by lucky coincidence the couple were in love as this pair were reputed to be.

For about half an hour after dinner Sultan Ali and Sultan Saleh sat talking together, withdrawn from the general circle. Seen side by side like this, Ali's expensive silk shirt and immaculate trousers next to Saleh's tribal khaki, the contrast between them was striking: the contrast between the old and the new type of ruler, between the would-be modern and the necessarily feudal, and made even more striking by the fact that they were both young men of about the same age, and both very handsome. Saleh's face was the more determined of the two, almost ruthless, the face of the man of action, while Ali had the look of a dreamer. Both Sultans had about them the air of inner emotions suppressed by the habit of training and by the necessity for a ruler to keep private thoughts safely concealed. Ali had learned to hide this constant tension beneath the veneer of Europeanised social chit-chat which Saleh would probably scorn anyway. There was no burning intensity about their talk together. Rather it seemed the familiar, desultory exchange of two brothers, friendly rivals with vastly dissimilar problems and certain views on which they had agreed to differ.

I was realising already the chief difference between them. It was that, for various reasons, Ali's was a two-sided personality with all the neuroses and torturing self-criticisms of such a division, whereas Saleh, although always deferential towards the acknowledged Protectorate leader, was basically independent and at one with himself, with an instinctive unquestioning certainty about the rightness of his actions.

Later on when Sultan Ali came and sat next to me, he made the situation even clearer. I felt I knew him well enough to ask what he considered to be the main difference between himself and Sultan Saleh.

He thought for a moment and then said slowly, 'I suppose you might sum it up like this. Quite soon there will be no such thing as a Sultan here. We shall all be swept away and my comment would be—a very good thing too. Because, you see, to be a nationalist is to be a republican. But for Sultan Saleh such an outlook would be impossible. His is the old way, ours is the new.'

He went on, 'Of course, our situations at the moment are completely different. His present task is, to use the Government phrase, "freeing his land from the Yemeni invaders". My own people have passed that stage of the proceedings. The invaders from whom they want to be freed are the British. And my task is to persuade them that it is not necessary to go to extremes about it. Being a man of peace I believe that mutual understanding and co-operation can solve any problem. But at the moment I am walking a tightrope between my people and yours.'

I knew that the current cause of disagreement between Ali and Government centred around the scheme for a Federation of the Protectorate states. Some of the rulers approved the idea, others felt it to be an encroachment on their independence. Ali stood for those who would prefer federation on a wider Arab basis along Nasser's lines than co-ordination into a British-group which could only exist for a limited time.

'Why then do some of the rulers still prefer the plan for a British federation,' I pressed him.

'A few of the weaker ones do because it means a continuation of their own power which is in danger of being overthrown by the will of the people in favour of another. But mainly for practical reasons. If you examine the response to the scheme you will find the support comes generally from those states bordering the Yemen. For these people it's merely a defence organisation dependent on the British. Impersonal ideals of political progress and unity just don't come into it.'

I felt then that if Federation was to become the crux of British policy in the Protectorate this would be a more important breach between Ali and Government than anyone yet realised. I knew by now that in Government opinion the Sultan of Lahej was extremely obstinate—or staunch—depending on which side of the argument one found oneself.

Ali himself sighed and closed his eyes for a moment. 'You know, I am becoming very tired with this increasing pressure on both sides. Perhaps one day it will be impossible to keep one's balance any longer.'

He got up quickly and went over to where Sultan Saleh was sitting alone, in his usual self-contained, faintly aloof fashion, turning over the glossy pages of one of his host's automobile magazines with an expression of unwilling admiration on his face. I watched him pass Sultan Ali's expensive cigarette case over to him. He smoothed the black and gold surface between his fingers as he did so, and looked across at me with a quick rueful grin.

Sultan Ali lit his cigarette and became the host again, talking about the forthcoming marriage of the family poet. Apparently it was to be a triple wedding. The two other young princes were to be married at the same time, 'So much less expensive.'

Someone asked him how much the whole affair would cost him.

'About five thousand pounds,' said the Sultan. 'It is the time when the women rob us of everything.'

I learned later that this was about one-sixth of the Sultan of Lahej's annual income most of which came from land and cotton revenues.

The five thousand pounds would include the cost of the ceremony, the food and drink and the entertainment for the celebrations, and also gifts of silks and jewellery for the brides from the Sultan.

Before we left, local superstition and magic became the topic of conversation. Sultan Ali told us that although a Lahej mother would nowadays take a sick child to a qualified doctor, she would still firmly believe that a *jinn* locked up inside the child was causing the illness and she would probably visit the all-wise guardian of the local *wali's* tomb for a traditional remedy first. The Arab guests regaled us with stories of a certain Aden magician who turned pebbles into sugar. This sort of transformation scene was apparently a favourite one with magicians in this part of the world.

'What about the tomatoes at a season when there were no other tomatoes in the country?' cried Abdullah.

'That was the one who could turn himself into a black serpent.' 'And the hot meal flying in through the open window?' from Farid. ('Thrown in, you mean, of course,' murmured the materialistic American wife.)

'I myself have seen a bottle of pure water, tested and acclaimed ordinary water, produce the smell of any perfume requested,' declared Emir Ali solemnly. 'Hypnotism? Auto-suggestion?' the Count asked.

We went away happy with Sultan Ali's promise that we would see the sugar-into-pebbles genie on our next visit to Lahej and judge for ourselves.

For most of our time in Aden I was the correspondent for *The Daily Express*. For the *Express* and practically every other popular newspaper bad news was good news. Apart from 'trouble' stories the Colonies were a bore. And so every now and then I cabled off the appropriate facts concerning the occasional labour strike, the once-in-a-while inter-racial riot, the latest border clash, the court case with a political background, while the readers in Bacup and Llanfairfechan clucked their tongues over the breakfast teapots at the violence of life out East, said they didn't know what had come over the Empire these days and turned to the sports page. But there were some things impossible to translate into a ten-line cable. Such things as the changing tone and texture of everyday life, the subtle off-key tensions of atmosphere in the shops and streets where nationalism was not just a rude word in the Tory editorials but a new and powerful creed with a hero called Nasser and a special appeal for any corner of the Arabic speaking world still 'under foreign domination'. When something extra special happened, the gods from Fleet Street would descend in person. The ten-line cables became quarter-page features but reality seemed just as elusive.

Human dynamos with expensive new tropical suits, high blood pressure, stomach ulcers and a rubbery resilience to rebuff, they could squeeze a juicy story—guaranteed no artificial colouring—out of the most unpromising situation and polish off the Protectorate in such a single phrase as 'the country of blue men and yellow-faced women'. Off duty they dined together on expense accounts at the leading hotel in an atmosphere of lynx-eyed bonhomie and electrified the torpid club bars with their bird's-eye solutions to the Aden Problem and dashing personal anecdotes of world affairs. Life was always flat for a time after they left.

Not that the local press was inactive. There were two English weeklies and about half a dozen newspapers in Arabic, some daily, some weekly, and most of them written, edited and printed by small bands of enthusiasts in shabby upper rooms in the middle of Crater. Both English weeklies had Arab editors and staff and were a lively mixture of local reporting, foreign news and items of Hollywood gossip. As a concession to English tastes there was a whole page of 'Wit and Humour By : Jove!' type of cracker—gags and much detailed reporting of social events ('The band played, Mrs X radiated beauty in a white tulle gown and was kind to her guests.') The editorials were well written and quietly reasonable in their attitudes to Government policy. The Arab papers were much more excitable. They were usually called 'Dawn' or 'Awake' or something similarly stirring. They did not translate well into cold-blooded English, especially when the later press restrictions made their declarations even more vague and roundabout than usual. As a result the earnest English reader would find himself submerged in a welter of accusations about 'the poisoned dagger plunged into the bosom of Arab nationalism' and exclamations to the effect that 'The Age of Tyranny and

Delusion has gone—The Age of Light and life has broken forth brilliantly' and other poetic effusions peppered with capital letters, O's and exclamation marks and calls on Allah and sinister little trails of dots. . . .

The writers of these screeds were usually intense spectacled young men, unfailingly polite to meet, and not in the least voluble. My *Daily Express* connections may have aroused strong suspicions on the part of Government but they at least gave me an opportunity of talking at length to political leaders at official functions without being considered too eccentric by my fellow-English. The elected members of the Legislative Council represented a completely new type of Arab at these events, quite unlike the traditional representatives of their country, the grave robed *sayyids*, the aristocratic and religious leaders, who clustered together on the fringes of the gathering, aloofly dignified, sipping their squashes and murmuring polite formalities to any European who approached them. The new politicians were usually successful business men in the town. They wore double-breasted suits and boasted with the bravado of emancipation about the number of whiskies they could consume in an evening. They were on shoulder-slapping Christian-name terms with their English fellow members and were much given to quoting the latest pronouncements of Mrs Barbara Castle and Aneurin Bevan. They were energetic, intelligent and pleased as children with their new power. The political party to which they belonged was the Aden Association, the influential urban faction, the leading political group in the Colony and the most moderate. Its aim was internal self-government for the Colony within a given time.

There were two other political groups in Aden. One was the extreme left National United Front whose stated policy was the setting up of an independent state consisting of the Colony, the Protectorate, the Yemen and the Sultanate of Muscat and Oman. They also called for the reform of the present Yemen government, and had a certain amount of control over the local trades unions. But generally its supporters were so busy arguing among themselves that their unity was only nominal.

The other group was the South Arabian League which was never very strong, flourishing mainly in the Protectorate states bordering the Colony. They had a high-sounding, misty-eyed sort of programme involving in a vague sort of way the union of the Colony, the Protectorate and the Yemen. Its adherents rejoiced under the romantic title of 'Sons of the South'. They, too, were admirers of Barbara Castle and Aneurin Bevan but in addition to quoting them, they addressed long and fiery cables of protest to them whenever they thought the situation demanded it. The guiding spirit of the League was the Sultan of Lahej's Chief Minister, Sauyid Mohammed Ali Jifri, a member of one of the Protectorate's most powerful families, a handsome, extremely intelligent man with the personal magnetism of a born mob leader, fanatical, but not embittered, and, I thought, genuinely idealistic. Wearing his flowing *qadhi's* robes and embroidered cap and his customary disarming beam, with the look of a naughty boy dressed up as an angel for the school play, he was a familiar figure at a number of official functions and I always enjoyed talking to him. Then Mohammed Ali was seen no more in Aden when, to use Government's courteous euphemism, he was 'excluded' from the Colony for seditious activity.

It was at one of these functions that I first met Nabiha who was to become one of my closest Arab friends. She was a striking, middle-aged woman, with cropped blue-black hair and strong features of the aristocratic Persian type, who always wore the latest European fashions and make-up. I had always taken her to be an Egyptian visitor or perhaps Lebanese. 'Oh, no,' said the person to whom I was talking. 'That is Nabiha. She is the first Arab woman in Aden to come out of *purdah*.'

Later on I asked Nabiha, whose husband I had learned was one of the leading Aden business men of a well-known family, how she had done it.

'It was just like this,' she told me, speaking in a style of English that was not so much broken as splintered, with an exclamatory, highly dramatic effect. 'One day I am walking to the other end of the street to visit my sister. Suddenly I want to take off my veil to breathe some fresh air and see the sun—and so, pouf! I take it off! And that is that! Except my sister nearly fell out of the window when she see me coming with a naked face.'

'And what made you do it, you, in particular I mean?'

'*Purdah* is easy for women who live all their lives here in Aden. But I travel abroad with my husband and for me is very hard to live once more under the veil after I am free in Cairo, in Italy, in London.'

'And have you suffered at all, because of what you have done?'

'At first my husband's friends do not speak to me at parties. "Who are you?" they say. "I am Nabiha, wife of Jawad," I say. "Oh no, you cannot be the wife of Jawad otherwise you would not be behaving in such a shameless fashion," they say. But I have a good husband and slowly things become more easy. Now they say—"Oh, Nabiha—well, she is a bit crazy anyway you know." '

I asked her if any of the other women had followed her example. 'The other women in my family,' she said. 'Others like to but they are afraid—not from their husbands, but from their fathers and their husband's fathers. Soon it will be better. Things are changing slowly—under-the-ground-movement, you understand me?'

One evening Nabiha and her husband invited us to their house in Sheikh Othman—it was a wonderful evening, an evening out of so many other similar evenings that for some reason remained crystallised in my mind, caught whole and perfect and clear-cut in every detail. Perhaps it was because I was the only English person present and felt for the first time that it was possible for me to be absorbed into the Arab pattern of life and accepted as an Insider. Ronald was struck down by the Aden Scourge, amoebic dysentery, at the time, and I went on my own in a car they had sent for me.

They lived close by the house where Sheikh Mohamed had entertained us to a luncheon party. Once more a servant unlocked the tall barred gates and the car moved on up a drive overhung with shrubs and trees, dark and spongy in the shadows. The shabby columned front of the house gleamed coral-white ahead of us, with darkened sockets of arched doorways and upper windows where the moon couldn't reach—a great glistening balloon of a moon stuck on the topmost branch of a date-palm.

Everywhere seemed deserted. Where was our host—and the guests? As the car drew up, Nabiha appeared on the steps carrying a paraffin lamp and embraced me in a cloud of French perfume. 'Come—we are on the terrace.' And on the other side of the house was the terrace with about twenty people sitting in the moonlight and the soft butter-yellow glow of more paraffin lamps.

My arrival as the English guest stirred up the smooth pool of familiar company for a moment like the flop of a stone. But gradually the ripples subsided. I was ensconced among the ladies in the semi-circle of deck-chairs at the far end, there was English conversation on either side of me, but otherwise the Arabic rolled on as before, with the private whispers and laughter that always go with it.

'Why do the Arabs whisper so much in company?' I had once asked Sultan Ali.

'But that is *hashush*,' he replied surprised. 'A kind of gossip, private talk. It is polite because that way one avoids disturbing the general topic of conversation with a minor theme.'

The men in turbans and traditional dress were sitting on the ground where carpets and cushions were spread everywhere, some leaning against the low terrace wall, others grouped around Sultan Ali in front of the steps and pillars of the porch. The moonlight lay in fine turquoise flakes on the dark hands and faces, lamplight gilded the reclining silhouettes. At the Sultan's feet his favourite musician sat cross-legged, a grave, grey-bearded man, with a mandolin, shining like a mahogany pumpkin, a drum and a pair of tambourines scattered in the shadows beside him. The whole scene had the quality, static and theatrical, of some eighteenth-century painting entitled 'Oriental Scene'. One could almost lean forward and touch the rich satiny gleam of varnished oil and canvas.

I could distinguish the rotund figure of Emir Ali in earnest conversation with little Sheikh Ahmed. On either side of him were two young men I had not seen before, both wearing the long Laheji turbans, one thin and foxy-looking, the other plump and handsome with a narrow moustache.

'Those are the Bridegrooms,' whispered the young girl next to me, a niece of Nabiha's, in tones of awe. 'They are both Princes.' For a moment it was like living in one of Grimm's Fairy-Tales.

Sitting on my other side was a slim dark-haired young woman whose air of quiet assurance marked her out as an emancipated Cairo wage-earner—a school-teacher, in fact. In contrast, Nabiha's sisters and nieces, newly out of *purdah* and often scorned because of it, were still distinctly uneasy at finding themselves in mixed company, inclined to be self-conscious and gigglish in their manner. I watched them gesturing delicately with their hands as they chattered, antique bracelets and ear-rings shivering together ill at ease with the brash new European skirts and blouses, a dozen different scents striving valiantly with each other, and thought that all of them, old and new types, had something in common—that traditional modesty and grace of bearing which seemed instinctive to every Arab female.

After supper an expectant hush fell over the party. The night breeze of the cool season had sprung up, creaking through the batwing leaves of the palm trees high overhead. The stars glittered densely behind the dark shape of the house roof. One by one the ladies brought out their wraps and settled back in their chairs. The Sultan had flung himself down on some cushions out of the circle of the lamps and lay there in a listening attitude, his head supported against his hand, his gaze turned away towards the garden. In the centre of the group the musicians sat silently, waiting for the signal to start, the grey-bearded singer, Emir Ali with his lute, a small boy with a flute at his lips.

Slowly, imperceptibly, a few thin notes wavered out on the stillness from the flute—to western ears an introductory bar, a sort of wispy preliminary flourish. But the same thing is repeated by the *oud* and continued.

'This is a lovely one,' murmurs the young girl and we are obviously in the middle of a favourite melody. The very strangeness of Arabic music is the inconclusiveness of it. This is a language all its own. We are in a strange country and the signs are unfamiliar. The frail minor notes thread themselves backwards and forwards with spider's-web delicacy, each phrase trailing away seemingly half finished with a dying fall. It is a perfect match for the shadowy, random moods of the Arab conversation, for the thin-spun desert air around us, the fragile elegance of the setting.

Out of the plucking of the mandolin, the alternate quiver and pulse of the tambourine, comes the voice of the Sultan's singer, high-pitched, melancholy, undulating. He sings with closed eyes, eyebrows raised in a yearning expression. Otherwise he sits absorbed and motionless as a statue, straight-backed, his hands resting on his crossed ankles, while the voice trickles out with an uncanny, clairvoyant effect of tranced detachment.

'What are they about, these songs?'

'These are *ghazal*—love songs. What else is there to sing about?'

Now we clap our hands in complicated counter-rhythm to the beat of the music, the hollow-sounding Arab hand-clap made with cupped palms, not the European polite applause version. A sense of excitement grows with the shared rhythms. Suddenly the Sultan springs to his feet and taking the handsome bridegroom by the hand leads him into one of the traditional Laheji dances in the centre of the ring. In some ways the physical pattern of the dance can be described as a combination of Scottish reel, English country dance and French minuet, except that there is about it a passionate undertone, a sensual suppressed *volupté* completely alien to any western product. Turbans fluttering the two men move barefoot across the carpets with high, neat delicate steps and sidesteps, the upper part of their bodies held proudly rigid, heads lifted, eyes cast gravely down. The patter of the drum follows them closely as a shadow. Now they advance to each other, now they retreat, now circle each other like moths round a candle, right hands clasped, left hands at their dagger hilts.

There is no formal end to the dance. Out of breath and laughing the men retire and the ladies take their place. 'Come, you must come too!' they say, drawing me in with them. Suddenly I am relaxed, absorbed into the movement, part of the pattern. Too soon the flute falters and the drum dies away. But somehow in that moment another barrier crumbled. And in my mind the music goes on, the dancing goes on, the moment preserved against time like a fly in amber.

6

The Black Veil

An Arab husband regards a European woman who wishes to make friends with his wife or wives in much the same way as the Russian government looks on visitors from the West. The risk of unfavourable comparisons between the two ways of life was something to be avoided as far as possible.

'Some time,' an Arab friend would say, mentally putting off the evil day, 'some time you must come and meet my family.' 'Family' was always the polite pseudonym for 'wife' in conversation with Europeans. Among Arab friends the reference was even more veiled—'How is your house?' was the traditional way of putting it.

And so for a long time Arab women remained a mystery for me. In the streets they never stood together gossiping in groups in the way of women all over the world but slipped through the crowds like shadows, swathed completely in black silk *sheddas* or shawls apart from a glimpse of a sandalled foot or a henna-ed hand clutching the garment more closely about them. Sometimes one glimpsed a friendly, inquisitive gaze through the black gauze of the face veil. Occasionally it was possible to exchange a smile of greeting inside an Indian shop where a daring customer would half unmask to inspect her purchases more closely, one corner of her veil caught between her teeth to reveal an intriguing triangle of face. Always I found myself wondering what were their lives really like, what sort of ideas and feelings did they have? Most of the European wives I knew dismissed the subject with 'Poor things! But they've never known anything else—they're happy enough. Otherwise they'd do something about it.'

This overlooked the fact that the idea of rebellion was something quite alien to the feminine oriental nature; that in all the other forward-moving Arab countries such as Egypt, Sudan, Lebanon, Syria, Jordan and Iraq, reform had been instituted by government legislation; that in Aden, almost the last bastion of the *purdah* system, such legislation was impossible because government was in the hands of the British, ignorant infidels, whose any attempt at change would be seized upon as an assault on the sacred law of Islam.

I also knew that the domestic law administered in the courts by my husband was still based on a learned Moslem work of the thirteenth century called the Minhaj, and that the application of these inflexible rules often gave rise to much misery and unhappiness. Whether drunk, joking or dying, an Arab husband had only to utter the magic word '*Talaq*' (I dismiss) three times for a divorce to be effective. Most of the upper classes seemed to find it easier to remember the Prophet's injunction that 'of all permitted things divorce is the most hateful in the sight of God'. But the incredible fact remained that for every ten recorded marriages in the Colony, between seven and eight divorces were registered in the Divorce Register. This made Hollywood sound like a haven of cosy married bliss.

Apparently the divorce rate reached an all-time peak soon after the visit to Aden of an Arab crooner who was Egypt's answer to Frank Sinatra. This event rallied the women as no slogan of emancipation ever could. Against all admonitions, chiefly from aged fathers and the religious leaders of the town, they swarmed in their hundreds to glimpse their idol through their veils at an open-air performance, and later reaped the time-honoured punishment for such disobedience.

And what were the other rules which governed the lives of any one of these mysterious black-veiled shadows in the street? To begin with, her husband would be selected by her father on grounds of social and financial eligibility. Unless they were cousins they would not meet until after the separate ceremonies. She might be one of four wives but she had two traditional rights on which she could insist—adequate maintenance and a separate apartment. Otherwise it was a man's world with a vengeance. On

divorce by her husband she would lose her right to any maintenance at all. If she remarried she would have to give up care
and custody of her children. Throughout her marriage she would
have no right to petition for divorce on grounds of cruelty or
infidelity.

Taking these facts into account it was not surprising to learn
that about seventy per cent of the prostitutes in Aden were
divorced women. For these women, without either a value in the
marriage market or training for employment of any kind, it was
the only means of existence.

But all these things were still nothing more than printed facts
to me—a strange and complicated creed reduced to a series of
statistics which however impartial always seems to have a tone of
bewildered western disapproval about them. My husband often
described to me scenes of distress involved in a number of the
domestic cases which came before him. Even so I sometimes wondered whether courtroom episodes were a true mirror of everyday existence in any country. It seemed probable that the truth
lay somewhere between the ominous-sounding legal records and
the 'They're-happy-enough' summing-up of the European wives.

Oddly enough, it was at a birthday party for a Parsee lawyer
that I had my first insight into the real meaning of Moslem marriages. The celebrations were held in the gardens of the Parsee
Fire Temple, a rambling pillared building with polished expanses
of tiled floors glimpsed through half open doors. 'Inside there is a
sacred flame. It is always kept burning—it represents the spirit of
Good, you see—that half of the world against which we believe
the Evil is for ever in combat.' So our lawyer friend told me. But
from outside the flame was not to be seen and I was not invited
to go in. Next to the Temple was the home of the Priest, a shabby
cream-painted house with a white cockatoo swinging and shriek-
ing from a top verandah. The party was the usual thing—lots of
different-coloured lights, drinks and faces; long singsong speeches
laden with those 'fun-book' jokes so dear to the hearts of Indians;
much nudging and giggling among the plump sari-ed ladies;
scores of children in stiff white dresses and shirts, with freshly

oiled liquorice-black hair, whining heavy-eyed around their mothers' skirts and being urged to 'keep awake and enjoy the party'. The general gaiety seemed unaffected by a sinister silhouette which loomed close by. This was the Tower of Silence where the bodies of the Parsee dead are left to be picked clean by the vultures. This was the final fate awaiting most of the prosperously dressed figures around us.

Apart from this macabre note the evening was a dull one until I was introduced to an Arab insurance agent which sounded even duller but proved to be fascinating. He was a short, plumpish man of about thirty-five, wearing a well-pressed suit and a sober tie. He had a kind, intelligent face with a neat V-shaped moustache and coffee-coloured eyes, earnest and prominent behind his spectacles. He told me that next week he was getting married. Like all bridegrooms he was nervously expansive on the subject, eager to discuss his destiny with anyone who would listen to him.

'How do you set out to choose a wife under *purdah* conditions?' I asked him.

'Listen, I will tell you.'

An Arab schoolmaster I knew quite well had joined us—he was also the bridegroom's closest friend. So three chairs were drawn up at a table and we sat down while the insurance agent told us how he had fallen in love with a Cairo girl a few years ago. He wanted to marry her. But this would mean bringing her to Aden to live under *purdah* conditions. She had wanted to come.

'She said she would be content to live on bread and water under any circumstances as long as she was with me. But I told her—that is because we are in love. In a year or two you will be wanting to go out, to the cinema, to the dances, as we do in Cairo. It will never work.'

So he gave up the girl, came back to Aden and decided to remain single in hopes of *purdah* traditions becoming less rigid as in other Arab countries.

'I waited four years. Still conditions were the same. Then I thought I will go mad unless I get married. My nerves were becoming worse and worse.'

'You must remember the Arab bachelor is a very rare species,' here interjected the schoolmaster in a grave voice. The bridegroom leaned earnestly forward across the table.

'So how to go about it? Well, the usual way—I started making enquiries among the women relatives of my family, my mother, my aunts, sisters, nieces, sisters-in-law. Could they recommend a suitable girl? Beauty was not important. I wanted someone of good family and education who could cook well, run a house efficiently and bring up a family as I would wish.'

'And younger than you, of course?'

'Of course. Eventually I had a list of nine candidates with detailed descriptions of face, figure, voice, personality, etc., and I started to make my preferences. Can you imagine how difficult this is without having set eyes on any of them? Talk about this American blind date! Then I came across another dreadful stumbling-block. No sooner did I choose one above the rest, than the sponsors of the other eight would immediately start denying her a single good quality. "But she is fat; have you not been told? She is so fat . . ." "And that one is cross-eyed—don't be fooled. Also very lazy . . ." And so on, until I thought I was going mad again with all the women-folk in the house squabbling among themselves.'

The schoolmaster sighed heavily. 'How I recall the very same scenes myself. One wonders if it is all worth it.'

'Anyway, in despair, I approached a Palestinian girl I knew, the wife of a friend of mine, and out of *purdah*, of course, on account of her nationality. And she produced a tenth candidate for my list. Well, you know, in place of photographs which are strictly forbidden, it was my custom to lie upon my bed in the dark and summon up a mental picture of each candidate. It sounds incredible I know. But in time each girl became a real, clear person in my mind. And it was always with this last tenth girl that I felt most at ease. After three sleepless nights in succession I finally made up my mind.'

'So you wrote her a letter?' I asked.

'Good gracious me, no! This is what we do. The next day I

asked my best friend to approach the girl's father. He is a well-to-do dentist in the town. Then the following day I make an appointment to see him myself—not for my teeth but for his daughter, of course! By this time he had obtained all particulars of my character and career and seemed agreeable to my becoming his son-in-law. "But first I must consult my wife," he said. A week later he told me the thing was settled and the marriage contract was arranged between us.'

'How much did you pay?' asked the schoolmaster conversationally.

'Five thousand shillings on the spot and another five thousand at a later date.'

The schoolmaster whistled. 'Almost a record I should say.'

I asked what the usual figure was.

'About three thousand,' said the insurance agent. 'Oh, all the other bridegrooms are furious with me.' He laughed. 'But the fathers of the unmarried girls of Aden are delighted!'

'And what happens to this money?'

'The first five thousand shillings will be used by the bride's family to buy her trousseau and personal things. The deferred dowry is usually kept in case of emergency—divorce, or the death of the husband,' he went on. 'The marriage ceremony takes place in three weeks,' adding proudly, 'One thing about we Arabs, we have none of your long engagements!'

I didn't like to point out that as he was unable to see his bride-to-be even through a window, hospital-style, there would be little point in such an arrangement.

He told us that he would be having a party for about five hundred men, while his fiancée would be the centre of celebrations among the women in her family's house. Then she would be taken to the house of her new husband the following day.

He hesitated for a moment and plucked indecisively at his neat little moustache. 'I don't want to offend you in any way but I feel I must speak of certain matters in order to make my outlook quite clear to you. You see, I do not intend to consummate the marriage on the first night according to custom.'

'It is a cruel practice,' agreed the schoolmaster. 'Too sudden for the poor girl.'

'Yes,' agreed the bridegroom with the pride of a liberal man. 'My family may be furious but, never mind, I shall let her get used to the idea of a husband first. After all, why the hurry? I have married her for life.'

'For life,' he repeated to himself, a sudden expression of anxiety on his face. 'One can't help wondering about her . . . after all, she has seen me by now—a peep through a shutter when I went to the house, or something like that. But for me—not even a snapshot.' He shrugged his shoulders. 'Well, it's a lottery. One must accept one's fate.'

I found myself remembering this conversation when a week later I was invited with a friend to the women's celebrations of another wedding. They were being held in one of the merchant's houses in the middle of Crater. Standing outside on the pavement we could hear above the noise of the traffic the sound of the women's ululations—lovely word for that ecstatic trilling sound they could produce somewhere at the back of their tongues for special occasions.

Just inside the dark little doorway our host left us. 'I can come no further,' he said. 'Now it is women only.'

As we climbed three flights of narrow stairs, past mysterious doors and sounds and smells of cooking, the warbling grew louder until in a small room at the top of the house we arrived at its source. The door was open, the room crammed to the threshold with Arab women of all varieties, shapes and sizes—brown faces, ivory faces, young ones, old ones, some pure bred, others, mostly sewing-women, with strong traces of Javanese or African blood. At the sight of strangers there was a general fluttering movement like a startled aviary. Then a stout middle-aged woman in a long velvet robe, with a pair of steel spectacles perched incongruously on the end of her nose and the anxious expression of brides' mothers all the world over, came weaving her way through towards us. She kissed hands in the usual graceful way of welcome and gestured us to two small upright chairs standing uncertainly in the middle of the room in our honour. We said, many thanks, we would prefer to sit on the floor with the other guests where there were low couches and rugs and cushions laid. So the chairs were whisked away again amidst a murmur of approval.

'And the bride?' asked my friend, whose Arabic was more accomplished than my own.

I had supposed the cause of the celebrations was to make her appearance later. But the mother, forging on ahead of us, waved aside a cluster of women to reveal a small shrouded shape crouched on a brass bed, in the corner of the room. This was the bride.

'The enthronement ceremony,' my friend whispered as we went closer. 'In the old days she would sit in state like this any time up to ten days. Now it is only about two.'

There was an indefinable atmosphere of awe about this sacrificial figure on its altar of pillows. Of all the women in the room she alone was veiled. Her dress and shawls glittered with embroidery and over her head hung a canopy of tasselled damask. She neither spoke nor moved as we stood in front of her, merely remained in the same seated pose, her head meekly inclined as though under the weight of the heavy silk and the invisible burden of ceremonial. The problem of greeting was solved by the mother who lifted the bride's black face-veil a discreet few inches and gestured us to look beneath. From the shadows the face of the statue smiled wanly back at me, then was covered again. Finally our hostess uncovered first a hand, then a foot, both equally motionless, for us to admire the intricate patterns drawn in black henna-like lace mittens.

Then we rejoined the general throng sitting in a rough circle facing the bride who continued to remain aloofly detached from all the proceedings. The chatter was terrific with much tossing of plaits and flicking of stoles and fluttering of painted hands, each movement giving fire to the wonderful ceremonial jewellery— the carved gold belts, the pearl-stranded necklaces, the long swinging ear-rings and clustered rings. Very strong in the room was a feeling of delighted freedom, the heady, unrestricted lightness of release—uncovered faces, raised voices, a sense of importance. Such a feeling would be impossible amongst a similar group of European women.

To them an all-female gathering would be just an item in the day's programme, and a rather dull item at that. For Arab women this sort of thing was a major part of their lives, and a very significant and exciting part. The streets outside seemed unreal as a dream, detached as a back-cloth, a confusion of masculine noise and energy. Here they were free in their small rooms, their women's world, and they were happy.

And now the drums started, small drums made of goatskin. In the far corner of the room squatted the players, four African slave-women, two of them of seemingly incredible age. They wore long loose robes of brightly-patterned African cotton and round their ankles heavy bracelets of antique silver hung with bells. Unfalteringly they beat out a complicated cross-rhythm with the flats of their hands, flinging back their heads, rolling their eyes, mouthing the old mysterious verses in a joyful state of trance. They told me that some of the songs were in praise of the bride, some in praise of the guests and some in praise of the Prophet. After each verse came a chorus—'*Hudaeyani wa hudani wa hadum*,' which like most choruses meant little but rolled effectively off the tongue.

On one side of the drummers sat an ancient great-grandmotherly figure sucking contentedly at a long striped hookah with an elaborate silver base. On the other side a blind woman squatted with her back to the wall, swinging her head from side to side with the music and clapping her hands with rising excitement.

All at once the drumming reached a peak of energy. One by one the players rose and advanced towards the bride on her canopied bed, finally beating out the rhythm almost against her face with a kind of savage relentlessness.

There was a general movement of all the women towards her and supported by them, like some brightly-coloured plaster saint in a religious procession, she disappeared through the doorway, preceded by the mother.

'Now she is going to be bathed and dressed in new clothes,' said someone.

Behind them came two maidservants carrying soap, towels, rose-water and armfuls of fresh silks, and at the rear of the procession two women with silver trays of smoking incense—a scent which would never leave her during the days of celebration.

Hustled along in the general stream we came to a large landing two flights down. The bride had already disappeared behind a small door opposite and while we waited the dancing began, first in pairs, then in groups of six. Sometimes weaving their long plaits, sometimes extending a shawl with one delicately poised hand, they moved to a simple gliding step with a fascinating mixture of feminine assurance and traditional modesty. Around the walls the older women sat gossiping, clapping idly in time to the drums or smoking hookahs. Eventually the English women were drawn in, protesting of course, but to no purpose. As the rhythm grew louder, the protests became weaker, the layers of polite dignity succumbed to the universal beat, and soon the white Sunday-Church hats were bobbing more or less in time with the smooth black heads and the music raced faster and faster.

At a signal from one of the guests it stopped. In the middle of the breathlessness and laughter there was a hush. Through the door appeared the small puppet figure still heavily veiled but in different colours, and supported as before by the procession of close relatives and maidservants. As she passed us on her way upstairs again she stopped for a moment and a hand that trembled slightly emerged from the draperies to adjust the pendant on her head. Then she moved on again.

A pretty young Arab woman next to me murmured, 'Poor thing, she is terrified to death already. Well—that is how it is to be a bride.'

I asked how old the bride was.

'Fifteen, two months ago.'

This time the party had assembled in another room—one of those dim scented town rooms typical of a wealthy merchant's house, full of Victorian furniture and pink satin beds. Here the bride would receive gifts of money from the guests.

As for us, we made our apologies and slipped away down the stairs again. Through the open door of the kitchen they were busy dividing loaves of freshly-baked bread, meat and fruit on to the stacked dishes. I could have stayed, missed the lunch party where I was due if I could manage it. But beneath the warmth of the welcome we were still strangers in the house among the old customs and emotions. Perhaps it was better to go after all . . .

The Sultan of Lahej's family was, I suppose, a world of its own in this country of contradictions—a country where class levels remained rigidly fixed in an antique pattern, yet where 'privileged' members of society could eat and sit with their servants without loss of dignity to either party in a way that made 'democracy' a superfluous word.

On the day before I went to tea with the Sultan's harem at the Aden palace, Sultan Ali warned me with gentle irony, 'No doubt you are expecting the usual thing—hundreds of dancing girls with few garments, marble pools, sherbet, oh, and, of course, all those great fierce eunuchs on guard at the doors.' He clicked his tongue disapprovingly, 'Honestly, all you people know of Arabia when you come here is the Hollywood version of *The Thousand and One Nights*, not to mention *Scheherazade*. Do you even know what the word harem means?' I shook my head apologetically.

'It is simply the plural of the Arabic for woman, that is the womenfolk of the family. As you know I have one wife only, but,' he rolled his eyes heavenwards, 'hundreds, more than hundreds of relations.'

'Then as for . . .'

'Then as for anything else you may be thinking of in your decadent western fashion, please remember three things. That this is a very poor, therefore a very moral part of Arabia. That modern times anyway would not permit me to follow the habits of certain of my ancestors.' He grinned, 'Also, that women very much scare me . . .'

Even so, there was still a drama about the way the front doors of the Palace were slammed to by the servants and bolted and barred behind me as soon as I had crossed the threshold the following afternoon. The Sultana was coming downstairs to meet me first—a rare event—and all precautions were being taken against the horrid event of surprise callers on His Highness.

Sultan Ali was waiting in the main reception room and at his side a fat youngish woman wearing the traditional Laheji dress, sleeveless and loose from shoulder to hem with a gauzy embroidered shawl over her head. My first impression was of the strangeness of seeing an Arab husband and wife standing side by side and of the introduction.

'This is my wife, Miriam—Miriam, this is June.'

So far Farid was the only Arab I had ever seen with his wife.

Then we shook hands and inspected one another while exchanging polite greetings through Sultan Ali, her English being very limited.

'June,' she repeated carefully, sounding the J like a G, then gave up with a smile.

'I told you this was a difficult word for Arabs,' said Sultan Ali.

Her face was plump and powdered, with dark-red lipstick to match her nail varnish, and the Jewish-type features one noticed in so many Arabs—shrewd dark eyes, curved nose, small pouting mouth, and pencilled eyebrows. She had a sweet smile and an air of calm self-possession, remarkable for a woman who had never travelled outside her own district and rarely outside her house. Two long shiny plaits emerged at her waist from beneath her shawl, tied together with a jingling circlet of gold coins.

She was wearing her best jewellery, all of it, matching and otherwise, heavy gold bracelets, superb emerald ear-rings and pendant, an elaborate many-stranded necklace of pearls and rubies, and on her right hand a single enormous diamond. I recognised this from a description by Sultan Ali a few weeks before—'She pestered me and pestered me for it—a merchant brought it to show me—and in the end I gave in. It's a good family investment anyway.'

After a few minutes we left the Sultan and I followed her down the draughty Victorian corridor and up a flight of stairs. The Sultan was right. There were no eunuchs standing at the entrance, only a couple of small children swinging on the nursery gate at the top step, who tottered rapidly away in the opposite direction with cries of alarm at the sight of the strange visitor. Inside the main room there was a quantity of gilt and tapestry furniture and a circle of women chattering over the teacups in an atmosphere that reminded me strongly of a Women's Institute meeting—not a regular meeting, the Christmas fancy-dress party admittedly— but nevertheless the resemblance was there.

I was sat down next to a young girl I had already met at Nabiha's, a niece of the Sultan's called Ahmina. She had lost her shyness with me and spoke English well. For the first ten minutes she struggled to untangle the intricate web of family relation- ships surrounding us. Out of a bevy of cousins, mothers-in-law, sisters-in-law, two women stood out. One was an animated handsome person with proud features and a wonderful Rossetti neck who looked far too young to be the mother of the Sultana. The other was an elderly woman of great dignity sitting on a chair of honour, a figure out of Chaucer in her black-velvet snood head-dress, which framed a face of parchment elegance and severity.

'That is the aunt of the Sultan,' whispered Ahmina. 'She is a spinster and she is very strict. It is she who makes the law for us here, you know.'

'But how?'

'Everything in the house is decided by her. Who is to marry whom, what is to be the name of the new baby, which material is to be used for our *Idd* dresses, what recipe the cook shall use for our dinner—we all eat up here on our own of course, never with the men.'

'Has she travelled outside Aden at all?'

'Once she visited England—against her will, of course, but she had to accompany one of the children for an operation. Do you know, she wore her Laheji dress and her *purdah* shawl over her European clothes; she said there were far too many people in London, and shut herself up in a house in Brighton until the time came to travel again. She even refused to answer the telephone—in case there was a man at the other end of it! You are lucky to see her today—it is only lately she has agreed to meet women outside the family.' She heaved a sigh of mock despair. 'We spinsters! What a fiercesome lot we are.'

Poor Ahmina, who had just that year reached the ripe old age of seventeen, was obsessed by the thought of a fate that was to an Arab woman nothing short of disaster. Of all the young girls at the Palace she was the only one so far unbetrothed. Shy and spectacled and pretty, she looked a model secretary in her English skirt and blouse. This time last year she was living in Russell Square, London W., waiting for her sister to complete a course of medical treatment. Now she is back in *purdah* again with no eligible young man left for her.

'You know, it is not the Sultan's fault,' she told me. 'He is progressive in his ideas and quite willing for me to marry anyone of suitable standing and character. But these old women! They refuse to let an outsider into the family, and so it has to be someone of our own blood. At least that gets around the *purdah* conditions and one can meet one's future husband beforehand because he is a relation—but even so! Everyone knows what a bad thing these inter-family marriages are—the Sultan himself has said so. But what can he do with so many women against him?'

Apparently, with the support of her father, she did win one small victory. According to custom, even today unmarried women are not permitted to attend the bridal ceremonies at Lahej but she appeared in European dress and stayed—despite the barrage of criticism and insult from the older women. Her father was so infuriated by the obstinacy of the women that he gave her official permission to attend all such celebrations in future.

'Sultan Ali married outside the family, of course,' she said. 'That was politics, you see. Her family are very wealthy and powerful in the state and there was a lot of trouble going on when he was made the Sultan.'

Then she took me into the balcony corridor and showed me the highly organised system of vantage points for inspecting visitors—peep-holes and window-cracks sprinkled strategically through the women's quarters where one could safely see and not be seen.

'And what do you do all day?'

'Oh, English lessons in the morning, rest in the afternoon, drive in the evening when it is dark in a closed car of course. And then there is singing and dancing and cards and *hashush* and playing with the children. It is best of all when the men of the family come up to see us and tell us the news.'

We rejoined the circle. I sat next to the Sultana on an Empire couch with the Rossetti-like mother on the other side, who spoke a little hesitant English. She told me they were just discussing Elizabeth Taylor's new hair-style, and pointed to a pile of glossy American magazines on a nearby table. 'Sometimes we see a film in the Palace,' she said. 'But not very often.'

I started telling them about a film with Elizabeth Taylor I had seen yesterday evening, while they all listened eagerly to the highly-inaccurate translations by the mother and Ahmina combined. 'And what else?' they cried as soon as I had finished. 'Tell us what other news. What about the party at Farid's last week?'

So I related what the ladies wore, what we ate, who was there and they sat intrigued as children listening to a bedtime story, *kohl*-ringed eyes huge in their pale faces.

'And what school is Prince Charles at now?' 'Is it true violet is the fashionable colour in England?' 'How much is the dowry of an English bride?' 'And how many rooms are there in Buckingham House?'

I would have been reduced to a state of collapse in a very short time but for a fortunate intermission when the Sultana remembered she had to send a message to her husband downstairs to make an appointment to see him after tea, and everyone rushed around looking for a pencil and paper.

Then two of the brides-to-be came shyly in. They were twins of fourth-form age and had obviously just completed their elaborate toilette, consisting of identical taffeta skirts, lace blouses and velvet cummerbunds. After them appeared a nursemaid with the latest baby to be dandled and admired in his frills and flounces, a gold locket on a chain round his fat neck containing an inscription from the Koran, and a curl of hair. By this time the light was fading, the lamps were lit and half a dozen slave women had crept in quietly in the far corner and started an unobtrusive accompaniment to the chatter with drums and tambourines.

'Now dancing!' cried the handsome mother of the Sultana, with the enthusiasm of someone hitting on a completely novel idea. One of the younger women seized a tambourine and put it in her hands—'And the *oud* for the Sultana!'

The next minute the usual swaying, hand-clapping ring was winding its way among the tea-tables, flying veils and skirts missing the Crown Derby by inches.

Then as swiftly the whole atmosphere changed. We were invaded. Lounging into the room came the two young princes, in tribal dress but bareheaded, to be deluged by a wave of eager welcome from everyone except the betrothed twins. At the first glimpse of their husbands-to-be they had disappeared through the other door in a flurry of muffled giggles and high-pitched protest, like fourth-formers fleeing the wrath of two prefects whom they secretly adored. Their mother, a good-looking woman in an advanced state of pregnancy, shook her head with fond indulgence.

'They are stupid,' said Ahmina to me disgustedly. 'They have seen these boys all their lives. They are cousins. And now they must pretend to be so modest.'

Everyone clustered around the visitors chattering. The Sultana's mother swept up to me and announced: 'Now the bridegrooms are here. Now you will see Haifai.'

'Who is Haifai?' I asked rather dazed. 'The third bridegroom?'

This remark she greeted with upraised hands and peals of laughter, passed it around the circle in Arabic where it was received with the same delight. Eventually Emir Mohamed took pity on me and beckoned me over to an alcove where a new radiogram reposed, monumental and glossy. 'This is Hi-Fi,' he said, stroking its shining flanks proudly. He took out a stack of brightly-coloured American records from the cabinets, 'What shall we play—Rock and Roll?'

There was an immediate stir of enthusiasm, which brought even the modest twins back into the room.

'Yes—yes. But first you must show us how to do it properly, June,' said Ahmina who was the only one who had successfully mastered the English J sound.

I demurred. But excitedly everyone gathered round and took up the cry at the tops of their voices.

'Goon, Goon!—rockintroll, rockintroll!'

Thus commanded there was no alternative. With a rigid Emir Mohamed as partner, I did my best, heavily inhibited by the dignified furniture, the family portraits and in the background the expression of stupefied disapproval on the face of the aunt.

When I left the two princes and their betrothed were performing a grave minuet to the vibrations of Elvis Presley. It was a sight I shall never forget.

7

Best of Both Worlds

By this time I knew I was some way out beyond the mysterious boundary marks laid down by the European camp in their connections with those people in whose country they were living. Being a good Colonial wife of course entailed the duty of being-nice-to-the-locals. It was the white woman's share of the burden. But it need not involve anything more strenuous than an inter-racial cocktail party once a year, an occasional lunch to which one invited one or two of the jollier Arab notables and a squire's-wife type of appearance at the odd tea party which after all often provided hilarious material for bridge-table anecdotes the following morning. ('—and the food, my dear, you couldn't tell the flies from the currants!') For many of the commercial and service wives life was even more restricted—an Arab was simply that irritating creature in the kitchen who always forgot to put the salt in with the potatoes or someone who took two whole days to mend a simple leak in the bathroom drainpipe.

And here was I visiting the houses of Arabs regularly, making close friends among them, ploughing across that dreary desert to Lahej where as everyone knew there was nothing more to be seen if you had been there once. And the Sultan was definitely 'dangerous'—politically, of course. It was obvious I showed every symptom of becoming that unspeakable embarrassment, the Arabian addict. Ahead of me lay the usual grim fate—long beads, folk-weave smocks, obscure lecture tours—to the accompanying drum-roll of comment, 'going native' or 'losing one's standards' or 'giving the wrong impression, if you know what I mean,' which I never did anyway.

Not that I stood alone. Among the small group of Arab enthusiasts, divided by the other women into the 'do-gooders' and the merely 'odd', my favourite was Isabel, the middle-aged wife of one of the leading Government officials. My first glimpse of her was from the verandah of someone's house soon after our arrival in Aden, when I was watching a religious procession, known locally as the Fishermen's Feast, wind its way through the streets below. 'I can't think where Isabel is,' remarked my hostess irritably, 'she said she would be coming up to get a good view for a sketch.'

'Good Heavens! Surely that can't be her down there,' exclaimed another guest, pointing an indignant finger towards the very centre of the throng now surging towards the doors of the mosque. Out of a sea of bobbing turbans I picked out one that looked different—it was a feminine European version of a turban in an elegant dove grey, and beneath it an attractive face in dark glasses, and a slim figure in a matching linen frock. Smiling and chatting with vague charm, the unknown lady threaded her way through the press, pausing now and then to jot down a sketch on a large drawing-pad and finally settling down with a portable easel on a nearby hillock encircled by a milling mob of admirers but as composed as though alone in her studio at home. Obviously the sun didn't worry her either. It wasn't until about half an hour later that she nonchalantly arranged a parasol over her head, and she was still at work when I went away.

I may have left the boundaries of the main European camp behind but that didn't mean I was already fully ensconced behind the opposite frontier. Often I had the disconsolate feeling of being lost somewhere in between in a sort of no-man's land. Those Arabs I knew best treated my enthusiasms with a kindly cynicism which was partly justified. In actual fact I was busy trying to have the best of both worlds. And as a would-be Arabist I had a number of glaring faults. I was lazy about learning the language, lazy about reading the histories and putting up with physical discomforts; I admired without discrimination and in a shallow two-dimensional way—a modern prototype of those nineteenth-century travellers of the Grand Tour, ready to swoon with delighted sensibility at every 'picturesque' ruin and 'romantic' view; with Arabs I often showed off in my role of Sympathetic English Friend, unconsciously posing myself to advantage in the foreground of every new impression; I had a huge appetite for Arab flattery which I swallowed whole. An elderly newspaper editor with a flair for phrasing summed it up—'You are eager to skim the cream of sensation but it is the milk of fact which is more nourishing—and infinitely more digestible.'

Yet these Europeans who only met Arab people at official functions could hardly be blamed for their lack of enthusiasm. Such occasions were usually marked by a rarefied atmosphere of strain and artificiality—like the first five minutes of a children's party extended for two or three hours. It was unfortunate but obviously true that both people were much nicer on their own.

It was about this time that the European team was dramatically enlarged by the arrival of a new oil refinery.

A few miles out of Aden was the tiny fishing village of Bir Fukum. One day the surrounding desert was barren, the next it had blossomed in a way the Bible writers could never have imagined in their wildest dreams. Out of the sand and the moon-like rocks and craters of that desolate corner of Arabia a highly-organised town of four thousand inhabitants sprang up at mushroom speed. Oil towers rose skywards, roads unrolled like magic carpets, housing estates fell into line with parade-ground precision. Government watched the progress of this monument to British and American engineering with the grudging admiration experienced by parents towards the over-forward child prodigy next door.

A great majority of the refinery employees were local-born Arabs. They formed a new industrial population, many of them young training apprentices who in the future would constitute a unit of considerable influence in the political scene.

From our house I watched a road growing in the sea, the new causeway linking Little Aden, as the refinery was known, with big Aden. Obviously faith wasn't the only thing which could move mountains. Every day half a dozen giant-mawed pieces of machinery would gnaw another hunk out of a convenient rocky slope nearby. The hunks would be carried away in lorries, broken up and added with ant-like industry by scores of coolies to the end of the miniature peninsula which was to be the road to the refinery. It expanded like a telescope until it finally touched the shore of the opposite bay and the link between the two Adens was complete.

Thereafter it became the fashionable thing to spin along the sleek ribbon of tarmac for a late afternoon drive. With the blue of the water so close on either side and a new receding view of the shore behind, the causeway had the romantic quality of an English seaside pier. Sometimes an obliging school of flying fish would somersault out of the waves or a pelican or flamingo wing its way slowly upwards. It was also an irresistible temptation for speeders, and the roadside was always littered with upturned cars from which the drivers had miraculously escaped uninjured the previous night. The road pointed directly west and the best time for a drive was at sunset—the fabulous Aden sunset—when one seemed to be caught in the very centre of a great slow-folding fan of light and colour along the opposite horizon.

The oil town itself was half an hour's drive beyond the causeway. For most Europeans in Aden it was a heaven-sent extension to the cramped confines of the Colony. It soon became an enviable thing to have 'friends at Little Aden'. Driving up at night one saw it lit up and glittering in the distance like a skyscraper city. In daylight it was more mundane, a child's meccano set left behind in a sandpit. By night and day the orange flame of the oil flare roared above the refining tower, a landmark for miles around.

'It never goes out,' said our host in the same proud tones as the Parsee at the fire-temple. But I hardly liked to ask him whether or not it represented the Spirit of Good. Everywhere there were large notice-boards, directions in two or three languages, neatly wired off pathways, rows and rows of utility bungalows, some of them with gardens and husbands in shirt-sleeves clipping the hedges because it was Sunday afternoon.

'They're even going to send us out lawn-mowers now,' our

friend told us. We also passed two churches, large-scale bungalows with a peaked gable and a cross, one Catholic and the other Protestant—an open-air cinema, a hospital, a school, a sports ground, and a vast and bleak-looking recreation hall, all steel and plate glass. Around the communal-housing lines strolled Arabs, Indians and Somalis, most of them in European clothes and looking a little lost amongst so much order and efficiency. The general atmosphere was a mixture of a working Butlin's Camp and an English village with the Manager's wife as lady of the manor, stepping out of a black Daimler to present the cups after the sports and receive another bouquet.

Like every other guest we oo'ed and ah'ed at the Wellsian wonder of the vast refining plant with all those intestinal pipelines throbbing away in a special barbed-wire enclosure of its own. Like every other guest we admired the compact lay-out of the bungalows, the magazine kitchens, the over-efficient air-conditioning system which sometimes converted the place into a cosy residential 'fridge. Like every other guest we drove away sweating normally again and murmuring, 'But thank heavens we don't have to live there.'

As one wife explained, 'It's just like living on board a big ship. . . . The same gossip with the wives at the shop after breakfast, the same games session in the afternoon—tennis, not deck-quoits of course, the same feuds and friendships among the passengers, the same drinks in the next-door cabin or the first-class lounge before dinner. The only difference is we're not going anywhere!'

Once or twice we went to dinner with the General Manager which was always a very grand affair and much more luxurious than Government House. They lived a few miles beyond the refinery town in a large ultra-modern villa which perched with a startling Daliesque effect on one of the prehistoric crags surrounded by a waste of rock and sand and sea. Inside there were suites of fashionable blanched furniture, fitted carpets from Waring and Gillow, small refrigerators in every guest bedroom, spring daffodils flown from Devonshire on the dinner-table, and frozen caviare from France to eat. After dinner we trailed out in our long dresses on to an enormous terrace where, joined by the men, we watched an Alec Guiness comedy and ignored the moon rising over the desolate lunar landscape all around us. Altogether an object lesson for those who talk of the decline of western civilisation.

After the Refinery, the Alhambra Night-club was Aden's most important new institution. It was Aden's first night-club ever and caused a stir of controversy and discussion. If by the term night-club one imagined clustered tables, a cosy pool of polished dance-floor under the discreet glow of lighting concealed within pink satin walls, then the Alhambra was something of a shock. It was an open-air arena of dusty concrete under white neon strips adjoining an Indian cinema and set up by the enterprising Indian manager. The pallid glare picked out like a searchlight the faces of the clientèle sitting around the dance space—a closely-packed wall of all the known colour graduations between brick red and pure black. It picked out the Italian band on their gaudy little platform flashing gilt and ivory smiles and instruments, the grubby check table-cloths and in the background the trellis-work surround of faded green. The bar was suffused by *crème-de-menthe*-coloured illuminations which gave a Toulouse Lautrec effect to the groups of local tarts and pimps lolling over their drinks. Undertones of Indian singing and sudden wild shouts of dialogue from the adjoining cinema accompanied the chatter and the dance music but nobody seemed to notice. Rhinestones sparkled on coffee-brown décolletés, perhaps a real diamond or two on fat, moist Middle East fingers. People were gossiping in Arabic, Hindustani, Somali, Dutch, French and Italian.

Then just in time for the famous floor-show the visiting English élite ambled in, parties of government officials, service officers, business managers and their wives, pink and talcumed and after-dinner-looking. The Alhambra might be a shady-looking place with a faintly naughty reputation—everyone knew what those girls really were—but still one was given the seats of honour, cushioned, and it was all very 'amusing'. Besides it was escapades like this that provided the light relief at the dinner-tables after the usual talk about 'Are we losing our grip on the place?' or 'How to deal with those dangerous half educated types', and so on.

There was always some dismay when 'those girls', or Les Girls as they were billed, finally made their appearance as a band of healthy bouncing peasant women in a Greek folk dance, eminently respectable and rather long. To the relief of the audience, this was followed by individual acts in which the plump, jaded-looking but still enticing proportions of the ladies were revealed more fully. Most of them were Greeks and they were at the end of a tour of the Middle East, but their spirit and energy was undiminished. One of them walked the slackwire, a teetering hourglass in black velveteen tights, spinning coloured rings in mid-air and catching them between clenched teeth, the powdered face tensed in a mask of anxiety, finally flopping from a height of ten feet into a splits position, graceful, triumphant and exhausted. Another brunette, tightly bound in white satin, sang sentimental French songs with throaty sighs and languid sexy gestures which drew enormous applause, especially from the back rows. Clinging fiercely to her position as star of the team was a middle-aged lady who ogled us, pekinese-like, with a kind of desperate pertness over the top of an enormous fan of scarlet ostrich feathers. But the favourite of the evening was undoubtedly Dominique. She was very large and exuberantly curved with a dead-white face, square and handsome, her black hair oiled into a chignon that made her look like a practical French housewife, a kiss-curl plastered on each temple and a black beauty-spot on each cheek. Dominique's speciality was to hurl her vast frame into a non-stop circle of incredibly light, absolutely soundless cartwheels. There was an uncanny effect about this lack of impact, almost as though she were bouncing through space like a big white balloon. At the same time she disrobed herself of each frothy garment except two, dispensing them on her way round to favoured admirers. The first time we went to the Alhambra was the opening night, in aid of charity and dignified to everyone's surprise by the presence of the Governor, a confirmed bachelor. Dominique, however, was undaunted, and it was only due to the alacrity of the A.D.C., a famous catch-fielder at cricket, that a pair of pink lace panties just failed to land in His Excellency's lap.

After the cabaret the girls reappeared in evening dress and joined those tables where men were sitting on their own to drink champagne. The band started up and the dancers re-emerged from their caves in the shadows to trace their patterns on the concrete once more. Couple by couple, the English would leave for sleep and daily boredom again, the women tired in creased dresses, the men bleary about the eyes, dimly aware somewhere of the old vague disappointment after the razzle—those whiskies had tasted most peculiar too, and could that smell really be 'just the harbour' after all. As for the girls, they were no chickens, definitely tatty, perhaps embarrassing too when the wives were there . . . perhaps that was the whole trouble. Still, it was all splendid fun they declared in their loud, stock voices. We must come again—and of course, they did, because as in all Colonies one had to take what entertainment there was.

Distinguished visitors were always top-rank entertainment especially when a full-dress reception was laid on at the Crescent Hotel and the guest of honour was a head of state like Marshal Tito. For weeks beforehand, the ornate invitation cards were prominently displayed in the living-rooms of the fortunate few and affected or nonchalant enquiries made about the composition of the protocol list by the unfortunate many. (—'I mean, good heavens, we couldn't care less about not going ourselves, but it does seem absurd that the X's have been missed out, doesn't it?')

We were invited by mistake and made the most of it. Someone had had the brilliant idea of arranging the reception to start at 6 p.m., an unfamiliar time when the roof-terrace had a sort of theatrical glamour about it with its sweeping view of the harbour and the Arabian coastline beyond. As everyone assembled, the tower clock, in working order for once, struck the hour. Punctually the sun set with a prima donna obeisance into the glow of fading footlights, flanked at either wing by the cardboard silhouettes of stage scenery islands. The lights had not yet come on. While we waited the sky was magically bare for one brief moment

—no sun, moon or stars—just a polished shell reflected pale blue-green in the sea below and the marble floor of the terrace. There was little conversation or movement. No drinks could be served, no cigarettes lit. On our best behaviour, we stood waiting in a solemn circle, the women over-dramatic in the last of the daylight with their evening make-up, gauzy dresses, carefully preserved furs twitched over sun-peeled shoulders, the men strangely sinister as the dimness grew, in their black tail-coats and dead-white fronts. There were little glowing blobs of decorations on their lapels pinned on before leaving home by wives who nervously cursed their gloved fingers and queried the correctness of the kitchen clock. Here and there one of them ran a finger round a stiff collar that chafed like the devil—but never mind—this was an Occasion, something big for Aden, something special to write home about next week.

Suddenly a breeze sprang up, a framework of coloured lights sparked into life around us, and the buzz started that Tito was here. As master of ceremonies the Chief Secretary gestured us into a closer ring and made for the entrance with confident ring-master strides. A fanfare from the two red-turbaned buglers standing on either side of the archway over the entrance broke the silence. Without further ceremony a short thickset figure in the familiar white uniform tufted with gold walked through on to the terrace with the Governor. A party of six men in evening dress followed them. They all looked quite ordinary as they stood there making and receiving the usual preliminary courtesies—the Marshal, broad, tanned and blue-eyed, more like a farmer than a totalitarian ruler, his entourage of a different type, dark and intellectual-looking. And yet something magnetic emanated from them—the faint but unmistakable aura of power. They looked disconcertingly young to British eyes, these national leaders. Not one of the Government heads appeared to be more than forty and even the Marshal at sixty-two somehow gave an impression of youthful middle age.

Introductions took place with the Marshal seated on a dais with a chair on either side of him. The ladies made a bob, the men a sort of compromise between a bow and a nod. Then, wreathed in smoke from his famous pipe-shaped cigarette-holder, the great man waved the couple to be seated for a moment and bent a leonine head to each side in turn in polite conversation. The waiting queue was all agog, particularly the wives, rattling their fans nervously, eyeing the earlier introductions with lynx-like watchfulness and a mental picture of the precedence list. After all, it was something to shake hands with a real live Communist dictator, a good one, of course, and a Communist on a large scale, not to be confused with the unshaven creatures at Hyde Park Corner.

The Foreign Minister, the Secretary General, someone with the title of Chairman of the Executive Council of Serbia, and the others, strolled around informally. They all radiated confidence and vitality and an unhibited national pride, injecting a spontaneous brand of propaganda into every conversation. There were also a number of Yugoslav journalists present. One of them said to me over his third white-lady cocktail, 'Now you know that we don't carry knives between our teeth and wear rings through our noses after all. . . .'

With the winter season arrived a new distraction in the form of a series of monthly race meetings. These were held at the Sports Club, a low cluster of white bungalow-style buildings about a mile into the 'desert', that is about a mile away from the nearest European housing estate at Khormaksar. Alongside the club-house a sprinkling of tee-flags denoted that the sandy waste was in fact a golf-course where every Sunday morning a dogged band of enthusiasts stroked, and plodded and dreamed of Frinton and St Leonards. Behind the club stood the stables where half a dozen horses were kept. Every Sunday afternoon they were led out for the ceremonial game of polo in which half a dozen devotees took part watched by a small group of wives, children and enthusiastic Arab bearers from the bar. The polo had become a sort of mandarin ritual, a sadly-fading relic of imperialist days struggling for survival against a new background of R.A.F. landing strips and refinery towers. The amount of money spent on the horses was always a subject for bitter criticism at the volcanic annual meetings of the club but the pro-horse group was always vindicated with a flourish on the four days out of the year when the races were held.

The first race meeting was in October and this was the 'must' of the social season. Some time before the date, hostesses would rack their weary, heat-ridden brains for suitable eating partners, and invitations for lunch parties 'And the Races' were sent out in all directions.

The lunch parties follow a time-honoured routine—two gin-and-tonics, chicken in aspic, fruit salad and coffee, liqueurs for the men while the ladies disappear to adjust their rarely-displayed hats, gloves and stockings. Then into the cars to the Club where the parking ground is already full of shiny-backed, petrol-and-leather-smelling monsters basking in the sun. Flags fly, crowds gather, in the distance a brass band snorts and whinnies. More hats, gloves and stockings among the ladies—one of whom distinguishes herself further by having a Somali *ayah* walking behind to carry her mink coat—and among the men, pork-pie hats, slung binoculars, an occasional light tweed suit (the sun is cooler in the winter), even the odd shooting-stick sported with a slightly self-conscious air of defiance.

But the British are not the only ones in national costume. Crowding alongside into the paddock are the tribesmen from up-country and the Arab levy soldiers off duty, small, wiry, gleaming men with their cotton kilts in dazzling checks, bare shoulders, daggers at their waists, and head-cloths of orange, green and violet binding their long hair. They study the horses and the Europeans with much interest, displaying a somewhat amused, condescending attitude to the latter, especially to the females, as though to say, 'All these ornaments, bare legs and arms and faces, all this freedom—but we know what you really are—slaves to we men like all the rest.'

Each race takes about five minutes, twice round the white-railed sandy track in front of the Club. There are five races, including a camel race, and the afternoon lasts from 2.30 until

5 p.m. So most of the time is spent walking in the intervals, walking between the paddock ring and the tote shed; walking around the miniature grandstand where behind a galaxy of silver cups sits the Governor and anyone else who may feel they deserve the privilege of a more comfortable view; walking along the club terrace where rows of chairs are set out in school-sports fashion and a well-known winner is greeted at the post with approving applause and cries of 'Well done, Finlayson!' Like the school sports everyone has a fairly accurate idea of the results of each event. There are rarely more than five horses running in each race, perhaps two belonging to the Club, two to Sultan Ali (although Farid sometimes wangles it that his name appears on the card as owner), and another to some up-country sheikh or a wealthy merchant in the town. As a result it is unusual to get back more than double the amount one had laid on the two-shilling tote. Despite this, and the Koranic disapproval of gambling, the tote windows are thronged between every race—Arab business men and English army officers impetuously waving ten-shilling notes, country tribesmen and Government wives digging into their purses for sixpences. Detached from the crowd the half-dozen Rulers who have travelled in from all parts of the Protectorate and stand in an elegant group together, with their expensive Cairo-tailored jackets and gold brocade turbans, sip Coca-Cola in the shade. Equally detached are the *ayahs* in their white shawls, fluttering around a flock of small children playing in the sand outside, and the amateur film enthusiasts perched on walls and roof-tops trying to cram the whole throbbing scene into one small camera. Strong tea and cucumber sandwiches are laid out on tables in the club-house. And after it is all over people gather for drinks in the members' bar, a small dark room full of bits of old harness, and pictures of horses and past presidents usually indistinguishable from each other. Here the talk is all of the success of the afternoon. Everything has gone well they repeated—no tiffs at the weighing-in, no dreadful rumours of poisons or stimulants administered by rival owners in the horses' feeds, no accidents with the nervous ones at the starting-line, no unpleasant disagreements

between the judges, those noble trilbied men stranded at the furthest corners of the track, keeping faithful duty in the beating sun. This is the summing-up, identically the same after every other meeting. But for me the races always summon up a picture that has nothing to do with any of this. There is the smell of sand, the shimmer of heat, and Gilbert and Sullivan from the levy band; above it all remains the moment when Ayesha with handsome Abdul the syce bent double in the saddle and his bare feet kicked free of the stirrups, chestnut mane and white turban flying, streaks first past the winning post with a cry of sheer triumph.

With the cooler weather everyone seemed more energetic than ever. The opening gambit at cocktail parties about The Cure for prickly heat was exchanged for a boasting session about the number of blankets one could sleep under at night—'Positively freezing, my dear!' On Christmas Day we were able to wade through roast turkey and plum pudding and carols with the temperature only slightly above that of an English south coast heatwave. The Indian shop windows were plastered with tinsel, frost and cotton-wool snow while we wistfully hankered for the slither of real town-slush underfoot. On New Year's Eve sober Legislative Council members became St Trinian's schoolgirls, frilly-legged Financial Secretaries danced a can-can and we all gnawed our fingers in a frenzy of suspense as His Excellency, lightly disguised as an eighteenth-century gentleman, awarded the prizes at the traditional Club ball. Every weekend, we went to see cricket or football games in which the referee disputes always provided the most exhilarating moments. One memorable evening we conga-ed to a Latin American band round the rugged masts of a replica sailing ship of the Brazilian Navy.

At least once a week we tramped the rubber corridors of one of those less romantic vessels, referred to by superior travellers as 'floating gin palaces', in search of some elusive traveller referred to in a letter from home in such terms as 'Old Mrs X—you remember you met her nephew two years ago—on her way to Australia, would love to see you . . .' In the meantime the unknown Mrs X would be tramping the Steamer Point streets acting on advice from the same source at home just to 'ask any policeman where to find them'. I think at home they must have visualised the scene differently—one small row-boat gliding into an isolated little bay with ourselves waving a welcome from an overlooking window to the solitary English figure in the stern. The fact that Aden is the second largest British port in the world surprises most people who have never been there.

Soon after Christmas we sported our hats and gloves again for the official opening of Legislative Council with the Governor in plumed helmet and gold braid, the Chief Justice drooping like a lamb for the slaughter in his curled white-wool wig. The programme of procedure was rounded off with a brief excerpt of Council business, a sort of exhibition match, usually as inspired as it was well rehearsed.

In the women's clubs we salved our consciences in a number of good causes, dividing enormous bowls of powdered milk at the clinics among the battered tin pots and kettles thrust forward by the queue of ragged under-fives and pregnant mothers, doling out free meat and rice at an annual feast for the older children. On a more fanciful level was the good-works enthusiast who volunteered to teach Arab women Scottish dancing and Swedish drill. The cynics were baffled by the zeal with which the students flung aside their veils—after a thorough search had been made through the building for any sign of men—and sprang into an eightsome reel. The exercises were less popular though one member of the class told me she had demonstrated them at home and her husband thought them very pretty.

Women's clubs and societies were open to every race. All seemed to run smoothly enough apart from the famous incident at a combined meeting when a rebel splinter of Arab representatives staged a walk-out and set up a rival group in protest against the election of so many European members to the Committee. 'Arab nationalism raising its ugly head again I'm afraid,' commented the chairwoman afterwards with a sad shake of her head.

All this was Aden, and somehow it still wasn't enough. 'Best of both worlds' had a hollow ring about it these days.

8

The Coptic Cross

It was about this time that we flew to Asmara, capital of Eritrea, for a week's holiday. It was only about a couple of hours' journey away, but when we stepped out of the plane we felt as light-headed as space travellers emerging on to the moon's surface. The sun was shining but the air was like champagne, chilled and dry and intoxicating after the sodden humidity of Aden. In this rarefied atmosphere every surrounding detail stood out in crisp focus as though one were short-sighted and had just put on a pair of new spectacles. The lawns and flower-beds outside the airport buildings glittered with unnatural brightness, even the people looked more vivid, moving and speaking at a different rate of tension. In the Customs department everyone was recklessly expending surplus energy in a spate of argument and indignation.

'I'm afraid it is more chaotic than usual,' apologised our Aden friend, the Italian count, who lived in Asmara and had come to meet us. 'We have just handed over the administration to the Eritreans—but they will settle down eventually.'

A customs officer in brand-new military-style uniform chalked the necessary cross on each piece of baggage with the reluctance of one marking the plague-sign on his own door, another leafed through our passports, and we were out. We were staying in a cottage in the grounds of the American Consulate, kindly loaned us by the Consul. Our meals we had with the count whose own small villa was full of family on holiday from England. The Consulate had the sheltered calm of some retreat—smooth lawns, regularly groomed with automatic sprinklers, gravel paths, blonde secretaries driving past in silent elongated cars, the purr of air-conditioners. In the cottage we spent the first half-hour unpacking and joyfully exclaiming on the coldness of everything we touched.

Asmara itself might have been a continental town invaded by large numbers of polite, sepia-skinned, woolly-headed people. Or so it seemed to the visiting, cockily upside-down European mentality, forgetting that this was 'their' country and taking in only the superficial Italian veneer. This was still very much in evidence though cracking rapidly.

The Eritrean men had an impressive style of dress—long trousers, tight as jodhpurs, white shawls draped like togas and broad-brimmed felt Garbo hats. The women wore ankle-length cotton robes, the same shawls and a bizarre hair-style as formidable as a hat itself. This consisted of dozens of wiry plaits strained back from the temples and released at the nape of the neck in an exuberant black fuzz. The whole thing is dismounted, washed and re-styled with elaborate ritual once a month. Their faces were generally plain, strong-featured with little negroid cast of countenance.

Trees lined the pavements of the town, and every other building was a café or a bar. Here one could sip little cups of hot chocolate by the hour under the striped awnings or inside, behind those sinister film-type doorways which are screened from the street by a swinging curtain of tiny chains.

But the place had a half-deserted air, like a party drawing to a close. Since the hand-over by the Italians and the federation of Eritrea with next-door Ethiopia, the Europeans had been leaving in scores. Said the wife of the British Consul, 'I'm glad we're going. It's sad to see something one's fond of dying a slow natural death.' At these words a depression settled over their traditional Sunday lunch-table—roast beef, apple tart and cheese amidst flowering chintzes and Regency-striped silk curtains and the scent of herbaceous borders under the open windows.

The most thriving institutions in the town seemed to be the native schools. In the European shops business was almost at a standstill. Many Italians had stayed on, of course, holding positions of use and importance in the community, mostly doctors and other professional men. They lived on the outskirts of the town in charming villas with long white shuttered windows, gardens glowing with fruit trees and flowered shrubs, terraces laid out with wicker sun-chairs, cocktail trolleys and umbrella-shaded tables. Small Italian children in very short frocks and trousers and very long immaculate socks played near the tall gates of ornamental wrought-iron, which were always kept padlocked and opened by a servant at a ring of the bell.

From behind the unimposing façades of the local restaurants wafted the glorious smells of Italian cooking. Inside among the international beer advertisements and the fly-blown Coca-Cola calendars there were pyramids of freshly-baked crescent rolls, real Italian ham, red Chianti bottles nested in straw and mountains of grated Parmesan for the minestrone. At an elegant reception at the Italian Consulate, some of the wealthier wives sported the newest fashions from Rome. The sound of Italian voices rippled out everywhere, through doors and windows, in the streets and gardens and cafés, swinging to and fro like the bells of the two churches, the Ethiopian Coptic and the Roman Catholic cathedral, undulating as the country roads that spiralled the green mountains behind the town.

On one short drive along these roads we saw wild monkeys, baboon-size, ducking down in the undergrowth and peering out again as we passed. Also a chameleon crossing the road in uncertain, splay-toed fashion and changing colour again as he reached the green of the grass verge with an almost audible sigh of relief. We tasted prickly pears from the ubiquitous cactus bushes growing along the mountain slopes, crushed eucalyptus and pine leaves between our fingers for their scent, and saw gladioli growing wild and foxgloves and small blue mountain flowers of an unknown name.

Once we caught sight of a remote monastery on the edge of one of the highest hills. Here according to the Count (Vittorio or 'Toio' for short) a collection of ancient Coptic manuscripts were closely guarded and visitors discouraged. Another time he pointed to an overhead cable slung high above the valley for carrying

quarried stone and told us about the English army officer—
'Mad, like all the English'—who had crossed in it for a bet and
capsized to his death just a few yards from the opposite side.

We were on our way back from a visit to one of his farms about
ten miles outside the town. Toio, who was the son of a fanatical royalist, land-owning family from Piedmont, was a brilliant
agriculturalist. During the war he was semi-released by the
British to organise food supplies for the people of Eritrea. Now
he had a prosperous coffee estate in Kenya and a number of
farms around Asmara producing fruit and vegetables to be sold
in Aden, where he owned the main cold storage depôt. Tall and
beakily handsome, he marched happily in his old khaki shorts
along the lines of pickers in the tomato fields, dispensing his
dynamic charm in all directions, stooping to run the soil through
his hand, pausing to prod the ripe fruit with an expert finger, and
talk with Mario the tenant, a young peasant from the same part
of Italy, about the dry weather. The buxom wife and I sat on a
settle in the front porch drinking black coffee out of thick rose-
patterned cups, while she told me what a wonderful man the
marchese was. This was the sort of thing people always said about
Toio. We played with the new baby, who had nothing on but the
crucifix round his neck. He was a plump black-eyed replica of
his father, and she showed me some snapshots of her family in
Italy. The hot afternoon sun splashed through the ragged leaves
of the vine which twined along the porch trellis. A few hens
scratched drowsily in the dust. In the silence a bee mumbled in
the mug of honeysuckle on the window-ledge. She told me they
were poor but happy and that they wanted six children, four boys
and two girls.

Driving home we talked enviously of the pleasures of a rustic
existence, so simple, so placid and undisturbed. About an hour
after we arrived back the idyll was shattered. The police tele-
phoned Toio to say that the farm had been attacked by bandits
a few minutes after we left when the labourers had gone home
from work. Mario had been shot in the arm for refusing to open
the door behind which he had locked his wife and son. Help had

arrived before they could kill him. People told us these bandits were a common occurrence on the roads leading out of the city where they would stage hold-ups for money. No one would drive into the countryside once it was dark. 'Now you see,' they said, 'life is not all honey here.'

Two days before we left we went to see the famous ceremony called the *Maskal*, after the yellow flower that grows everywhere in Eritrea at this time of the year. The ceremony was held in a large open field near the centre of the town. A three-man-high pile of wood had been built in the middle of the field and bound with white strips of cloth, mummy-style, into a pyramid shape. From early in the morning people had been streaming in, moving close to touch it for luck and then gathering round to watch and wait.

When we arrived in the afternoon the sun was shining in a cool blue sky. Native drums pulsed gently, steadily from one corner of the field. From another corner a European brass band clashed in with a programme of vaguely military-style pieces. Italians swarmed up from all sides in tiny gleaming Fiat cars. Chevrolets of various vintages disgorged well-dressed American families. A number of American soldiers, off duty and not so well dressed, rattled into the parking ground in their jeeps and emerged languidly to view the female scene. The prettier Eritrean girls were flaunting European frocks and their flashiest jewellery and smiles. Most of them disregarded the local youths who lounged with cigarettes in the corners of their mouths, hands in their wind-cheater pockets, nonchalant under the disapproving gaze of their toga-ed elders. Flies and small boys selling chewing-gum clung with leech-like persistence. Through the soft wash of foreign speech a pure English voice was occasionally heard slicing through, unyielding as sharpened steel.

Soon the onlookers were standing a dozen deep in one big ring at a respectful distance from the mystic pyramid which was now encircled by the brilliant ceremonial umbrellas of the priests, silk and velvet, green, red and yellow, fringed with gold and silver embroideries. Here and there the gold of a Coptic cross, delicately ornate, glittered in the sun. Originally an old pagan ceremony of thanksgiving for the crops, it was not until later that the *Maskal* was combined with a Christian festival celebrating the legendary introduction of the true Cross of Christ into the country.

A few minutes later a large maroon-coloured limousine, flying the Viceroy's standard, nudged a path through the crowds. To an awed silence, an impressive-looking Ethiopian stepped out, tall and stoutish, a long grey cloak swinging from his shoulders over a European suit, a pearl-coloured Homburg in his hand. This was the Ruler of Eritrea, son-in-law of the Emperor Haille Selassie. Somebody told us he had been an ordinary business man, of good but middle-class family until, like the fairy-stories, he married a beautiful princess and won a throne. He was reputed to be unusually clever and a very firm governor. At his side was his nephew, a small boy in naval uniform who saluted the crowd with dignity. Everyone rose to their feet and the Viceroy gazed around him, a mild but regal gaze. Then he walked out to inspect the pyramid and bless the crosses. On the way back he took the hand of the small boy who politely disengaged himself and walked stiffly alone, slightly behind his uncle.

No sooner had they taken their seats on the dais than a shout broke out. A flame flickered at the base of the pile—a puff of smoke rose up—and the fire was kindled. Soon the wood was one enormous cone of orange flame, a visible shimmer of heat enclosing it like a halo. And now the Eritrean troops broke ranks and came running from the far corner of the field. The solid khaki mass resolved itself into a twining, swiftly-moving wheel around the fire to the thud of bare feet and the pulse of drums. Each man brandished a long leaf-crested branch above his head like a lance and together they chanted in their own language. 'God keep us safe until the next crops.' One soldier started to leap away in a dance of his own but the crowd roared their disapproval. No one was allowed to break the circle—it symbolised an uninterrupted year of good fortune. Then when they could run no more they stopped for breath and flung the branches high into the flames.

But the excitement went on growing. Brightly-dressed horse-riders kept back the crowds as the fire reached its climax. 'What now?' growled one G.I. irascibly. 'Don't tell me we have to wait till this phony bonfire goes out!'

'Which way? Which way?' chanted three small Italian boys jumping up and down on the bench in front of us, and now the whole crowd was shouting something and bobbing up and down with suspense, eyes fixed on the blaze. 'Everything depends on which way the pile collapses.' explained Toio. 'One side means a good season, the other a bad one.' But he couldn't remember which was which. Not that it mattered. In the end the fire sank straight and steady to the ground, leaning neither to the left nor the right, leaving the future for this year veiled in mystery.

The Governor drove off again, waving and bowing. The priests processed out under their umbrellas, preceded by the cross-bearers. The soldiers stamped proudly away behind the flags, and the band and the crowd broke up. Only the usual small boys stayed behind to drag from the embers the still-flaming branches which the passer-by had to jump over, 'for luck'—and a few cents.

But it was the last day of our stay that must remain stamped for ever on the memory. For no apparent reason I was suddenly in-fected by a mysterious attack of Colonial Etiquette. Conditioned by Aden's mandarin rituals I started behaving like any well-trained robot. I said that of course we couldn't leave the place without Signing the Book. What book, asked Toio? The Gov-ernor's book, of course—that is, the Viceroy's. Toio seemed vague about the procedure but politely prepared, as usual, to humour the mad English. So on our way back from our last picnic the three of us drew up in the dusty little Fiat outside the Palace gates. The two armed Eritrean guards on either side went on standing stiffly to attention, their eyes fixed in front of them. Toio turned to me and enquired gently, 'Where exactly do you expect to find this Book of yours?' I said feebly that such a thing was usually kept in a sort of kiosk near the gates.

'A sort of kiosk,' he repeated in the same patient way, leaning out of the window and peering through the spiked iron bars. '*Scusate*,' he said at last to the guards. There was no reply. One of them flickered an eyelid and twitched the rifle on his shoulder irritably. On the third and loudest *scusate* another soldier came running out of the guardroom behind the gates. 'No tourists allowed inside,' he announced in Italian.

'One minute, please. We wish to sign the Book.'

The man's jaw dropped. 'Eh?'

'The Book.'

Again a blank look. 'Wait.'

He turned and disappeared into the gardens. While we waited the sound of singing stopped in the guardroom and interested faces appeared grinning at the windows. Toio wiped his forehead with a silk handkerchief. The next minute the soldier arrived back accompanied by an officer in elaborate uniform who marched up to the gates and demanded, 'What is this, please?'

In low demented tones Toio repeated, 'Some English visitors wish to sign the Book.'

'The Book?' An expression of bewilderment was hastily covered with one of brisk intelligence. 'Ah—the *Book*! Wait.'

There was another interlude. The faces left the windows and reappeared with bodies in the doorway to have a better look. Down the drive came the officer again. With a triumphant gesture he thrust through the bars a tiny notepad—the sort used by housewives for their shopping lists. Reverently we accepted it and pondered our message. Eventually we just wrote 'Senior Magistrate and Mrs Knox-Mawer, Aden' and the dates of our stay in Asmara. With sighs of relief we handed it back and prepared to drive off.

'Stop!' cried the officer, holding up his hand, 'you must not leave.'

'What's that?'

An irritable twitch of the rifle to our right. A shuffling movement outside the guardhouse from the soldiers who had stopped grinning and now looked disapproving.

'Wait.' One officer disappeared again.

This time both Toio and Ronald turned on me. Did I realise where my stupidity had led to? This wasn't a British Colony. Anything could happen. If only they hadn't given in to me. And so on. We were still arguing when the officer appeared panting at the gates once more. He drew himself up and announced loudly, 'His Highness will see you now.'

There was a horrible silence inside the car. The soldiers were pulling back the gates and the officer was waving us through impatiently. 'You may drive up.'

The Palace itself looked imposingly palatial. Before we got out Toio attempted to rub off his shorts the last remnant of the salmon mayonnaise that had been the highlight of the picnic lunch, while Ronald was struggling to fasten his sandal buckle with an old piece of string. I for my part was at least thanking my lucky stars that I had put on a skirt instead of my slacks. 'He might not recognise me like this, of course,' Toio kept repeating. Slowly we shambled up a flight of steps as long as St Peter's and presented ourselves to the footman at the top who looked us up and down and handed us over to another servant. This one led us down a number of corridors and finalled installed us in a reception-room with the words 'The *Bidwedet* will be a few minutes.' *Bidwedet* was the Eritrean title for Prince.

The room was mostly red plush and cut-glass, very large, with a view of the gardens through the french windows. There was an enormous portrait of the Emperor at one end, and a number of signed photographs of English royalties on small tables. Between the Mountbattens on the mantelpiece, I furtively powdered my nose in the mirror and wondered what an Expressman from head office would do under the circumstances. But Toio was now in charge of the situation. 'You had better leave the talking to me,' he said. 'His Highness understands only a little English.'

While he was speaking the door opened unobtrusively, and the tall, stoutish Ethiopian of the *Maskal* came into the room, wearing the same dark suit but without the cloak and the homburg. He greeted Toio who performed the introductions. Then he explained that he couldn't let the Aden visitors leave without first greeting them and asking if they had enjoyed their stay in his country. We made apologies for our appearances, but His Highness waved these aside. He mixed us all an expert dry Martini at the cocktail table, and from then on things went with a swing. Conversation was half in French, half in Italian, with a few kindly interludes for my benefit conducted in slow English by the *Bidwedet* who said more than once he was afraid I must be bored. He told us that the Christian element in the *Maskal* fire ceremony could be traced back to the legend of Queen Helen or St Helena. The Queen dreamed that at the point where the smoke from a great fire first touched the ground again would be found the remains of the true Cross, and the dream proved true. He also talked about historical relics in Eritrea, the Aden political scene and the proposal to ban *qat* from the Colony—most of Aden's *qat* was imported from Ethiopia. I kept thinking what a magnificent Othello he would make with his heavy, handsome features and deep oblique-set eyes.

At one point the small nephew came bursting in and ran up to the *Bidwedet* to whisper something in his ear. The *Bidwedet* listened, then waved him sternly away. Disconsolate in his white sailor-suit he stood a few feet away pulling his hair and gazing with huge eyes at the great man. I smiled with a gesture of consolation which sent him off in such a panic that he caught his finger in the door on the way out and royal wails resounded the length of the corridor as the footman carried him away.

After about forty minutes Toio signalled it was time to leave. Could we not have dinner with him one evening, the *Bidwedet* asked? Then we could meet the Princess who was returning from Addis Ababa tomorrow. Unfortunately we were flying back to Aden the next morning we said.

'What a pity. We could have gone riding too one day.' He turned to Ronald, 'But if you like my country, why not take up a legal position here? English professional men are always needed.'

Shaking hands, we said at least we would return for another visit as soon as we could.

In the plane going back I thought that to leave Aden now

would be like losing a half finished book—the mysterious book of Colonel Jacobs. It was no longer sealed, but like a child I had looked at all the pictures first. Reading in a strange language was requiring more concentration—still so much to find out, so little time in which to do it.

Talking to the elderly Arab merchant sitting opposite us, I asked him what was the Arabic for 'I am glad to be going back again'.

'*Ana furhan arja thani marra,*' he replied with a smile.

'*Ana furhan arja thani marra.*'

I repeated it off and on to myself all the way home.

9

Carpets in the Sand

Once again we were driving out through the desert to Lahej. Once again the dry singeing smell of dust in the wind, the cry of a hawk exploding high up, high in the blue air, the freedom of a sea-flat world meeting an arched sky in a circle that was unbroken as far as the eye could reach. Here everything was reduced to essentials. Each object protectively assumed a common shape and colour, submissive in the violent, unrelenting clutch of the sun's rays. Even the few trees sagged close to the ground, parched branches brushing the shade in the same humped outline as a sand-dune or a resting camel or a crumbling village.

Through the deserted landscape Farid roared ahead with the erratic panache of a drunken madman in a heavy traffic area. Swerving, braking, accelerating, bouncing all over the place he shouted excitedly to the passengers in the back. 'See how we find our own track! Nobody drives in the desert better than Farid! Just the same way as I handle a frisky mare!' Feeling rather sick we nodded back dumbly, the American Consul, his wife and ourselves, wondering if we would now be arriving too early for Sultan Ali at the Husseini Gardens.

Nearing Lahej there were patches of green springing up everywhere along the track, miniature crops of corn planted in the puddles after the recent day of rain and drawn up at hot-house speed by the strength of the sun. The avenue of trees leading to the gardens was the same strange bright green—a tunnel of jade over the rutted, dusty road. In the maize fields on either side the men and women were singing, 'because there is so much water now,' said Farid.

Just outside the gates to the gardens we saw a tree covered with

133

white blossom. As we came closer the blossom seemed to stir and flutter as though caught in a sudden wind. Then the whole tree shook as a cloud of flamingoes detached themselves from the branches and rose flapping into the sky, pink legs stiffly extended against the cotton-wool whiteness of their feathers. Farid told us they nested in great numbers around Lahej. They always perched close together, covering an entire tree, or two together if there was not enough room on one.

Sultan Ali, Sheikh Ali and Hassan were waiting for us on the verandah of the pavilion—Toio arrived a few minutes later with his wife Vanda and sister-in-law Luciana who were all in Aden on holiday. In a corner of the immense, untidy old garden English tea had been set out, all Worcester china, lace cloths and silver services.

The usual bevy of white-uniformed servants appeared to minister to our needs, and as we solemnly consumed tea-cakes and jam among the pink and white oleander bushes, Farid took photographs. Farid was always taking photographs. He had at least half a dozen cameras, none of which actually belonged to him. His method was to contort himself into an incredible variety of positions—once he appeared from under the table-cloth which caused Sheikh Ali to draw his dagger with lightning speed. Then he would snap away without warning at the rate of about ten a minute. Some of the ones that came out were horribly realistic.

'I am the only person who can take really *natural* pictures,' he kept exclaiming with a frown of concentration. When he had finished he grinned all over his large horse-bag face. 'Wait till you see these—they will be mag-*nif*-icent.' It was this enormous enthusiasm of his that was Farid's greatest charm, also his kindness. Otherwise he was noisy, bombastic, irresponsible, excitable and a disconcerting mixture of stupidity and shrewdness. But we loved him anyway.

'Now I am going to be chauffeur,' Ali announced after tea, getting into the front seat of the Chevrolet. He liked to drive and did so with a flourish though not particularly well. 'I will show you another house of mine.'

This was an old deserted building a few miles further on at the end of the *wadi*. From the high mud walls which enclosed the terrace we stood and admired the view of the Yemen mountains and the greenness of the surrounding countryside with two oxen tilling the field below, the farmer plodding behind to guide the rough hand-plough. In the garden some men were loading a muzzled camel with the latest crop of bananas. While the Sultan stopped to talk with them, a small boy standing nearby waited his chance and then crept up and whispered some request to him. Ali told us afterwards it was for a shirt 'if you have one to spare some time'. This was promised and the petitioner fled with a smile of rapture.

Then we walked down to the *wadi* itself which was running high and full of brown rushing water. Everyone took off their shoes to paddle except Farid who seized the opportunity to stretch out on the back seat of the car and snatch a short snooze. The stones were hard and uneven under the feet but the water was wonderfully cool and fresh.

On the way back we passed some small mud houses I had noticed before. The front walls had been painted by their owners in formal, archaic designs of flowers and leaves in white. It was growing dark and the surrounding palm trees reverted to cut-out silhouettes against the dissolving apricot light from the west. In silhouette too were the fields of cotton on either hand, the line of women walking in rows along the roadside on their way back from the wells with pitchers on their shoulders, the tired camels trailing their loads of long grass behind them like peacock's trains, slow, stately and undulating. By the time we reached the *suk* the short dusk was over and the paraffin lamps had been lit everywhere in the shops and houses, throwing a net of shadows around the vivid gleaming faces, the wet table-tops, the bales of coloured cloth, the corncobs roasting on orange embers, the trays of sliced melons pink as water-lilies among their shiny green skins. Above the noise of radios someone was ringing a bell down the side-streets as a sign that the new Egyptian film at the picture-house was about to start.

Through the gates of the Palace the garden paths were deserted. The smell of jasmine was heavy in the air and the stars were brightening but there was still no moon. Ali led us on past the main palace through a second gateway where the smaller 'summer palace' came into view, sugar-white, like a fairy-tale, in the lamplight behind the screen of trees. It was a breath-takingly beautiful building, designed by the Sultan's father. It had one long low storey with a tall-pillared entrance and another cluster of white pillars supporting a circle of Moorish archways around the terrace which separated the sleeping-rooms from the living-rooms. Dark red bougainvillaea drooped in garlands over the columns and the main doorway. The whole effect was a mixture of an American Colonial mansion and a Greek temple in a miniature style of the most delicate kind. We sat in a circle of low chairs under the trees facing the Palace. Somewhere behind us a fountain was playing. The flower smells expanded and mingled in the warm stillness. The bearers moved softly backwards and forwards between the house, ice clinked against crystal, the talk was low and idle. Suddenly someone made an exclamation pointing towards the rooftop where a flamboyant full moon came gliding into view. Tranced for a brief moment in the glow the ring of faces tilted to watch the magic lantern drift ever so slowly higher in the sky.

'Now we must go,' said Ali, breaking in, 'now is the time to go.'

Down to earth again the ladies retreated indoors to a modern and luxurious bathroom suite to powder their noses. Like children we exclaimed at the efficiency of the lavatory flush, the hot and cold water taps—'in the middle of the Arabian desert'—and explored into the main bedroom, all vast pink satin bedspread and innumerable scent bottles behind glass doors.

Back in the cars, we drove out of the town across the sand tracks we had bounced over with Farid earlier on. Near the long low buildings of the cotton ginnery we turned in and stopped. This was the place that brought an annual revenue of twelve thousand pounds for the Sultan. In the day-time it was a hive of activity. Now it was deserted, as eerie looking in the moonlight as the sand of its name—The Ginnery—which in my mind always conjured up a weirdly-mixed association of Arabian *jinns* or devils and a Dickensian liquor-distilling den.

Beyond the buildings the soft sand of the desert began again. 'Now we climb here,' said our host mysteriously, pointing to the high sloping sand-dune in front of us. So we took off our shoes and climbed, digging our feet into the cool sand, reviving incongruous memories of summer-holiday beaches and the cloudy days of an English summer. And there just at the top we stopped and gasped at what we saw. A natural shelf of sand had been transformed into an immense divan, strewn with rugs and backed with cushions, long enough for all eleven of us. As we flopped down, the embroidered pillows exhaled waves of musky perfume and incense—'The wives of the overseer have prepared these specially for us,' remarked Ali. All around the moonlight lay like water on the desert with the dark line of town rooftops and palm trees in the distance. Below us at the foot of the slope the white-clad minions had appeared again like stage-hands in the wings of the opera. One by one a circle of wood-fires flared up out of the shadows, glittering in the faint wind; then the smell of meat cooking and the clatter of pots and pans. Tonight it was kebab, with rice, bread, honey and fruit, accompanied by the usual silver trays, carved finger-bowls, even fruit-knives, all carried up in pilgrim-like procession by the bearers, while we sprawled like lords surveying the Sultan's desert beneath us. Finally there was tea in small glasses and rose-water with fluted jugs and silver bowls and fine linen hand-towels. Then a replete silence, followed by a happy belch from Hassan at one end and an introductory snore from Farid at the other and desultory conversation among the rest of the guests. Ali threw bones to the humble, mewling, prostrate crew of wild dogs who had collected around us and related all the *hashush* I had missed while I had been away.

'There is something else I want to tell you.' He spoke in low tones, leaning on his elbows away from the others, looking down at the thread of carpet fringe he was twisting between his fingers, 'Something about myself.'

It was difficult for him to talk. I waited and he went on, 'Perhaps you know I am not pure Arab by blood.'

I said I had heard talk about this.

'But never from me. Yet you are my close friend and this is the only way to understand me properly. You see, when my father had been Sultan for some years his wife was growing old and she told him he must take a second wife. She was a very intelligent woman, my step-mother. So, because he was devoted to her, he obeyed her wishes and chose one of the African slave-women from the Palace as was the custom of those days. I was born. My mother was very proud. Although my father already had sons another boy was always a great thing in an Arab family.'

'And she is still here in Lahej, your mother?'

He nodded. 'This is why you have never met her in the harem. I love her very much and every time I go to see her I must kiss her knee because she is my mother. But she is still an ignorant old slave-woman.' He remembered something and laughed. 'Once she met a European woman who understood no Arabic. My mother spoke very smoothly to her and the woman smiled, thinking what nice things this old creature must be saying. And all the time my mother was cursing her with the utmost violence to protect herself from the evil spirit of the infidel. It was very hard not to laugh!'

I asked him if he had grown up in the Palace with the rest of the family.

'I was always treated in exactly the same way as my father's other children. But of course no one ever expected that I would be the Sultan. Perhaps it would never have happened if my step-brother had not had that shot wound through the eye as a young man. It didn't kill him but many people say it affected his brain. When he was Sultan it was all drinking and women and so on. And then the night of my wedding! Then he went quite mad!' He pointed to the track-road through the sand leading to Aden. 'If you could have seen us rattling along as fast as we could for

Aden in the middle of the night in an old truck full of crying womenfolk and a couple of guards and any belongings we could snatch, escaping from this man who had in the middle of the feast seized his gun and started to fire among the guests. He was crying out that all of them, friends and family alike, were plotting against him. Fortunately all the English ladies who had come over from Aden for the ceremony had left in the afternoon.' He closed his eyes, and shook his head. 'I tell you it was the worst day of my life. I can never, never forget it.

'Then, while we were at the Palace at Crater, the British stepped in with force, had him removed to another country, and put me up for Sultan. I was selected by the body known as the Electoral College, who formally deposed Sultan Fadl. That is how it is done under such circumstances. But even from the beginning it was never a happy time for me—I suppose I was an unwilling Sultan. One half of my family was pleased, the other furious. In the same way many of the Lahej people cheered me when I drove through. But it is the others I cannot forget—the ones who shouted after me, "*Ya abd, abd,*"—"the slave, the negro slave." ' He smiled wryly and looked up, 'Now perhaps you know me a little better. See me more clearly.'

I nodded. But suddenly I was seeing everything more clearly— not just Ali, but everything else took on a mysterious new meaning and unity, the last sparks whirling up in the smoke from the dying fires, the streets of Lahej in the lamplight, the ruined villages in the sand, the crowded colour and turmoil of the Crater *suk*, Arab faces and places I had still not found.

'Now I have made you depressed,' he went on, in a schoolmaster voice. 'Listen! One more lesson for the day—What are the ninety-nine names for Allah?'

I laughed. This was an old joke, 'All I know is that only the camel has learned the hundredth,' I said.

'Correct. But why ninety-nine? Have you ever thought?'

I said I hadn't. He held the palms of his hands to the moonlight. 'See, the Prophet has written it here. On one hand the Arabic signs for 18, and on the other 81 . . .'

Outside the ginnery buildings lights had appeared and people were moving about. 'They have arrived for the dancing. *Yalla—let's go!*' Everyone got up and stretched, then down the slope we plunged again, ankle-deep in the fine, sugary drifts.

Now we could hear the thudding of drums soft but insistent like the rain on leaves, joined by the sound of flutes. 'It's the last day of the cotton season,' Ali explained. 'This is a sort of end-of-term party for the pickers and the ginnery workers.'

When we reached them we saw that the crowds were split up into half a dozen groups, each group surrounding a different dance. In the centre of the nearest cluster of people a man and a woman were dancing together. This is something that is never seen inside the Colony where the *purdah* restrictions are inflexible. But once in the Protectorate it is a common sight to see men and women working side by side in the fields, and only the upper-class ladies are kept closely veiled. The two dancers wove their patterns with a striking grace. His right arm supported her waist, her head drooped on his shoulder as they circled round together with that gliding, dipping two-step movement that seemed to be the basis of all the local dancing. There was a movingly simple directness and dignity about the pair of them—he wearing an ancient *futah* and turban with pride, she extending with her right hand the ragged shawl round her head in a gesture of classic ease. Near by a group of four young girls were dancing with an absorbed delight, their hair unbound and swinging to their waists. I thought of Binyon's 'Little Dancers'—

> Holding their tattered frocks, through an airy maze
> Of motion lightly threaded with nimble feet
> Dancing sedately: face to face they gaze
> Their eyes shining, grave with a perfect pleasure.

At their feet sat the musicians, a man beating a drum with the flats of his hands, thin bird-like hands, and a small boy with a dusty close-curled head piping away at a reed flute and staring throughout straight in front of him, eyes glazed with concentration. Behind them an old woman rocked happily backwards and forwards shaking and slapping a tambourine high in the air. Crowded around the tiny dancing space—not more than three or four feet across—the intent watching faces hovered like moths in the glare of the paraffin lamp, hands clapping out the rhythm of the drums in the ardent excited way of children, elbows close together, outspread fingers a few inches from their faces. At regular intervals a sound arose like the long quavering shriek of an express train in the distance, a wave of ululation from the women who modestly veiled their open mouths and the bell-clapping tongues that produced the effect.

After a while we moved on to another group where a string of half a dozen men were dancing on their own, arms linked advancing and retreating to the beat of the music like chorus-girls, but with stern engrossed faces turned downwards and none of the smiles and nods and glances and general audience-awareness of European dancing. They might have been dancing alone on the moon, grave and self-contained, for all the attention they paid their onlookers.

At the arrival of the Sultan the crowd swelled, and when the dance was finished there was a shuffling excited movement near by from which a tall lean figure emerged and took up his position in the centre. This was the local poet, or rather the leading local poet, for every other tribal Arab is an amateur composer in his own right. For a moment he stood silent, eyes flashing in his sharp, wrinkled face, his hair falling from his turban in long black strands to his shoulders, while the audience waited respectfully. Then raising his hand, he declaimed the first line. This was immediately taken up by the crowd while the dancers formed up in two lines on either side of him and fell in step, backwards and forwards with the chant. Each line was repeated in this way, the poet bobbing up and down between the two rows conducting the performance with gestures of passionate encouragement. The favourite theme seemed to be one which began, 'O Postman take this letter to the girl with the beautiful eyes.' There was another which ran,

'The ginnery is happy because of the good crops this year and I am happy too . . .'

On the outskirts of the throng some children started up a rival chant, playing an old Laheji game,

'*Khatam as-Sultan dhaa—dawira luh ya abid.*'

(The ring of the Sultan is lost—search for it, O slaves.)

But the squeaky chorus died away at a sharp reproof from some of the elders standing near, for such disrespect to the poet.

Apart from the poet, the outstanding figure of the gathering was an enormous old slave-woman with a round flat beaming face who waddled rhythmically to and fro in a scarlet-flowered garment, shapeless and flowing, exuding social goodwill, nodding encouragement, exhorting the performers to even greater efforts like some oriental Elsa Maxwell. When she caught sight of the Sultan her enthusiasm knew no bounds. Prostrating herself on the ground she crawled towards him on all fours and greeted him in the traditional way, flinging her arms around his legs, kissing both his knees, and calling on Allah in a commanding croak to bestow every known blessing on her lord and master. Slightly embarrassed the Sultan patted her on the head laughingly.

'She was born at the Palace—her mother and father were our servants all their lives,' he explained, adding with a sigh, 'Of course I don't really approve of this form of greeting. I'm trying to change it, but it's very difficult. They wouldn't understand, you see.'

At that moment one of his bodyguard came up and whispered something in his ear. Ali turned to us and announced, 'This magician you were anxious to see. He is ready for us now, waiting in the ginnery.'

'In here?' I asked as we climbed up to the deserted work-room by the light of a paraffin lamp. 'Wouldn't it be better in the moonlight?' I couldn't help sympathising with anyone, even an established magician, who had to produce fresh vines of grapes and black serpents among all those rows of machines and bales of cotton stamped 'Liverpool U.K.' Perhaps he felt so too because when he appeared, a small dour-looking figure swathed in a dilapidated *futah* and shawl, he merely shook his head sourly and muttered in Arabic something to the effect of, 'Only the sugar tonight—I'm not in the mood.'

So we grouped ourselves awkwardly around him in one corner of the room away from the machines. Scowling all over his wrinkled walnut face, he grudgingly revealed first of all from the folds of his *futah* a handful of small pebbles. These he replaced, carefully twisting the material tight around them again. Next— horror of horrors to any self-respecting magicians' trade union— he calmly proceeded to turn his back on us and walk away to a distance of three or four yards. There was some fumbling in his *futah* and then he turned round and rejoined us. After some gentle persuasion by the ginnery overseer, who was stage-managing the performance, he sulkily unfolded the top of his *futah* and brought out a handful of lump sugar, not the familiar European cubes but the small rough squares looking like marble that are used in this part of the world.

Despite a sinking feeling of disappointment we all made polite exclamations of amazement, reaching out to sample the miraculous products. Somewhere a childish hope flickered—there were pebbles and now there is sugar, one cannot see any obvious hiding place for the pebbles—there is an eerie effect about the silence and the shadows of the machine room, also there are sworn legends about the man and those small black eyes of his are oddly hypnotic when they stare back at me . . . It was disconcerting to look up and glimpse on the Arab faces the expression exchanged among parents at a children's conjuring display. But perhaps I was mistaken about that too.

One thing was certain—it was obviously an 'off' day for the magician. Leaving us the sugar for souvenirs he tottered down the steps again leaning on his stick without so much as a word or a backward glance, only a prolonged irascible mumbling to him- self. But the performance was not yet over. As we passed through the door outside again we heard a shattering series of low groans coming from a group of figures standing in the shadows. Among them we could distinguish the magician, half bowed to the ground and supported by two youths, presumably relatives.

'He will be sick tonight,' one of them remarked reproachfully.

'Is it true?' asked the wife of the American Consul in anxious tones.

'Who knows whether he might recover too?' added the other.

The overseer bustled them away indignantly, and we walked on, longing to laugh it off but full of a vague remorse. 'Perhaps he really does suffer nervous stress after these exhibitions,' Mary-Jo Lakeland went on.

'That was why he wouldn't do big things tonight—he was frightened,' the overseer admitted. 'He says if he does something really big one of his family dies, and even if it is fairly big, then someone falls sick.' Which hardly reassured us. But someone else put in with a laugh, 'He's just an old hypocrite. And he makes money out of it too.'

The overseer led us back to a large open tent where the head workers and other local people of importance were waiting to receive the Sultan. We sat ourselves on the usual cushions and rugs and sipped Coca-Cola.

Discarded scraps of *qat* lay all around like hedge-clippings. Sheikh Ali selected some fresh bunches and instructed Mary-Jo and myself on the best pieces, the juicy inner leaves—'and one must eat a lot, of course.' But the first few mouthfuls were enough. It still tasted just like privet. Suddenly we were aware of the disapproving eye of the white-bearded notable seated opposite, taking in our disgraceful levity towards the custom, and even more so, our white Englishwomen's legs stuck out in front of us from under our cotton frocks. There were very few Europeans who could sit with their legs tucked neatly beneath them for any length of time without getting severe cramp, and I was not one of them, though for an Arab it was obviously as easy and graceful as folding one's arms.

After the ritual exchange of courtesies and gossip it was time to leave. Soon we were in the cars again, bumping our way over the sand homewards with a wonderful last glimpse of the desert— a wild fox crossing our path, standing transfixed by the glare of the headlights for a split second, and then disappearing into the darkness on the other side once more.

The day after the next was to be my birthday. As we turned into our drive the Sultan's car followed us. A minute later Ali appeared mysteriously at the driving window and handed Ronald something small with the instructions that I was not to open it until the proper time. But of course I opened it there and then. It was a brooch, a perfect three-inch replica in gold set with rubies of a traditional Arab *jambia*.

Into a way of life which had been as formal and restricted as that of his father and grandfather, Sultan Ali was now cautiously introducing a number of innovations. Most of these were looked on by the older members of the Lahej governing council with the same suspicion with which they regarded most of his proposals for the development of modern governmental institutions—proposals which had nevertheless made Lahej the most politically advanced state in the Western Aden Protectorate.

Apart from riding regularly, he played in a weekly tennis four on the Crater club courts with Farid, Ronald and a well-known Indian player, and often came with us to the cinema at Little Aden or Steamer Point. Most daring of all, he even joined our party for the occasional charity ball. But not all the persuasions of the other European women would lure him on to the floor, either at a public or a private dance, though he loved dancing and always looked forward to the decadent western tangos and quick-steps he could indulge in on his visits to the Continent. Neither in Aden nor abroad would he ever drink alcohol in any form. He once said the very smell of it seemed to sicken him. On these two points he was inflexible and, under the circumstances, rightly so.

Despite this he was subjected to a great deal of personal criticism both from his own people and from leading Europeans—all of whom accepted his invitation to an *Idd* reception at the Aden Palace. This was the biggest innovation of all, the first mixed gathering on a large scale the Sultan had ever given, and he discussed the idea anxiously with us for weeks beforehand. In my showy, journalistic way I suggested that this grim old barracks of a palace should be made to look as picturesquely Arab as possible and the whole thing sentimentalised just a little to conform with the general European idea of a Sultan's reception. Thus the morning of the party saw Nabiha and I, Emir Mohsin and Emir Mohamed and, of course, Ali himself, plus a small army of servants moving out all the 1930 Harrods' furniture, laying down dozens of Persian carpets, including reinforcements from the Lahej palaces, over every available inch of floor space, and some of the walls too, bringing out the wonderful family portraits from the seclusion of the dining-room, arranging huge bowls of flowers from the Lahej gardens, and playing over a radiogram some records I had found of *Scheherazade* and Gustav Holst's *Suite Orientale*—genuine Arab music would render most of the English guests to a state of intense irascibility after about ten minutes. Grumbling, Sultan Ali said that the next suggestion would be that the ladies of the harem should entertain the guests in Hollywood costumes with the dance of the seven veils. I said that only the thought of The Aunt's face deterred me. Every now and then Sultan Saleh, visiting Aden for the reception, looked into the room with a slightly sardonic smile at such frivolous preparations. Much scampering and sounds of excitement were also heard coming from the harem quarters overhead, with servants constantly on the run between the two parts of the house carrying news to the women of the latest activities.

The party itself was a great success. As a host Ali was far more relaxed, much less shy than as a guest. Only Arab food was served, and the fruit drinks were so varied and exotic that nobody seemed to mind the absence of alcohol. There were Protectorate Sultans in elegant new turbans and *futahs* for *Idd*, Sheikhs in flowing *abbas*, French, American and Italian Consuls, English business managers, and Service officers and Government officials. One of the highlights of the evening was the appearance of the new Parisian wife of one of the sons of the famous French millionaire wearing, in modest Arab style, a gold embroidered shawl draped over her elegant blonde head. For most of the Europeans it was their first visit to the Palace and for some their first opportunity to speak to this Sultan of Lahej, of whom there was so much sinister rumour.

It was about this time that his unpopularity with the more dogmatic sections of Government was particularly marked for a number of reasons. Firstly, he was a frank admirer of Colonel Nasser and had openly admitted that he was in sentiment an Arab nationalist. Thus, according to the same dogmatic sections, it was more than probable that he was also a full-blooded Communist. Secondly it was extremely irritating that due to a long-founded family friendship with the Imams of Yemen, his was the only border State free from frontier attacks and internal fighting among dissident tribesmen. It had even been suggested that he was responsible for an arms-smuggling campaign through Lahej into Yemen. And now when *qat* had at last been prohibited by Legislative Council in the Colony, he obstinately refused to ban it in his own State so that all along the frontier at Sheikh Othman an enormous *qat* market had been set up to which all the Aden population flocked, and *qat*-chewing went on for most of the night in hastily improvised huts and sleeping quarters. In addition they found him hyper-sensitive to criticism and suspicious of any move by the British which might be interpreted as outside their advisory capacity.

We sometimes discussed these things with him when we were with him informally at the Crater palace. Lahej was his working headquarters to which he travelled every day, often staying overnight or for prolonged visits of two or three days, but Crater was his place for relaxation. Even so, there was always a couple of hours of paper-work to be done there before setting out for Lahej each morning, with perhaps a meeting at Government House or a conference with the British Agent or some visiting Sheikh, and in the early evening the front wall of the Palace was always lined with squatting petitioners awaiting his return from the Protectorate. For many Arabs democracy may be a new word, but its meaning is as old as the hills. It is the first duty of a Ruler to be available whatever the hour to any subject who might wish to see him.

Ali's favourite retreat at the Crater palace was his 'Bachelor's Den' as he called it, and this was where we usually sat with him. A small room half-way along one of the downstairs side corridors, it was the one place where he could escape from the eyes of the servants—and the harem spy-holes—and while he was away it was always kept locked. Inside there was some shabby white-painted furniture, a sofa, an ottoman couch, a few old armchairs, some good rugs, a few modern flower-paintings on the walls, a magnificent radiogram, and littered everywhere the usual impedimenta of any young man's room—old papers, long-playing records, a couple of ties across the back of a chair, a half-opened tin of cigarettes. Some things were missing, of course—no female photographs were to be seen and an air-conditioner took the place of a fireplace. And some things were different. Over the chest of drawers hung a complete framed text of the Koran in microscopic print and a pair of heavy rifles and ammunition were stacked in the corner. At the far end of the room were two divans for resting after lunch, one for himself and one for the friend who might happen to be with him at that time of day—it was here that Farid spent most of his somnolent afternoons. Ali also slept here whenever his wife was away as it would not be considered correct for him to continue sleeping upstairs in the women's quarter's in her absence.

Here Ali would be wearing a cotton sweater and linen slacks while the radiogram played Louis Armstrong at a discreetly low pitch. Emir Mohamed and Emir Mohsin would be in the same sort of clothes. Only Sultan Saleh, a frequent visitor, retained his familiar khaki *futah* and bush-jacket, his turban under his chair, studying the gleaming Cadillacs in Ali's automobile magazines. At a rock and roll recording though he raised his hand in a stern, banning gesture, and replacing his turban on his head, left us with a regretful smile.

This particular day, I remember, after he had gone, we started discussing politics. I took the plunge and asked Ali whether he was an actual Communist or not. Without any hesitation he answered, 'I am a Moslem and I believe in a divine power. I am not interested in Communism. It is a materialistic doctrine.'

He added that the Arabs generally were not interested in Communism except in so far as the Communist countries might aid them in their national struggle. 'But after Arab independence is established that will be the dangerous time. After that many Moslems might be tempted to seek a new ideology.'

Someone asked him whether the Arabs realised that the Russians would use nationalist aspirations as a weapon for their own ends.

'But what evidence have we so far that Russia has any imperialistic designs on the Arab world?' Ali said. 'What about the French Army in Algeria and the alliance of Britain and France with Israel to attack Egypt? These things contrast rather unfavourably with the words of peace and protection from Moscow.' He lit a cigarette and shook his head. 'But don't worry—we can look after ourselves. We shall find our own way all right.'

'And Colonel Nasser?'

'What is this Nasser bogey that has been built up in Britain?' Ali exclaimed impatiently. 'It is surely time to face the fact that he is no Communist, and never has been. If this distorted picture is allowed to continue it can cost the British dearly. And there is still time to restore the Arab-western goodwill which existed in the past. It would mean so much good to both sides.'

'Then you wouldn't describe yourself as anti-British?' I put in.

'Anti-British! This is the label they always hang around my neck. I am not anti-British, I am merely pro-Arab. Is that so unnatural? Does the one thing have to imply the other? Surely it is right for every self-respecting young Arab to long for a return of the greatest influence we had in other centuries. And this can only be done by unifying all the different national elements into a workable whole.' He paused, then went on slowly. 'Do you know it is a fact that the majority of Arabs would far rather accept western co-operation than Russian aid. It is only essential that co-operation should be offered as between equals, in genuine friendship and mutual respect. We are a very proud people, you know, we Arabs.'

I changed the subject and asked him about the *qat* problem.

He laughed. 'Problem? What is the problem? and, by the way, how would the British manage their Empire if they had their whisky taken away from them? As things are I am making a lot of money for new hospitals and schools and the people are happy because they still have their *qat*. Now isn't that a sound business proposition?' Then, more seriously, 'Besides, I personally do not feel I have the right to take away from my people this consolation for a hard life. Do you know I found something on the very subject by your Dr Johnson in a book the other day—he said exactly that thing and very well too. But don't worry—it can never last, this ban. It is against nature. *Qat* will be back in Aden.'

He jumped to his feet. 'Now let us have the other side of the Louis Armstrong—I like this man Armstrong you know. It sounds like the voice of an old slave grumbling to himself.'

10

A House on the Frontier

A few weeks later a group of British and American press representatives from *The Daily Mail*, *The Daily Telegraph*, *The Times*, *Life* magazine and other leading publications left Aden for a visit to the Yemen at the official invitation of the Imam. Government had advised that, under the circumstances, it would be extremely unwise for the wife of a Government official to be among the party. Perhaps they visualised me held as hostage in some lonely tower while below the Imam dictated his frontier terms to an anxious British peace delegation led by Ronald.

Anyway I stayed at home feeling frustrated and disconsolate until Sultan Saleh came to dinner at our house one evening and remarked casually, 'Now when can you visit my country—next week, perhaps?' He added, as an afterthought, 'Only little fighting these days, everything peaceful for the present.'

Ronald said it was unfortunately impossible for him to get any leave at the moment, especially as we were going back to England in a few months' time, but he would be delighted for me to go. I turned to ask Nabiha who was having dinner with us if she would come with me. She, however, shook her head rather nervously and said hastily that she had some relatives coming to stay at the house. Later she confessed to me in private, 'It is the noise of guns, popping all the time—it makes me very frightened.' Finally it was decided that Fatima, the adopted Arab daughter of our crocodile-owning neighbour, would be the ideal companion. Educated in England, she spoke perfect English and with her knowledge of Arabic and Arabia would also be able to be interpreter and general guide to the harems.

Within a few minutes Saleh had the whole thing organised.

There was an empty house ready for us at Mukeiras, the central town of Audhali State. Usually Nabiha and her husband stayed there but it had not been used for some time. It was only a hundred yards away from the Palace and he would put a detachment of his own armed guards on duty there day and night. Servants and food would be arranged. We were to stay as long as we liked—he would show us everything of his country we wished to see.

'I had better bring this with me,' I said, holding up an antiquated Arabic-English textbook I had found in somebody's house, bound in musty green leather and redolent of the faded past of British rule in Aden. Saleh looked through it with keen interest and found it most amusing. Slowly he read out some of the sentences for beginners—'Boy, that punkah is not fanning sufficiently quickly,' and 'Order the carriage for me at once, groom.' When he came to 'Sahib, if you do not wake at once you will be late—this is the third time I call you,' he burst out laughing. 'I do not think you will need this,' he said. 'We can teach you better than this in Audhali—we are up to date there. And I will improve my English too.'

I asked him if I brought my painting things with me would he consent to sit for his portrait though I could not promise a good likeness as I was very much an amateur? Saleh graciously nodded his agreement, then glancing at my modernistic version of Sultan Ali on the wall, added politely, 'The likeness is not too important, but I would prefer my face to be the same colour all over please.'

As he left, Sultan Saleh asked Nabiha's husband to stress to me that the visit would not be a luxurious one—his conversation was still half in halting English and half through interpreters. At a careful pace, pausing to select the right words, he added with a grin 'I have jeeps . . . I have donkeys . . . I have no Chevrolets.'

'And the Yemeni situation—it will not be dangerous there?' Ronald asked. Saleh squared his shoulders, the very embodiment of strength and reliability. 'Do not trouble. They are in my hand. Government cannot forbid.'

And, of course, Government did not forbid, though they obviously disapproved of the idea of the expedition. So did most of my friends. So did the 'plane which twice refused to land us there. On two successive mornings we watched the Audhali plateau swing into view veiled with rain under the old Dakota wing-tip. Each time we swooped low over the muddy airstrip only to rise again over the mountain rim opposite as the fair-haired English pilot turned round to us with a shake of his head and a rueful smile. Now would I see sense? everybody enquired petulantly. It was a clear warning by Fate explained the more superstitious. But I was obstinate. Audhali 6,750 feet above sea level, its frontiers adjoining those of the Yemen, was still one of the wildest corners of Arabia and I would be the only English-woman in the country. I knew it was a unique opportunity and some kind of strange compulsion was urging me on, telling me it was the last chance. Also, three was my lucky number.

The third morning dawned clear and sunny. Once more Fatima and I fastened our bags and set off for the airport. In the waiting-room the same passengers had gathered, the tribesmen returning up country, the Levy soldiers, the veiled women laden with Aden purchases, with two new additions, a middle-aged Arab who was suffering the supreme indignity of having to travel with his wife. Muffled from head to foot in black velvet she was bundled quickly through into the 'plane, while her husband followed some distance behind with an air of resignation. Inside the 'plane the general confusion was as great as on both the other mornings and the heat more intense than ever now that the sun had come out. When the ladies filed meekly in the smell of mixed perfumes and incense became almost overpowering.

Only the unfamiliarity of a strange situation can take away the dignity of Arab people. Here in this modern machine from the West they looked oddly displaced, their pride dissolved, nervously cluttering up the gangway, fumbling over parcels and precious belongings, crumpling awkwardly into their seats with looks of trapped apprehension.

Once more the old man sitting opposite removed his turban and slipped a string of prayer beads over his grey-stubbled head. At first he sat motionless, concealing his fear with a kind of desperate self-respect, one hand twisted around the amber stones, the other gripping close the arm of his seat. He kept his stick tightly between his knees. Then as we roared into the take-off he closed his eyelids, wrinkled as a parrot's, his lips moved silently, the ragged shirt front rising and falling into quickly-taken breaths. Once safely in the air his son, sitting next to him, leaned over to undo his safety-belt with a few reassuring words and offered him a cigarette. Before smoking it the old man fondled it with the tremulous appreciation of one snatched from the very brink of the grave.

In the seat behind us a small brother and sister in brand-new clothes and leather shoes from Aden curled up together, perspiration beading their arms and foreheads, eyes bright with distrust, fingers plugged firmly into their ears. The lady in black velvet in front slipped aside her face veil and smiled shyly round at us.

Now we had left the sea behind. The 'plane swayed higher into the air and the kettles and cooking-pots rattled over our heads in the luggage racks. Soon we could see below us the country of Sultan Saleh. Mountain ranges, yesterday hidden by cloud and rain rose in tiers of petrified foam, prismatic in the sunlight as splintered glass. Under the flying shadow of our wings stretched lion-coloured patches of desert, tiny villages circled with oasis-green, narrow rivers carving a zigzag course through the rocks into the blue distance of an Italian Renaissance painting. It was a remote, barren and beautiful land.

'Look! The Palace at Zara!' cried Fatima pointing to the white-peaked turrets that rose glittering like a fairy-tale in the brilliant turquoise light from an overhanging crag far beneath. 'Now we are nearly there.'

A few minutes later the 'plane was circling the Mukeiras runway for the third time. This time the strip of stony turf was clear and dry and, amid exclamations of triumph and praises of Allah, we made a smooth landing. An eager crowd clustered around the doorway outside to greet the returned friends and relatives. It seemed to me that in the excitement the two newcomers could slip through unnoticed. But it is impossible to arrive unobtrusively when there is a four-foot gap to be jumped between plane and ground and when one is not only a stranger but a female *Ingleesi*. There was an unnerving interlude of rapid and intense scrutiny from a sea of upturned faces, indigo-stained tribesmen, white-robed merchants, village people in the striped *futahs* and flat toque turbans of Audhali. Then a tall Levy soldier extended a friendly pair of hands and swung me down and there were smiles, nods and words of welcome all round.

'But where is the Sultan's jeep?' someone cried.

'Here! here comes Mohamed,' shouted somebody else, pointing to a cloud of dust advancing along the horizon. It disappeared behind a bend in the track, then revealed itself again as a small grey jeep rattling towards us over the stones with a loud trumpeting of the horn. There was a screech of brakes and out sprang a thin alert young man with a European jacket over his *futah*. Cries of reproach for his lateness arose from the bystanders, but with a flashing smile he waved them all aside. In clipped precise English he introduced himself, 'I am the secretary of His Highness Sultan Saleh bin Hussein. I offer apologies for my lateness. And now I will take you to the house.'

So off we rattled again, leaving everyone to pronounce judgement on the Sultan's guest from Aden and the young girl with the plump, pretty Arab face, and the English clothes and speech.

The morning air was sharp and fresh as a lemon and dew still glistened on the pebbly fields on either side of the track. The countryside was flat and clear and green, bounded by rocky slopes. Everyone else seemed to be travelling on foot, or jogging along astride little grey donkeys as compact and hardy as the jeep itself but so small that the riders feet dangled a bare inch above the dust on either side. Over the ridge of the first hill we saw Mukeiras, the mud-coloured Arab houses seemingly moulded out of the sand itself with the worn crumbling look of yesterday's sand-castles on a holiday beach. The narrow winding streets, which were more like passages between the houses, did nothing to deter the speed of our driver. As we roared through chickens flapped from beneath the wheels, munching goats turned their heads to stare, and mothers snatched their children into doorways to wave and salute as the jeep went by. On the other side of the little town there were fields of green crops along the road again.

'There is the Sultan's Mukeiras palace,' said Mohamed. No glittering turrets this time but a big square house in grey stone set solidly on a hilltop with small barred windows and the air of a frontier fort. 'And this is your house.' He turned into a driveway opposite with two pillars at the entrance and a bank of yellow and red roses lining either side—real English-type roses and the first I had seen since leaving home. Equally surprising was the prosperous European-style house at the end of the drive—the whole thing was like the house and garden of a well-to-do English country doctor set in the middle of the Arabian hills. Three people were waiting lined up on the top step to greet us. In charge of affairs was a very tall, cadaverously-handsome bearded man of tremendous dignity. This was Abdullah, the general overseer, who in turn introduced Awadh the cook, a short good-looking young man with a shy smile, and Hassan, his assistant. Someone else came panting up to be included in the introductions, a shrimp-like ten-year-old with a huge red rose stuck in his embroidered cap and nodding over his eyes which were incredibly wide-set and slanting, as elegantly rimmed with black as a Paris mannequin's. 'And I am Abdu, garden boy,' he announced.

Proudly the four of them with Mohamed bringing up the rear processed us through the house, pointing out the virtues of the shining taps in the bathroom—both marked Cold—and the store cupboards crammed with tinned food. 'But better than this are the Mukeiras vegetables and fruit,' said Awadh. 'You will have them fresh from the gardens every day, you poor hungry people from Aden.' There were coloured sheets on the beds and tightly-wedged vases of flowers on every table. In the living-room there were cane chairs, a long dining-table, even a desk, and a radio which Abdullah bent over tenderly and turned on with a blast of music which practically blew us out into the garden again.

'But the terrace!—wait till you see the terrace!' exclaimed

Mohamed darting to the head of the procession and beckoning us upstairs. Through a french window at the top we stepped out on to a large square balcony with a tiled floor and a low surrounding wall topped with boxes of bright plants. There were cane tables and striped canvas garden chairs carefully set out in a semi-circle and the *pièce de résistance* was a luxurious swinging seat for three with cretonne cushions and a fringed canopy. Beyond the musical-comedy garden with its urn-topped pedestals festooned with roses, its handkerchief lawn and its flights of shallow steps, stretched the Mukeiras valley folded in by low rocky slopes and the blue Audhali hills.

'The Sultan came over to see that everything was as he had ordered soon after he had woken,' Mohamed said. He indicated the al fresco breakfast Awadh had laid for us complete with fine rosebud china and two large tins of cigarettes. 'Now I will leave you. His Highness will be coming down to welcome you in person later on.'

After breakfast we sat out on the lawn at the side of the house under the shade of the striped beach umbrella, as incongruous in this setting as an orchid in an English lane. From here we could see the Palace, a hundred yards away on the hill opposite. A band of singers and musicians had arrived to entertain the Sultan and were playing at the front entrance, wandering minstrels outside a feudal castle. They spend their time travelling from village to village providing accompaniment for weddings, saints' days and other feasts, in return for food and lodging for the night. From the hilltop the pulse of drums and the thin thread of flutes and singing voices floated down on the glistening morning air. And all the while the intermittent procession of visiting tribesmen, disputants, litigants, anyone with a problem to be settled, continued to climb the hill to the house, a moving frieze of indigo silhouettes, guns on shoulders, against the gauzy blue web of sky. Each new arrival would join the line of figures squatting against the front wall of the house, waiting their turn to see the Sultan. Faint snatches of their talk, an exclamation, a practice shot, echoed down towards us over the rocks. Otherwise everything was still in the sunshine. Silence here became a positive not a negative quality, flowing backwards and forwards between each sound like quicksilver.

From time to time a messenger came leaping down the path with a slip of pink paper fluttering in his hand on his way to the wireless station with a cable—events of mysterious urgency must be moving behind the stolid façade of the Palace. Once it was a slip of white paper, a message for us written by Mohamed and signed in green ink by Saleh to say he hoped to see us in about half an hour.

While we waited I brought out my sketch-book and we were soon surrounded by a throng of small would-be models. These were mostly recruited by Abdu of the beautiful eyes. For a moment he stood goggling over my shoulder. From then onwards he shouted out to every passing child—'See! Here is one who takes photographs with her pencil!' Some of the older girls were elaborately painted with a yellow powder made from a local herb called *hurid*, Fatima told me, with orange circles drawn under their eyes. Their hair they dressed in dozens of tight little braids with a short fringe over the forehead. Each one wore a straight robe to the ankles dyed blue-black with the traditional indigo, a head-shawl but no face-veil. Here *purdah* was a luxury reserved for the upper classes. After a while they remembered the errands they were supposed to be carrying out and drifted off again with shy backward smiles and promises to come and see us another time. All except one small girl, a pair of huge silver rings pierced through the tops of her grimy ears, who sat on, popping rose-petals with her tongue and languidly conducting a conversation about her family affairs. Her elder brother was helping her father in the next field but one. Her name was Miriam. She was supposed to be helping her mother wash at the well. Her baby brother was to have a new dress of red silk next *Idd*. She would like to have a husband as soon as possible. I was the first Englishwoman she had seen. Why had we no jewellery to wear—not even a pair of silver rings for the ears? And why could we not afford a dress to fit us—right down to our ankles? An angry woman's voice from behind the house brought these queries to an end, but she too promised she would not fail to return again.

Up at the Palace there was a stir among the waiting tribesmen. We saw them get to their feet and crowd around the entrance as a party of soldiers emerged from the shadows of the open door-way and started to walk down the hill. At the head of them was the Sultan, a figure in khaki slightly shorter than the rest, dif-ferentiated only by the commanding style of his walk and the silvery-grey silk of his turban, a colour which by custom only the Ruler was permitted to wear. At the gates of our house he turned to dismiss his bodyguard who sat down in the shade to await his return. Only his cousin accompanied him, at a respectful distance, because it would not be correct etiquette for the Sultan to speak alone with women in a public place.

He flashed his usual charming smile at us and shouted to us, '*Ahlan wa Sahlan*,' the traditional welcome, as he came up, but his bearing was more formal than in Aden. A gathering crowd of tribesmen watched with interest from the gate, and Awadh and Hassan rushed out from the house with a tray of cold drinks as soon as he sat down at the table with us, cocking a cynical eye-brow at the absurd umbrella. Conversation flowed easily with Fatima as interpreter. At this moment he was the man of affairs, the absolute ruler of twenty thousand people and the morning's news had disturbed him. He told us that a Yemeni raid had been made that night on a neighbouring village. Cattle had been stolen, crops had been fired, and most serious of all in this part of the world, the well had been blocked.

'Now I am going to inspect the damage and see what I can do,' he said, draining his glass. Then he added, seeing Fatima's anxious expression, 'Don't worry. This is not for you. It is some distance away.'

As he left he turned round and said, 'I would like you two ladies to have dinner with me tonight,' adding with the grin I remembered in Aden, 'And for June especially there is a surprise I think she will like—something to make her feel less homesick for Aden.

'Now today you must rest after your journey—tomorrow you will start to explore,' was his final command, before he stumped away down the drive again to rejoin the soldiers and climb into the jeep which had driven down after him.

Impressions of a place glimpsed from a car or train are a collection of snapshots. To watch a single setting in repose is more rewarding. Its real life unfolds like a film, a three-dimensional film into which one is absorbed as part of the scene.

That afternoon, and every other afternoon, the view of the valley from the terrace slowly ripened to gold once the sun had passed its highest point. The fields of maize and barley, the fig-trees, the threadbare outlines of a ruined village on the hill swam in the yellow light. On the far slopes sheep grazed indistinguishable from the white scattered boulders. Black figures moved among the crops which grew shoulder-high, the women in indigo robes and shawls working side by side with the men. In the field bordering the garden a man was ploughing with two yoked oxen and a wooden ploughshare. He stopped and shielded his eyes to watch his wife walk quickly and lightly over the furrows towards him, a bowl of food on her head, a kettle swinging from her hand. As she walked the sunlight glinted on the silver of her anklets and bracelets, on the hilt of the ploughman's *jambia*. Close to the house there was a stone well-head in a patch of shade. Backwards and forwards an ancient camel trod an unchanging path drawing the water up in a sheepskin bag at the end of a rope and pulley. Hour after hour the small boy in charge of him chanted a slight, monotonous, undulating song.

'We've got work to do, but let's get on with it today.'

'*Al-yon*,' 'today, today,' echoed across the valley, where new voices caught it up and tossed it back again.

Other sounds fissured the silence—someone crying, '*Ya* Hussein! *Ya* Hussein!' the crack of a rifle, the curious, pumping, despairing scream of a donkey, and once, from the direction of the frontier, the boom of an army gun, like a giant door slamming in the distance.

It had rained at noon for a few minutes. Now I could lean over the terrace wall and flick away the last drops from a solitary peach on the tree which grew alongside the house. Pink roses clung to the wall. A highly-polished beetle with a yellow and black back like a scarab brooch nosed its way into a wet over-laden flower and tumbled with the loosened petals on to the branch below. Somebody called, '*Ya Ingleesi!*'—a small boy perched on a rock behind the house. He waved in salute than produced from his shirt a flute on which he piped a sad little scrap of a tune for me. Then '*Ta kher betig,*' he suddenly cursed as he sprang off to re-capture one of the sheep he was supposed to be watching.

The light was fading now, and a trail of tired figures started to wend its way homewards across that poetic landscape which was to become to me more than a landscape, with some extra under-lying quality about it, mysterious as an allegory, poignant as a dream.

Fatima and I changed for the dinner party into cotton frocks with full gathered skirts, essential for sitting modestly on the floor. When we went downstairs Awadh was waiting for us with a fresh rose each, at his suggestion to wear in our hair—it was a special occasion to dine with the Sultan. 'I will come with you,' he said. 'I am cooking the dinner, you see.'

So we climbed the steep hill to the Palace, threading our way through the loose stones by the glimmer of Awadh's torch, which he insisted was far superior to a hurricane lamp despite its failing batteries.

'*Mesal kheir,*' said the two guards on the doorway politely as we passed inside. The hallway was bare and dim and flagged with stones, reminiscent in its sturdy dourness of a Scottish manse. Mohamed then appeared and waved us into a room on the right.

Here Sultan Saleh was sitting with the men of his family and a ring of masculine faces turned with the same expression of rapid, intense scrutiny as our welcomes at the airfield. They stood up when we came in with a sort of good-humoured deference to European custom but in the usual Arab way introductions did not take place at this point. Saleh merely shook hands with a smile, asked us how we were and indicated chairs near to his own.

Conversation trickled slowly but pleasantly by, dammed up every now and then with the accumulated efforts of translation and counter-translation, while overhead a pressure lamp flared and hissed at the end of a long chain from the ceiling, throwing heavy shadows on the patterned linoleum floor and the surrounding rectangle of cane chairs. Bowls of flowers, glasses of squash, and cigarettes—these hastily brought in and opened by a messenger a few minutes after our arrival, dotted the tables in front of us. From thick wooden pegs, protruding at regular intervals around the wall, hung a number of rifles.

As I talked to Saleh, telling him what we had been doing during the day, I was very conscious of the scrutiny of my neighbour, a handsome, elderly man with an expression of sly geniality. Over the usual shirt and *futah* he wore a richly-embroidered shawl and on his head a splendid emerald-green turban. Saleh told me he was the Governor of the neighbouring town of Ariab. In the middle of one of my enthusiastic, gesturing sentences I caught his side-long glance again and in it an expression of slightly sardonic amusement at the unrestrained ways of the European female—also a puzzled scrutiny of my dress and make-up. No doubt he too was reflecting sadly on the poverty of my ornaments.

On the other side of the room Abdullah, brother of Saleh, who was commander-in-chief of the Audhali forces, smiled encouragingly in my direction. Ahmed who was acting as Naib in the absence of Emir Jebel stared thoughtfully at the floor, obviously weighed down by the responsibilities of his new position.

After a while there was a shuffling in the hall and the sound of subdued voices. 'Here is your surprise,' said Saleh.

I nodded appreciatively, full of secret apprehension, and went on nodding, hypnotised, as no less than fifteen immense young Englishmen filed into the room one after the other.

'The Cameron Highlanders,' he announced with a huge wink in my direction and the ear-to-ear beam of a conjuror producing a rabbit out of a hat.

I had forgotten that the Cameron regiment was temporarily stationed just outside Mukeiras. The officers were as surprised to see me as I was to see them and, although I knew some of them well, we kept rigidly to the correct etiquette of procedure. Gravely and on their best behaviour they shook hands with the Sultan, then the Governor of Ariab, then the Sultan's family. Finally they greeted Fatima and myself, the Colonel hissing at me, 'What on earth are you doing here? Last time I saw you we were dancing a samba on the Crescent Hotel roof!'

Visions of not seeing another English face during my whole trip faded abruptly. Then noticing Saleh lean forward anxiously to judge the result of his surprise I put on my most pleased smile. At least I was still the only Englishwoman in Audhali, and their arrival certainly eased the conversational situation.

Eventually Awadh crept into the room and whispered something in the Sultan's ear. Saleh nodded then raised his hand. 'Now we eat, gentlemen—and ladies!'

By the light of a paraffin lamp we filed up the narrow winding stairs to an upstairs room. The Camerons were rather nervous of procedure. 'You must tell us what is the right thing to do.' But Fatima took charge of the situation. 'Take off your shoes,' she commanded in a whisper. In a flash fifteen pairs of brown polished shoes were ranged, hotel-fashion, outside the door of the eating room. Inside, an elaborate array of dishes was spread out over a long white cloth on the floor, flanked by rugs and cushions. I stood behind the men and tried to look as much as possible like a humble inferior woman in the presence of the all-powerful sex, but Saleh beckoned me firmly forward into the place of honour on his right, with Fatima next to me, and the Colonel on his left. The Governor of Ariab took his place at the other end with the same expression of sardonic amusement. Saleh whispered through Fatima that this was probably the first time he had deigned to eat at the same meal as another woman. Arab wives always have their food after the men have finished and usually in another room.

Fatima continued with her helpful advice throughout the meal. 'Your right hand,' I heard her murmur to the brawny sunburnt

Scots giant at her side. 'And please point your feet away from the person opposite.' The Colonel was more experienced and rounded off the last mouthful with a superb belch which brought the smile of a connoisseur to the face of the Governor.

Downstairs again, the atmosphere thawed even further as the young Captain and the Audhali commander animatedly discussed battle strategy against the Yemenis while Saleh told the Colonel about his proposed trip to Europe next year. The decision reached on this particular topic was that the Colonel would take the Sultan on a tour of Paris if the Sultan would provide the funds. '*All* the Paris,' Saleh reminded, laying a finger against the side of his nose with a wink of complicity. 'Do not cheat me, remember.'

When Fatima and I finally left it was almost midnight and Saleh reminded us we had a lot to see the next day. At the door he said in a hurried aside, 'The wife of the Naib would like to receive you for tea tomorrow at four—I am afraid the ladies of my family are in Zara.'

He smiled sheepishly. Then he gestured two of his guards to accompany us with Awadh to the house. 'Do not worry if you hear gunfire in the night,' were his last words.

We did hear gunfire in the night and at breakfast the next morning Awadh told us that a reprisal party of Audhali tribesmen had had an encounter with Yemeni troops near the border. 'We won,' he added as though he had been talking about a weekly cricket match—which is perhaps almost how the average tribesman regarded a situation which time and circumstance had made traditional.

After breakfast we went out to see the village women who came to the spring in front of the house every day to fetch water and do their washing. A group of them sitting by the edge of the stream gossiping got to their feet when they saw us coming and greeted us with cries of amazement and delight.

'Welcome to our country,' cried an old grizzled woman, drying her hands on her black witch-like draperies and beckoning to us. 'Come and talk.'

But first we inspected each other's dress and ornaments. Most of the women were young with slight graceful bodies, oval faces, smooth and tawny-coloured, framed in their black shawls, small fine features and white smiles. Under their shawls they showed us their hair-styles bound in dozens of long thin plaits, parted in the middle and topped with a tiny clipped fringe across the forehead, neat as the fringe of a rug and as essential a finishing touch. Their jewellery stood out with dazzling effect against the blue-black dye of their clothes. Each one was garlanded with silver coin and chain necklaces into which they tucked bunches of sweet-smelling herbs. They had silver rings on their toes and fingers, rows and rows of bracelets of coral and amber and cornelian and dangling ear-rings of the same stones, while their tattered dresses were caught in at the waist with carved belts of solid silver or linked coins, decorated with tiny bells. Like the little girls, their faces were powdered with yellow which gave them a not unattractive gilded look against the brilliant morning sunshine. 'It whitens the skin,' one of them explained.

Then they showered us with questions.

'Are you really an Arab like us?' to Fatima.

And to me, 'Where is your husband?'

'How many children do you have—a son? Praise be to Allah, you are fortunate.'

'I moan my fate,' said the old woman. 'I have just this daughter.' She pushed forward a plump, pretty girl of about sixteen who giggled protestingly. 'And she doesn't want to get married, so what am I to do?'

She heaved a sigh of resignation, they started to load up her donkey with old petrol cans full of fresh water.

'These are for the Sultan's house. Already they have drunk the load I have just taken—they don't think of my little donkey's back or my poor old arms.' She shook her head sorrowfully at the thoughtlessness of men, and the other women reminded of their own duties went back to pounding their washing on the rocks. 'We shall look for you tomorrow,' they said.

We were sitting out on the lawn again when a young man of about nineteen came up the drive. He introduced himself with a bow as the Sultan's nephew from Ariab. He was short and wiry like all the Audhalis, with a narrow mouth, a long curved nose, impressive eyes, and an air of self-confidence.

'This morning I entertain you,' he announced in English that was slow but sure. After the ceremonial drink of squash he confided to us that his chief ambition was to return to Aden—'Aden is very good.' There he would complete his studies at the Commercial Institute. Then he would set up his own business, importing fruit and vegetables from Mukeiras to the Colony. 'Thus I will escape the position that awaits me. The Sultan is a great man, but to be his secretary would be a restricting occupation, don't you agree? Also I like the city best.'

We admired his gleaming rifle, which he had placed carefully under his chair. 'You like it? Come then—we will shoot.' He sprang to his feet and pointed to the rocky hillside a hundred yards away. 'This is the best place for targets.' And off he went at a trot, over the garden wall and the ridges of sprouting barley beyond, Fatima and I following.

When he finally reached the spot to which he had pointed he waved us impatiently behind him and carefully lowered himself to a sitting position behind a small rock. Then he balanced the rifle on the rock in front of him, took aim at a cairn of white stones, some distance away, and fired. A puff of smoke arose where the top stone had rested and a triumphant voice exclaimed, 'Are I not a very good shot do you think, Mrs Knox?'

'Very good indeed, Saleh bin Abdulla.'

He nodded in a satisfied way, his eyes gleaming under the bright magenta silk turban perched toque-wise, level with his eyebrows. Then another doubt occurred. 'But my English. He is not so good, eh?'

'Very good indeed, Saleh bin Abdulla.' I had a sudden flash of inspiration and added, 'Much better than your uncle the Sultan. You should teach him.'

This was a great success. Saleh puffed out visibly and replied that this was true and he would indeed teach his uncle.

We shaded our eyes to watch a decrepit wooden lorry painted a

brilliant blue and red come lumbering down the track from Ariab.
It was top-heavy with a cargo of villagers, waving their arms and
singing at the tops of their voices to the accompaniment of the
lorry's horn, which was a musical one with a range of half a dozen
piercing notes.

Saleh suddenly slapped his forehead and exclaimed, 'I forgot!
It is market day. This is where I am supposed to be taking you.
Come—or we are late.'

As we crossed the stubble back to the track road he was silent
and then added casually, 'It may be that you will forget to tell His
Highness about our shooting after you have seen the market and
much else?'

I nodded reassuringly and nothing more was said. We walked
into the town in the wake of a family group led by an old man
who was dozing astride a patiently plodding donkey under the
shade of an old black umbrella. Behind us trotted a flock of goats
being driven to market by two young women in their best finery.

By the time we got there the entrance to the square was full of
people from all the outlying villages, mostly men, some women, a
vivid shifting pattern of indigo, yellow, orange, red and white.
Along the narrow lane into the market they were buying and
selling long bales of dried grass, feeding stuff for the camels and
goats.

Our entrance into the main square caused a general stir of
interest. Small boys were the first to spread the news that there
was a *nusuru* (Nazarene) in the market; the women clustered
round next to stare and smile and offer a few words of advice in
Arabic—'You like Mukeiras?—then stay with us,' and, 'Next
time your husband and your children will be with you we hope.'
Finally we were inspected by the men with a long, easy up-and-
down gaze, a salaam from the older ones, a grin from the youths
and always the greeting, '*Ahlan wa Sahlan!*' Having satisfied their
curiosity and made me feel welcome most of them drifted away
back to their own affairs. But a solid core of guides, gazers and
gabblers remained to accompany us on our tour.

Market business was conducted around the various piles of

goods laid out on cloths on the sandy trampled ground. A thin eager young man urged us to inspect the array over which he was presiding—a handful of peppermint lumps, a bunch of tobacco, two or three exuberantly patterned shirts, a string of plastic bracelets, bundles of pencils, mammoth-sized combs, ornately-framed hand-mirrors guaranteed to distort out of all recognition —all the minor flotsam and jetsam of Aden civilisation and each thing a luxury to the people of these places.

Near by they were selling local produce, sacks of corn and maize, stacks of rock-salt and unground sugar glittering in the morning sun like a jeweller's window display. In the shade of an alcove the town butcher was hacking his way through a leg of lamb with his *jambia*, surrounded by various carcasses lying in attitudes of supplication, forelegs bound together in mid-air. Half a dozen severed calves' heads, eyes mutely glazed, tongues extended in a last gasp, decorated the wall behind him.

On our way past we were drawn into a bargaining discussion with a tall bearded giant of a man who was selling woven baskets and hand-made shawls. We thought his prices high but used his wares as props for a photograph which pleased him enormously and drew an even bigger crowd around us. Eventually, after the ritualistic haggling demanded by tradition and applauded by our audience, he handed over a work basket to Fatima for three shillings instead of five with many finger waggings and sighs of martyrdom. Meanwhile an aged crone at the next stall sold me a similar basket for two shillings, a broad woman-to-woman smile on her wrinkled, orange face. Did my dress material come from Britannia, she wanted to know, stroking it appreciatively. It did? *Tamam, tamam*, that was good, she nodded. But not as good as the Mukeiras indigo cloth, I said, pointing to where an old man with a face like a prophet and skin stained the colour of gun-metal sat under a black umbrella, guarding the piled-up bales of shiny new-dyed cotton—the whole thing a static sepia silhouette in the midst of so much technicolour movement.

Whenever we stopped to take a picture crowds of enthusiastic 'walkers-on' rushed forward and wedged themselves together in front of the camera. Most of them were small boys, full of cocky good-cheer. The local warriors, tall and bashful in their bright toga-cloaks, leather fillets binding back their long curling hair at the temples, needed a little more persuasion to pose with their *jambias* and rifles and sashes of cartridges. Some of the older tribesmen obviously still regarded a camera with a strong superstitious fear. To them it was still the devil that took away a man's soul as well as a picture of his face. One of these die-hards stood in the background uttering shrill imprecations, his beard wagging with righteous wrath, until his relatives managed to calm him down and move him away out of sight. Even the women, though there were many not veiled, retreated into the shadows with gestures of affronted modesty and giggles of protest. Fatima told me it was because if their picture was taken unknown men outside Mukeiras, even Christian infidels perhaps, would be able to look on their faces without permission, whenever they so desired.

Most of the ground-floor rooms of the surrounding houses seemed to be shops—small, dim, pleasant-smelling places, with an atmosphere reminiscent of an English village grocer's. Here could be found the more sophisticated shopping items—tinned foods, washing powders, bottled squash, highly-coloured paper-backed notebooks bearing portraits of the various rulers of the Arab world—even rubber balls and chewing gum. While we made our choice the usual chair was hastily produced from a back room and whisked over the counter on to the few square feet of trodden sand on the other side. The cry of '*Jib kursi hina*' (Bring a chair here) always seems to go up automatically among Arabs on the appearance of a European, as though he might stop breathing if he didn't immediately sit down four wooden legs away from the floor.

After a courtesy five-minute sitting on this particular specimen, we moved on again, picking up the procession of the faithful, until we came to the house of one of the Sultan's soldiers where we had been invited in. It was the usual mud-packed façade, with the ends-of-the-storey beams protruding through the walls. There were the same tiny slit windows whose purpose was not to establish communication with the outside world but to let in the only bare essential of light and air while defying anyone to glimpse inside. We filed in through the narrow doorway and up the dark curling flight of stairs preceded by the warning cry, 'Any women about?' We passed two tiny landings and finally came out on the top storey which was open to the sky and encircled by a shoulder-high mud wall.

Peering over we could see the market scene revolving below in a vivid swirling mass of colour and movement, an impressionist blur of indigo flecked with the red and yellow, purple and emerald of turbans and shawls. By now the square was half submerged in a rising tideline of shadow thrown by the surrounding houses whose tall walls rose around the swarm like the sides of some sandy pit. One or two small faraway faces are turned upwards to look at us, a hand waves a greeting. From a neighbouring rooftop a woman's head peers out from behind the string of washing she is hanging out, then ducks hastily back again, as we look towards her. It was mid-day now and very hot. The air was heavy with the scent from a two-foot square garden of herbs growing in one corner of the rooftop.

We turned to shake hands with our host, a handsome man with a full black beard and a charming smile.

'What are they looking at down there?' he asked Saleh in mystified tones. 'Has there been an accident?'

'They are visitors,' said Saleh, but he was still obviously puzzled.

Lounging over to join us at the parapet, Saleh pointed to the narrow winding maze of streets behind the square. 'Do you know the real reason why there is not one straight street in Mukeiras? It is a safety-precaution for we fighting Audhalis—no man can take good aim at another with a loaded rifle down a lane as crooked as these.'

'Now there is coffee for us to drink,' said our host, coming over to us with Mohamed, the secretary, who mysteriously is here too in that haphazard overlapping of acquaintances and arrangements that is one of the delightful and sometimes maddening features of Arabia. 'This will be surely more refreshing than any view.'

He led us, not downstairs, but into a tiny penthouse built into one corner of the rooftop. Inside it was cool and dim with white-washed walls decorated with a central frieze of red and green painted patterns. Half the floor space was taken up with a Beihani rug, folded in two, and a pile of cushions. The men took off their rifles and laid them carefully on a narrow shelf set high into the wall where a pair of lamps and other family belongings were also stored, and we all sat down round a pot of steaming hot *qahawa*. This was a heady mixture of coffee grounds, ginger and herbs which was a great favourite in Audhali. After a while the in-evitable hookah was carried in by a small boy of the household who loaded it with tobacco and stoked it with hot ashes from a tin at our feet. Then it was handed round the circle, each of the men drawing a couple of long, bubbling, appreciative sucks through the wooden stem before passing it on. I politely refused it this time, so did Fatima, which was thought quite right and proper in masculine company.

After I had drained the three cups of *qahawa* demanded by etiquette our host asked us if we would not stay for lunch. 'The pleasure of thy company will only equal the humbleness of the fare.'

I said that much as we would like to we had to return home as the Sultan was coming for lunch.

'But first thou would see the ladies of the family?'

'I would be indeed happy to do so.'

The ladies were discovered in another smaller penthouse along-side which was obviously the kitchen. Three faces peered towards us out of the smoky gloom of the tiny cave. There was a servant girl stirring something in a pan over the fire, an old grandmother crouched in the shadows at the back, and the wife, a pretty young woman with a baby in her arms, who came forward to greet us shyly. We were sure we could not stay for lunch?—the food was nearly ready. Well, another time perhaps.

The husband drew her to one side and spoke to her earnestly.

Fatima told me he was asking her if she would not pose for our camera. He gave his full permission. But the young woman remained adamant. '*Aib . . . aib*,' she repeated, waving a small implacable hand, while the grandmother nodded vigorous approval.

'She says it would be shame on her,' the husband told us, regretful but helpless. 'Perhaps another day when there are less men about . . .'

We thanked him for his hospitality in the doorway where a goat's foot was hanging overhead 'to keep out the devil'. He plucked the bunch of dried flowers stuck in his turban and handed them to me with a gracious gesture. 'These will remind you of our country,' he said.

Back at the house Awadh had prepared an elaborate meal with all the Sultan's favourite dishes which aroused appreciative comments from Saleh on my prowess as a housekeeper. The other guests were two Arab officers of the Government Guards, one a huge fat fellow with a formidable barricade of white teeth and a ferocious laugh, the other slim and youngish with the same kind of good looks as Hussein of Jordan. Afterwards we drank tea— specially requested by His Highness who absently held his cup as though it were a coffee bowl, extending it for more minus the saucer. Then one of those long Arab silences descended on the company. To break it I suggested innocently, 'Shall we go up on to the terrace for our third cups?'

With remarkable alacrity the company sprang to their feet, taking their rifles with them. After a courtesy admiration of the view, the fat one could contain his impatience no longer. 'May we shoot, Your Highness?'

Saleh merely indicated me with a grin and I said hastily, 'Of course—a wonderful idea!'

And so the shooting party began. First, a boy was summoned from below to run across to the hill opposite and put up some white stones for targets, while the two officers roared instructions and mild abuse at him with what seemed to me the maximum volume possible for the human voice—even the Arab voice—until Saleh joined in too.

Then with ceremony the Sultan was handed the first rifle. Among the usual badinage and bets, he braced his stocky muscular figure absolutely still against the wall, the rifle hugged to his right shoulder, his small aristocratic nose wrinkled with concentration. The rifle crashed once, jerking back against his shoulder without moving it, then for a second time, and on the third explosion the white stone splintered in a puff of smoke amidst cheers all round.

No sooner had the first shots rung out across the valley than the garden was invaded by a stream of tribesmen and workers from the fields shouting their approval of the demonstration. News must have reached the Palace within minutes that the Sultan was shooting. One after the other the familiar faces appeared eagerly through the french windows leading on to the terrace.

'*Naqdar nudhbul?*' May we come in?

Soon the place was crowded and all the frivolous sun-lounge furniture pushed to one side to make way for more urgent affairs. The visitors clustered in line waiting their turn to shoot—the acting Naib wearing a smart maroon sweater over his *futah* to match the maroon turban which framed his long black curls and sharp features, the handsome young Commander Abdullah, an elderly cousin of the Sultan's with small heavy-lidded eyes and a great beak of a nose, another cousin in khaki jacket and shorts, a magnificent silver *jumbia* tucked in his belt, and all the usual court hangers-on, with their guards and servants. Everyone carried his own rifle and an enormous buckled sash of gleaming cartridges in leather sockets.

Fresh targets were set up and each man took his turn against the wall to fire a barrelful of cartridges while Fatima and I watched in a safe corner of the terrace among the boxes of geraniums. Saleh was undoubtedly the best shot of the lot. When he had completed his turn he came over to us and indulged in one of his schoolboy jokes. 'Look! I am wounded!' he groaned, clutching his right hand to his chest with a series of fearful facial grimaces.

Eventually he held up his hand for inspection and I saw to my horror that the little finger was indeed only a stump. I must have looked startled because he immediately added reassuringly, 'But that was five years ago.'

'How ever did you do it?' I asked.

'I was carrying my rifle so,'—he slung his rifle across his shoulders like a yoke, a hand hooked over each end in the comfortable way of the Protectorate tribesmen—'and the stupid thing went off by accident.'

He watched the boy setting up new targets on the hillside, 'You have never shot before—you would like to try?' Then he said hastily, 'No, no, perhaps not after all. I will take you another day where there are no people about.' He grinned and added in Arabic, 'After all he is such a nice young boy—who would wish his life to end so suddenly!'

Amidst the rattle of the fusilades and the volleys of back-slapping, laughter and shouting from the competitors the air grew acrid with the smell of gunpowder and cartridge shells littered the tiled floor. Only a sudden shower of rain dispersed the audience gathered on the nearby rocks and finally brought the party to a close. Otherwise I think they might have still been shooting at night-fall.

Later that afternoon Fatima and I walked up the hill to the Palace, which we had since learned was actually the Naib's house where the Sultan stayed while he was in Mukeiras. We were going to have tea with the wife of the Naib. As we drew nearer to the front entrance we were met by the unwavering survey of the bearded tribesmen squatting in line around the doorway, waiting to see the Sultan. Some smiled and nodded in greeting. The others merely looked solemn at the idea of one of these mad English-women and the Arab girl who was yet not an Arab approaching the residence of the Sultan from the front instead of through the women's entrance.

We were saved from this *faux pas* however by the sight of Awadh suddenly appearing from behind a corner and waving us furtively round to the side of the house. 'Did you not know this is the proper way to visit the ladies' quarters?' he whispered, irritated at the bad manners of his charges, and handed us over to an old crone who took us through a small door at the back of the house. At the foot of the stairs was the young daughter of the water-carrier. She beckoned us on to the first landing where, like the fairy-stories, a second messenger was waiting, a serving girl who led us up the last dark, winding flight of stone steps and through a door at the top.

It was a large bare room, carpeted in the same linoleum of which the Naib was obviously so fond, and dimly lit by three small barred windows. At the other end a tiny, delicately-featured woman, heavily pregnant, got up from her cushions and kissed our hands in welcome. It was obvious that we would only be able to exchange the briefest formalities without the aid of Fatima as our interpreter. Yet through all the constraints of translated conversation—the time-lag between question and answer, the impossibility of repeating an exact tone of voice, the disconcerting way in which trivialities became enlarged as under a magnifying glass—despite all this a spark of affection sprang up between Nur and myself within a few moments of our first meeting. We smiled as we greeted one another with a smile that meant the beginning of a friendship, bridging our two so-different worlds and all the barriers between them. Then she patted the cushions for me to sit next to her and I watched her as she asked Fatima the usual ques-tions—How long were we staying? Did we like Mukeiras? How many children had I? Did Fatima herself have a husband yet?

In her silk head-coif and her robe of dark green velvet falling to the ground in heavy folds from an embroidered sash under the bust she looked like one of those rich merchants' wives portrayed in early Flemish paintings. But the face was an eastern version of a Botticelli madonna, a pale, perfect oval with the same tender, resigned beauty and air of ethereal sadness. Her features were narrow and exquisitely drawn and she wore no cosmetics apart from the *kohl* with which she had rimmed her eyes, long and dark under heavy fluttering lids. Like all very small pregnant women she had a pathetically overburdened look about her but she still moved with touching grace and dignity. Her jewellery was an additional weight to her—heavy gold chains at her neck and wrists, cascading ear-rings of pearls and rubies. Her whole attitude was full of a modest tranquillity that had nothing to do with the West of the twentieth century. This was a Chaucerian world. The household keys swung from a ring on her sash; to the poorer villagers who climbed the hill every day to receive her dispensations of food and clothing she was *Ummi Nur*, our mother Nur; through the slit windows, bare of glass, she watched the seasons pass in the fields below the house where each man tilled and sowed and reaped his plot of the master's land.

At least part of Nur's contentment sprang from the fact that she was an only wife and a well-loved one. Her husband was the famous Naib Jabil, younger brother of Sultan Saleh, a small, handsome, wiry man renowned for his fighting courage and daring in this part of the world. At this time he was away in England where he was advised by his doctors to undergo a minor operation.

'He has met the Queen,' Nur told us. 'In a letter he told us her Palace is very beautiful. But best of all things in London he says is the moving stair and the underground train.'

A young servant girl with a bold gypsy face who had been adopted by the family brought in a tray of tea. Carefully she placed a cup and a small plate of biscuits in front of each of us. The five-year-old Feisal, Nur's only son, joined us for tea. 'This is our future Naib,' said Nur introducing him. He was a handsome little boy with enormous eyes, a pudding-basin fringe of hair and the spirited personality of all the men of the Sultan's family. He told us his two younger sisters were sleeping. Then he settled down to his tea, dipping each morsel of biscuit into his cup and devouring it with an expression of intense concentration.

'Now I would like another boy like this one,' said Nur.

'And when will the baby be born?'

'When? Who would know certainly?' She laughed at our

stupidity. 'Maybe one month, maybe more. It is in the hand of Allah.'

After the traditional hour of the first courtesy visit we stood up to go. 'Wait,' said Nur, reaching for a silver coin necklace which hung from a hook above her. 'This is for you,' she said as she fastened it around my neck. 'It was mine, now it is yours.'

I admired it in a small cracked mirror she held up for me. I wondered if the correct procedure now was to present her with something of my own. With some uncertainty I started to unpin a miniature gold brooch I was wearing but she waved her hand, declining gently.

'Then I will send you some material for a dress from Aden if I may,' I said.

Her face lit up with pleasure. 'Can you get velvet in Aden? It is so nice when the weather is cold here.' She indicated the chill rainy wind blowing through the shutters. The bare linoleum was clammy underfoot. The only other furniture was a bed in the corner, a cupboard and a stack of painted steel trunks. But poverty of possessions among such people only underlined the rich generosity of their ritual courtesies and her graceful farewell kissing of hands was a gift in itself, with the promise, 'Come every day—our house is yours. . . .'

As we walked down the hill to the house again we saw the Sultan's jeep waiting at the gates. Saleh looked serious as he waited for us. 'I have had a message saying the Levy C.O. has had a cable from Aden advising that you return,' he said in Arabic to Fatima. 'They say the situation here may become dangerous.'

'And what do you say?' I asked him.

'I say you are my guests and you are in my hand. Any news there is of Yemeni plans comes to me first and I am in the best position to take care of your safety.' He hesitated, then went on, 'This cable is the result of some news I sent to Aden telling them that a consignment of Russian arms has just arrived at Beidah on the Yemen border.' He pointed towards some hills in the distance behind the house. Then he smiled reassuringly, 'But at the moment all is quiet and I have special reasons to think it will continue so. Now I am going to talk to the C.O.' And settling his gold *jambia* more firmly in his belt, off he stumped back to the jeep, a square-built, powerful figure, his steel-coloured turban fluttering behind him, purple *futah* swinging, with an aura of invulnerability about him that made one feel this was a man to be relied on in any emergency, even the descent of all the hordes of Yemen.

Later that evening just as we were having dinner in the lamp-light, there was a knocking on the door. Fatima and I both jumped and Awadh nearly dropped the dish of rice he was about to serve. But it was only Saleh standing in the doorway. Awadh kissed his knee, then disappeared into the kitchen to listen with the rest of the household to the ensuing conversation. Saleh sat down on the edge of the table and told us to carry on with our meal. 'I have eaten,' he said, tentatively tasting a sample mouthful from the dish of curry, swinging his legs like a schoolboy.

But this display of oriental restraint was too much for me.

'What happened?' I asked impatiently. 'What did he say?'

'Oh, I saw the C.O. He gave me a squash—all your Englishmen were drinking cocktails.' He put an edge of satire on his pro-nunciation of this foolish word. 'It is agreed. You are to stay. If it becomes necessary you leave, it is my decision.'

He moved aside our effusions of delight and thanks. 'One thing is important. Once it is dark you never take a lamp on to the terrace. They might be too tempting a target. If you sit out in the evenings, you must sit by the light of the stars and the moon. You promise?—Otherwise—' he brandished an imaginary whip and grinned—'You will be punished.'

He stayed for a while to talk, exuding elder-brotherly con-fidence and benevolence. As he rejoined his bodyguard in the porchway he held his hand out to the rain. 'It seems Allah agrees with us. If he sends any more of this there can be no planes to take you back to Aden anyway. . . .'

11

The Turrets of Ariab

The next few days were fine and sunny. One afternoon soon afterwards we went to meet the harem of Sultan Abdulla, the Governor of Ariab and a cousin to Saleh. The jeep took us to Ariab, prancing and stalling playfully along the rough stony path which wound between the intervening hills. The slopes on either side were strewn with the ruins of old villages still inhabited, so Mohamed told us, by the last two or three families.

About half-way there we passed on the verge of the road a score of small rectangular plots, outlined roughly in stones. This was the cemetery of one of the villages. No names were written on the stones, though clusters of herbs and shrubs had been planted on some of them. Here the dead remained anonymous, their transformation into the dust among which they had lived was complete and perfect.

Through a gap between two hills we saw the turreted roofs of Ariab rise like a fabled town. Each house, whether of mud or stone, was a tower in its own right, a miniature fortress with the same eyelet windows, the same crenulated peaks at the corners of each flat roof. The white domes of two small mosques, built in honour of local saints, guarded the entrance to the town.

As the jeep roared its way in, swarms of children appeared from the entrances of every narrow lane and ran alongside the jeep with shrill cries of welcome and demands for a ride. Chickens fluttered away from the wheels, donkeys set up a snorting scream of disapproval at the rattle of the engine and women peered out from their doorways and shoo'd their babies to safety against the walls of the houses.

We drew up outside the largest building in the town, the tall white-stone house of Sultan Abdulla. Here Mohamed left us and young Saleh appeared to greet us. 'Now you see where I live,' he announced, then proceeded to conduct us at a racing pace up the curling stairway of the central tower. At what seemed to be the tenth storey we paused for breath and followed him into 'my room'. Inside there were no other people, as yet—in fact most of the space was already taken up by three beds. Two of them were ordinary iron bedsteads with patterned covers, but the third one was an epic of a bed, a four-poster complete with a crimson tasselled canopy, fitted at the head with a series of faceted mirrors and decorated at the foot with elaborate paintings of birds and trees. Around the edge of the floor was the usual border of rugs and cushions.

Fatima and I perched ourselves on one of the mundane beds, and at a signal in the doorway from Saleh, one by one the ladies filed in to be introduced. They made their entrances in attitudes of Byzantine formality, clad in ankle-length shapes of stiff flowered silks and metallic brocades, clasped in at the waist with solid silver and gold girdles of linked coins and tracery designs, with ornate tiers of necklaces and bracelets encasing their wrists and throats.

At first, each face looked alike under its ceremonial mask of adornment—white powder pressed over the etiolated complexions of airless rooms and *purdah* veils, heavily-rimmed eyes under an extended eyebrow line that met in a widow's peak at the centre, a beauty spot in brown paint on each cheek-bone, the mouth coloured a dark red. Then gradually one noticed the individual features. Sultan Saleh's aunt, a handsome plumpish woman of middle-age with an air of immense dignity, had the family nose, small and delicately curved. The beautiful teeth and classic profiles of the daughters were familiar characteristics, as were the long eyes and oval jawline of Saleh's sister whose beauty was of a heavier, coarser style than the others. Each face was framed by thick side-curtains of dozens of minute breast-length plaits with the narrow pelmet of the traditional fringe across the top. The hair was draped over with a short hand-woven shawl which emphasised the rectangular outline of the head. As they sat in line against the opposite wall, they were an Egyptian frieze come to life.

At first they spoke hardly at all, glancing at each other out of the corners of their eyes, exchanging subdued giggles, while Saleh guided the conversation from his lofty position on the bed of honour. Then gradually curiosity conquered their shyness. How many children did I have and where was my husband? How long had I been in Aden? Did I like it better than Britannia? They accepted my compliments on their dress and ornaments as a matter of course and examined my pleated skirt and sweater with a kindly air. Then the sister of Saleh whispered something in the ear of Saleh who repeated, 'They would like to prepare you for the party if you agree.'

With inward qualms I nodded enthusiastically, and couldn't help wondering what form would the preparations take. Fatima murmured reassuringly as we followed the ladies into another room that she wouldn't stir from my side throughout the operation.

I was waved to sit down on a cushion in the middle of the room while everyone else gathered in a circle around me. A tray of small pots and jars was brought in, and Saleh's sister sat herself face to face in front of me and studied me with an air of a high priest receiving a lamb for the slaughter. One of the young girls squatting alongside in the role of assistant handed her a tiny brass urn from which she drew out a dipper shaped like a pencil and tipped with powdery black *kohl*. 'You must close your eyes,' Fatima translated from behind me. Slowly and with infinite care she drew a thick line along the edges of the upper and lower lids. I opened my eyes and there was a ripple of amused approval from the hovering faces. 'It will sting at first,' Fatima warned anxiously. 'But it is really good for the eyes. Besides it looks lovely.'

The presiding genius then extended my eyebrows up to the temples and down in a widow's peak over the bridge of my nose with a sharp stick of charcoal while the assistant held up a mirror for me to watch. With her forefinger she placed a blob of brown paint on the centre forehead and on each cheek, and drew a fine semi-circle in red beneath each eye. She rounded off her operations by parting my hair in the middle and twisting it at the sides into a number of immature plaits, finally surveying me with half-closed eyes like a painter, leaning back to get the picture in better perspective.

I was turned around for general inspection. On the whole they seemed approving, but something was still wrong. One of them sprang up with an excited gesture and began rummaging through a big trunk. 'Now they are going to dress you,' announced Fatima.

In a second someone had tied a silk scarf over my newly-decorated face and willing hands removed my skirt and sweater over my head.

'*Ya maskin!*' said someone in a voice of pity, gently pinching my shoulder.

'What's the matter now?' I asked desperately, in muffled tones.

'She is only saying how thin you are,' replied Fatima soothingly.

Something smooth and shiny was slipped over me and I was unveiled to admire myself in a splendid robe of silver brocade, while necklaces and bracelets and a silver belt were fastened around me and a black embroidered veil wound over my head to conceal my skimpy tresses.

'*Mabruk?*' I asked, remembering the traditional phrase implying a blessing on a new item of clothing.

'*Mabruk, Mabruk,*' everyone cried happily, circling around me, clapping their hands at their creation. Only the sister of Saleh shook her head in a dissatisfied way and murmured something to Fatima who said, 'If there had been time they would have put henna on your hands and feet and painted beautiful patterns in black. Then you would have been perfect. But she says you are good enough.'

Now it was time to go to the party. We followed the ladies down the stairs again towards the sound of drums and singing and eventually came to a curtained doorway where a young boy was waiting to usher us in. The room inside was a long dimly-lit cave of colour and movement, crowded with about fifty women. The only light seeped in through three small barred windows and the walls were aglow with painted designs in crimson, yellow, green and purple. Everyone was singing, some squatting on the floor, some leaning shoulder to shoulder against the walls, and somewhere in the throbbing, swaying crowd a drum was beating out the rhythm of the song.

There was a brief pause as we were conducted to the far end of the room, and all squeezed down together on the pile of cushions reserved for us. Then a babble of comment and welcome broke out while everyone craned their necks to inspect the transformation of the English guest into a normal woman. Those sitting near me leaned forward to kiss my hand in formal greeting and my small stock of Arabic was almost used up in the first few minutes. A general consultation took place about the next song.

'This one, this one,' someone would cry, humming out the opening notes to the woman with the drum, a tall handsome creature with flashing eyes and a bold mouth. Finally she made her choice, striking out with the flats of her hands a kind of summoning, introductory double beat, insolent and thrilling. It was a big drum made of goatskin, and she carried it slung from a cord around her neck. As she struck the smooth stretched surface she radiated a kind of controlled ferocity that matched the violence of her playing. Her eyes followed the ring of singers but her face was preoccupied, expressionless, as though listening to a dictation of the rhythm from an outside source, compelled as a medium under trance.

The first dancers were, by custom, the newest brides. So the little doll-like wife of Salem and a beautiful statuesque girl who had just become married to his brother, took the floor with a fine display of modest protest. Stiff and self-conscious in their gold brocade they circled hand in hand like the painted figures on some musical toy, while the women clapped their hands and chanted the words of the song. Two less inhibited dancers took their place, servant-girls who glided lithely and freely as skaters up and down the narrow rectangular space, in the traditional pattern of steps, their arms around each others waists. Then a dozen women lined up on each side and performed an advancing and retreating dance, swaying backwards and forwards smilingly in time to the singing and the drum.

I was now experiencing a sinking feeling that sooner or later I would be called on to give an exhibition and I concentrated hard on the movements of the dancers' feet which looked deceptively simple. A minute later I was proved right, and a dozen willing hands pulled me to my feet with exclamations of encouragement. There was obviously no way out—the representative from Britannia had to show her paces. So I held firmly on to Miriam, the little serving girl from the Palace at Mukeiras, and with the sudden wild confidence of desperation launched into my nearest equivalent of the dance, a sort of subdued quick-step, which oddly enough matched the rhythm fairly well. After a few moments I began to enjoy myself and started showing off with all sorts of fancy variations. This was a mistake because the audience grew enthusiastic too and as soon as I showed signs of flagging another partner was thrust in my arms. 'They want you to teach them these English dances,' called Fatima above the hubbub. Once my shawl fell to the ground but another was hastily thrown over my head, while the singing rose to a deafening pitch and the drum palpitated faster and faster. My efforts were given official approval when first one bride joined me and then the other. Whenever I tried to draw to a conclusion, a group of small boys standing in front urged me on relentlessly with a fanatical gleam in their eyes and cries of '*Tamam! tamam!*' until with my last breath I managed to gasp to the drummer '*Khalas! Mashkur, mashkur!*' She gave a sudden nod of pity and stopped and the performance was over.

Claps on the back and kind words flooded round us as I was led upstairs again to be revived with *qahawa* and fresh grapes. But no one would allow me to change back into my own clothes, which were bundled up into a shawl and put in the back of the jeep when we left. 'They are for you to keep,' Sultan Abdulla's wife insisted. 'And this too,' said Saleh's sister, thrusting into my hand the little brass urn of *kohl*, 'so that you can wear it every day and return to see us again when you need some more.'

On the dark top-storey landing we kissed hands with them all. Then they disappeared into the bedroom again to watch us through the slit windows as we climbed into the jeep—my Arab dress causing a stir of comment from the menfolk sitting outside. We drove away waving to the faces we could not see but remembering their last words, 'Come again—be sure you come again. . . .'

Sultan Saleh did not forget his promise to take us out shooting. The next day he came to lunch, and sipping his tea afterwards remarked casually, 'Perhaps you would like to try your shooting now—if you are not too lazy.'

When we went outside we saw that the preparations had already been made for the trip. The little grey jeep was waiting at the end of the drive, with a stack of rifles in the back, and four guards standing to attention by the open door. Yet ordinary Arab pride would prevent him from presenting the invitation as anything but a sudden idle thought.

To my surprise he climbed into the driving seat and waved me to sit next to him while Fatima and the soldiers got into the back.

'I didn't know that you drove,' I said.

'Of course I drive,' he replied with a touch of indignation, then raising his eyebrows in a sly sidelong look, 'But a faithful jeep suits me better than a Chevrolet, I think.'

Put on his mettle, he roared the engine into a start and backed with a flourish round the circular flower-bed outside the front entrance. As we ricocheted out through the gates I glanced round at him, intrigued by the incongruity of that energetic Beduoin profile, and the gold *jambia* with left-hand drive signals and gear-boxes. But he merely wrinkled his eyes in a pleased competent half-smile and concentrated on the road ahead. Passing through the town he seemed unaware of the interest aroused by the sight of the Ruler driving side by side with an Englishwoman.

'Wouldn't you prefer me to get in the back with the others?' I asked uncomfortably.

'You will not,' he replied. 'This is the first time I drive with a feminine person in the next seat. I like this, it is something—novel! Also an honour,' he added recalling echoes of European courtesies to women.

Seeing Mohamed in the street he pulled up suddenly. 'We will borrow his rifle for you—it is lighter than mine.'

While Mohamed dashed into his house to get the gun, people crowded around the jeep. Two or three men pushed their way to the front with children on their shoulders so that the Sultan could pat them on the heads and ask about their welfare. 'This is *nasib*,' he explained. 'Like your custom of godfathers in England,' Fatima said. Mohamed had arrived back with the gun, and took up his official role. '*Nasib* means luck,' he went on in his best guide-interpreter's voice. 'Sometimes when a boy is born it is the custom to name him after the Sultan then take him to the Palace to be presented. Thereafter he has the right to ask food and clothing and lifelong protection from His Highness—a sort of insurance policy, in truth.' 'Then you must have many god-children,' I said to Saleh, watching the processional trail of infants up to the jeep. 'About half the children of the town!'

Then with a wave of his hand we drove off again. This time we turned away from the main track, bouncing over the turfy slopes while Saleh inspected the beauty of the wild, surrounding landscape of his country with an expression of proprietory pride.

He stopped near a cluster of rocks and we all got out. 'Now show them what it is to be a good shot,' he called in Arabic to the senior guard, an elderly bearded man with an expression of grizzled wisdom. Chuckling, the soldier took his rifle from his shoulder and aimed at one of the white stones, turning with a satisfied nod as he hit the target dead centre. Then Saleh took the lighter rifle and patiently showed me how to balance it across the boulder and fix my eye along the sighting piece, while the bearded one with an expression of weary irony at the nervous stupidity of women held it steady to that it wouldn't jump. I was still summoning up courage to fire when Saleh's forefinger came down over my own on the trigger at the crucial moment and a puff of smoke indicated a near bull's eye which deceived no one. Then Fatima was persuaded to try. After a while enthusiasm descended on us and we were firing off in all directions as fast as the guards could re-load until Saleh turned from his long survey of the Yemen hills to protest at the waste of good ammunition. 'Enough! More when you improve!'

So rubbing our sore shoulders but glowing with achievement we climbed back into the jeep and drove back towards town again, Saleh waving a reassuring hand to a party of tribesmen who were on their way to find out the reason for all the shooting.

On the way through the town we stopped to return the rifle to Mohamed. He came running up to the jeep window with a look of distress on his face and reported to Saleh, 'A Mukeiras boy has just had his hand badly injured, Your Highness. He was holding a grenade from the army camp and it went off.'

Trained from childhood to preserve a stony exterior in the face of all misfortune, Saleh asked impassively, 'How bad?'

'Two fingers blown off.'

'Then he must go to Aden for treatment.'

'But the father refuses.'

'Bring him to me.'

After an interval Mohamed returned with a very old man and a young man of about eighteen, who bent quickly in turn, to kiss the Sultan's knee and then stood with bowed heads at the open door of the jeep. 'This is the boy's father and his brother.'

Without any delay Saleh launched into a simple but decisive explanation why the boy must go to Aden.

'But they will cut off his hand,' the old man protested tremulously, moving out of sight of the strange Nazarene woman and turning his old troubled face into his shawl to hide his tears. The young man laid an embarrassed hand on his shoulder.

Saleh became more forceful but remained as patient as ever underlining his words with emphatic signs of command. 'If he stays here he will certainly lose his hand. But in Aden there are clever doctors. They will save his other fingers and make the whole thing heal quickly.' Sensing another reason for the old man's obstinacy he added, 'You know you need have no worry for the money for the plane and the hospital—all that is in my hand.'

There was an approving murmur from the crowd who had gathered round.

'Now you will put him on the plane tomorrow, eh?'

After a pause the old man sighed and nodded obediently. Then he wiped his leathery cheek with the back of his hand and made his way out through the onlookers, too numbed by his distress for ceremony, while the young man replied to the Sultan with suitable thanks and apologies for his father's behaviour. It was his brother's right hand you see, and how could a man defend his life without fingers to shoot with?

'The doctors will do their best,' Saleh replied.

The boy bent to kiss his knee once more in farewell, then raised himself and with a sudden passionate gesture of trust buried his face against Saleh's chest. He swiftly broke away again and turned and ran through the crowd to catch up with his father and carry the news to his brother.

'He would have made a good soldier too,' said Saleh with a shake of his head as we drove back to the house.

Sometimes in the evenings Saleh would come across to eat with us or sit for his portrait by lamplight, though he was not a good sitter and quickly grew impatient. Once there was great excitement because Naib Jabil was speaking in London on the B.B.C. and the talk was being relayed by Aden radio. Transmission in Mukeiras was poor and suspense rose to fever pitch as Saleh, Awadh the cook, Abdullah the houseboy, even Abdu the garden boy and two of the guards twiddled in turn at the knobs of the rather decrepit wireless to try and get the right wavelength. At last and just in time, a faint Arabic voice broke through the crackling. An intent silence descended on the listening circle. Afterwards Saleh grinned with delight at it all. 'He is doing well in London, that boy,' and the rest of the household went away shaking their heads in wonder at the mystery which enabled them to hear the voice of the Naib so far away in Britannia as though he was here in the same room—well, the next room anyway.

Many evenings we would sit after supper with the guards around their fire which they made in a low-walled corner just outside the front porchway. Stepping out of the shuttered living-room the night air was cool and unconfined, the rain of the after-noon still glinting in the starlight along the flagstones. The endearing, acrid smell of a new fire mingled with the scent of wet roses, voices rose and fell in conversation from the front of the house. Round the corner the circle of seated figures was already gathered round the impromptu hearth, their faces turned towards us like a string of gold coins in the blackness.

'Can we join you?'

'*Ahlan wa Sahlan*,' was the ever ready reply, the old greeting, polished with usage but spoken in the spontaneity of a freshly-minted phrase.

These were the guards who were off duty at this hour. At first there seemed to be four of them squatting cross-legged in the firelight. Then another figure wrapped in a blanket rose up at our feet to make way for us, a sixth moved along his seat on the low wall in the shadows of a rose bush, and yet another voice hailed us from above our heads. Looking up we saw Hassan, the clown of the party, curled up under a sheepskin on a wide window ledge.

They stacked their rifles together to make room for us and an ancient plaid rug was unfolded for us to sit on close to the fire. 'Because you have come from Aden where it is always hot.'

'And because the English always love fires, so they say,' put in Hussein, knowledgeably. He was a merry, laughing young man with a stock of repartee.

'This is my first fire for nearly two years,' I told them, while they watched me appreciating it with outstretched hands, glad as hosts are with a satisfied guest.

The fire was a small knot of flickering branches built on yester-day's ashes in the tin lid of an old box. It burned chiefly to make charcoal for their hookah. Once the flames had died out, with the ashes glowing red, the hookah became the focal point of the group. It was a rough-and-ready home-made specimen very unlike the Aden models which were all red-velvet coils and burnished brass. This one was made out of goatskin and tin cans with a long smoking stem attached to a small wooden cup at the top. The cup was first stuffed with a handful of tobacco and then covered with glowing embers picked carefully one by one from the fire with a pair of iron pincers. The expression of blissful satisfaction on the smoker's face was just the same as anywhere else though. So was the contented bubbling noise like a baby's bottle that arose from that section of the hookah where the water cooled the smoke.

They were all members of the Sultan's guard, the best warriors of Mukeiras. Some were young and in their twenties, one or two of them looked quite old with grey beards and lined faces. All of them were much taller than the average tribesman. As the flames died down someone lit a paraffin lamp and the yellow ray flickered over broad shoulders, muscular arms and legs, and encased in the folds of head shawls, lean, shy faces that were all cheek-bone and jawline and jutting nose with the gleam of deep-set eyes and the sudden white crease of a smile.

When someone made a joke they laughed quickly but not long, their faces transformed in a flash with expressions of undying hatred at some account of a suffered insult, or the firing of a neighbour's crops by Yemeni troops. And however linked together by tribal comradeship or mere physical closeness, they never quite merged into that inter-communicating, animal body of good fellowship which would characterise a party of, say, German soldiers. Something in the Arab blood held them apart. Each man was preserving deep inside himself a dark untouched pool of his inmost thoughts and feelings, with that final reserve, faint and undefinable, that individualism which is perhaps the basic essence of the Arab character. It is this individualism which explains why no genuine Arab could ever become a successful Communist.

They were laughing now, still a little self-conscious because of the Englishwoman, but gradually forgetting themselves. 'Who is the one that sings?' I asked. 'I hear him often at night, walking round the house on guard.'

'Not me!'

'No—not I, by Allah!' each one insisted, bashfully.

'Here, perhaps it is this one,' cried Abdullah, pointing to Awadh who had finished clearing away and had come out to join us.

'This one?' exclaimed Hussein. 'Why this one is only good for cooking—he hasn't even got a gun let alone a voice.'

Amidst the laughter, Awadh smiled rather ruefully and sat down in the shadows.

'No, this is the singer,' Hussein went on more seriously, pointing to an elderly man sitting quietly in the corner, a striking figure with a long curved nose and wide, slightly mad-looking eyes. He wore an eccentric collection of rags and sheepskins and his hair curled down to his shoulders, bound across the temples with a leather thong. Obviously this was the musician of the group.

'He is from the hills,' murmured my neighbour with a hint of apology in his voice. 'There they think the longer they grow their hair, the braver they become.' The speaker favoured the traditional Audhali hair-style, a neat nineteen-twenties bob, pushed back behind the ears.

'Yes, I am the singer,' said the man, whose name was Jawad. He came forward into the lamplight with a pleased smile.

'And you will sing for us?'

'I will try—but tonight, I don't know . . .' he replied with the traditional reaction of the artistic temperament.

A roar of protest broke out from the others.

'Commence! *ya Jawad!*'

'Gather your spirits, O foolish one!'

There was a general rustle as everyone settled down to listen. The tall figure of Abdullah the overseer appeared in the doorway where he remained standing, leaning against the wall with his arms crossed in the benevolent, patriarchal attitude suited to his position of authority. Someone leaned forward and stirred the ashes of the fire with a long stick so that the sparks flew up like fireflies.

In the centre, Jawad the singer rocked slowly backwards and forwards, sitting cross-legged with his ragged shawl bound round his knees and back, his head bent and his hands clasped over his ears, a frown of concentration knotting his brows. Suddenly a thin reedy voice emerged chanting, '*Dana, dana—ya dana*—the Arab la-la-la, a mere working-up of inspiration, an introduction to what was to come. This was repeated and taken up encouragingly by the circle—a short, undulating snatch of rhythm. And then Jawad's voice broke through again, waveringly high-pitched and nasal, completing the theme of the song, which went, 'When the Sultan's jeep goes over mud and stones, mind it doesn't splash you as it passes.' This was apparently a current local favourite. Awadh leaned over and told me that the composer had recently stolen a number of sheep and absconded to Yemen. Obviously song-writing was not a particularly lucrative profession in this part of the world.

It seemed here too that actual quality of voice had little to do with one's reputation as a singer, but rather with an ability to remember words and translate local events into simple phrases. Now Jawad was being urged to fresh efforts but somehow the muse had not descended on him that evening. He would croak out a false start and then stop again, shaking his head and tapping it exasperatedly. 'It won't come out tonight,' he kept repeating in lugubrious tones. After a while Hassan and Abdu, the garden boy, began to dissolve into giggles at these tremulous shreds of song, whereupon Jawad sulked, took umbrage, and eventually retired in silence back to his corner once more.

But once started, the singing was carried on by the others. The cheerful Hussein launched loudly into something about 'I am very happy because I have just paid two thousand shillings for a girl who is more handsome than the Sultan's jeep.' (The vehicle in question had by now acquired epic stature in Mukeiras and somehow insinuated its way into every other song.) This effort, however, was hastily suppressed, no doubt because it went into more detail of the lady's accomplishments than was considered fit in mixed company. A safe traditional nonsense song then followed, the circle taking up the theme introduced by Hussein as a chorus.

'There is a gap between evening and morning and
a difference also between an apple and a lemon.'

'Now one about an aeroplane,' demanded Awadh.
'This is the best one,' said Abdullah, stepping forward authoritatively and leading them into a rousing saga which ran,

'The guns shout from the border
And ours answer them.
We make cables for the British
And they send planes to destroy the enemy.'

There was a touching trustful note about this—a reply in a nutshell to those who said the British were not wanted in the Protectorate, so why didn't we clear out, get rid of this millstone around our neck.

The note of trust became positively imperialistic in the last item—'Make way for the cars of Government, for Government is all-powerful'—but perhaps this was especially for my benefit. If there was a rather more astringent follow-up to this proclamation, it was hastily suppressed amidst laughter and my presence politely indicated to the offenders.

After the singing was over, we stayed talking for a while. Two of the guards were turning over the pages of a glossy magazine I had given them, the others peering over their shoulders. With an exclamation of admiration they stopped at a picture of an officer in the Lifeguards in full dress. 'Just like us,' Hussein cried when I explained. But one of the bearded elder ones brought them down to earth, pointing to the elaborate headgear and uniform, 'But to sleep in such things! What sort of rest would that be?'

Another handsome young tribesman pored sideways over a pin-up picture of a protuberant blonde film starlet, 'And this woman here, so young with her hair already so white!' He clucked his tongue incredulously, then added to himself on closer inspection, 'Her form is surely most strange—can such things be true?'

I was interested to see how much impact Egyptian propaganda had made in this remote corner of Arabia and I asked them whether they preferred Aden radio or Cairo radio. A newcomer to the group, a guard just coming off duty, thought we were discussing the rival merits of Cairo and Aden and hastily struck in with 'Cairo? Aden? But Mukeiras is better than either of these places.' This was seized on by the others as a great joke, perhaps to cover a situation they realised might be a delicate one.

'Mukeiras radio! That's the one!' they shouted. 'That's the best of all, Mukeiras radio!'

And then more seriously, one said, 'All radio is very good. But not as good as our singing—this is what we prefer to listen to.'

We made our good-nights and thanks for their company and went back into the house. Locking the doors behind us Awadh still had his mind fixed on the joke made at his expense earlier on.

He hesitated then said with a grin, 'Perhaps if you give a good report of my cooking when you leave, the Sultan will give me a gun.'

'How much does a rifle cost?' I asked.

'More than a bride!' he exclaimed.

'Perhaps two thousand shillings?'

'And to whom does the Sultan give guns free?'

'To the bravest warriors, and those who live along the border.'

'Perhaps to a cook too, then,' I said reassuringly, although I couldn't imagine why, and Awadh went away beaming happily.

Through my sleep, I heard the guards singing again outside the house, the tune and words as familiar as if I had known them all my life.

When I was telling Nur one morning in the Harem about my visit to Ariab and how I was decorated with Arab cosmetics, she had merely replied rather primly that the ladies there thought more about these things than she had time to do. Still it must have been very nice for me. To console her I took with me on my last visit the day before we left a selection of Elizabeth Arden adornments—lipstick, powder, cream—so that she would have something new to flourish next time she visited the Ariab harems.

She received these offerings with a smile of pure delight, then questioned me intently about the correct procedure for each item. 'And how surprised the Naib will be to see me with a new face when he returns,' she murmured, fluttering her eyes demurely at her hand-mirror as she experimented with a beauty-spot of blue eye-shadow on each cheek-bone.

After a while she tore herself away to give directions about the lunch party the Sultan was giving downstairs for a visiting Sheikh. This made the eating arrangements for the household more complicated than usual. On this day four separate meals were served almost simultaneously—one for the Sultan and his guests downstairs, one for the men of the family in a room above, one for the women in another room on the same storey and one for the servants in the back-quarters, apart from the numbers of hangers-on of one kind or another, guards, messengers and their friends who could be found snatching the odd bite in a convenient passage-way.

The connecting link between all these groups was Awadh the cook. Cries of his name re-echoed from room to room from noon onwards. Other helpers might actually serve the meal but it was his mission to present special delicacies and to be on hand while they were sampled.

In between the other three meals he rushed into the harem quarters, flung a white cloth on the linoleum in front of us, then disappeared again while a small tousled boy staggered in with a load of plates. He dealt three of these to Fatima, Nur and myself, left a few more in the middle of the cloth, and vanished to dispose of the rest elsewhere. Another youthful lieutenant entered clutching a fistful of forks and knives but was so flustered that all he could do was to present them to me like a bouquet.

'This is the first time he has been in the harem,' Nur explained apologetically. In a flash, however, Awadh was back to restore order and to supervise the serving of the curry, rice and salad which Miriam brought in. As an after-thought he dashed out and returned with three joints of meat, carefully placing one in front of every plate. Then, with the air of a conjurer, he drew out from the covered basket on his arm three pancakes of bread the size of small cartwheels, carefully folding each one into four and adding them to our collection of food which now included large cupfuls of delicious hot soup. Exit Awadh, basket on arm, and re-enter the new boy, now more composed, with a basin of quartered lemons for squeezing into the soup.

Half-way through the meal we were joined by Nur's five-year-old brother. As an example of the confusing possibilities of Arab relationships, it should be pointed out that this midget was an uncle to Nur's young Feisal, who was his elder by two months. He greeted us with equanimity, removed a small pair of scuffed plimsoles and sat down to a large plateful of rice, curry and hard-boiled eggs. He murmured to his sister that he had become weary of the conversation of the men with whom he had started his meal in the room opposite. After a second course of fruit salad, he stood up, nodded in easy masculine fashion to us, kissed his sister's hand and disappeared again, taking the table-cloth with him and folding it up as he went.

Another visitor during the meal was a very old and dignified woman, who waved her hand in polite dismissal at the suggestion of food and squatted down on the floor near the door where she remained with a brooding expression like one of the Fates until we had finished eating.

'Who is this?' I asked in a cautious undertone.

Nur murmured something which Fatima nonchalantly translated as 'She is a lawyer.'

'A *what*?'

Nur then explained that this was one of the best-known personages in Mukeiras—she was a very wise and respected widow who had taken upon herself the duty of putting forward any cases of insult or tribulation brought by women of the villages to the

Mukeiras court. The court was an informal gathering presided over by Sultan Saleh every morning at the entrance of the Palace. She was, in fact, the recognised spokesman of the under-privileged female and as such was awarded a special place in society. 'She likes to come in here for some peace and quiet to think all these things over,' said Fatima.

I gazed with admiration at the Arabian Portia and would liked to have talked with her, but she suddenly left as unobtrusively as she arrived, with one hand uplifted in a benevolent blessing on the assembled company.

After the meal we stayed and talked for a while. Nur proudly displayed to us some jewellery we had seen before. 'Something modern, from Aden'—two ruby and diamond rings designed in the shape of aeroplanes. She wore one on each small forefinger.

I had been to see her every day since we arrived and I felt I knew her well enough now to ask her what she thought was the future for Aden women still under *purdah*. 'All right for some to come out of *purdah* but not others,' was her immediate reaction. Obviously the idea of freedom for all was something outside her orbit of thinking—the custom for upper-class women to be veiled must have seemed to her as permanent as a law of nature.

I asked her if she minded being unable to walk freely in the fresh air like the village women she watched from the windows. For a moment the essential truth of the situation came through, 'Sometimes one feels restless, of course, but what can we do about it?'

She added, 'Besides, it is the life one has known from childhood, not something that is put upon one suddenly.'

'And would you ever wish to travel to Europe, like some of the ladies of the Sultan of Lahej's family?'

Without hesitation, she replied with a faintly surprised, very definite shake of the head. And there was something grotesque about the picture of this gentle creature shopping in Selfridges at the rush-hour or stepping into the lift at her hotel—even more macabre to imagine her in our female European uniform and shorn of her beautiful yard-long plaits. Elizabeth Arden was in this case far better wasted on the desert air than transposed back to London.

For a woman of her rank it was an event for Nur to travel even from Mukeiras to Ariab. For her, life must remain fixed within its present bounds, a cramped but graceful pattern woven with the intricate threadwork of half-remembered, fiercely-guarded customs and traditions. She asked nothing more of it than to please her husband, care for her children, keep the household happy, and do what little she could to help the women who came to see her.

When the time came to leave it was hard to say goodbye. I kissed her hands and wished her a safe return for her husband, an easy time when the baby came and the second boy she desired. To myself, I thought: You have your rooms and your windows, I have the world. Yet you are contented, I am the restless one. There must be an Arab proverb to explain it somewhere—there always was—something about the deep pool and the shallow river? . . .

I also thought it was unlikely I should ever see Nur again. When we left Aden the following month we should probably not be coming back. But she said, '*Arja'a fisaa!*'—Come back soon. And I repeated '*Arja'a fisaa*' as though by saying the magic words one could break the spell of fact. She hesitated then said with a quick guilty smile—'And you know, for velvet, there is nothing I like so much as red!'

As we were going out of the door she came after us and put a basket in my hand. 'I know you like *qahawa*. These are the things you need for it and it is written down on a piece of paper how to make it—Fatima will translate it for you. Now you can drink it with your friends in England and think of us while you are away.'

We walked down the hill again, not looking back because Nur's windows were at the other side of the house. But a small boy, running behind us, caught up with us and panted a whispered message. We turned and saw for the first time Nur come out on to the top balcony in front of the house, a tiny figure shrouded in black, which waved once then disappeared into the shadows again.

Sultan Saleh came across to say goodbye to us later in the evening. For the first time, the strain under which he was living showed through in his manner and appearance. We were sitting out on the terrace with the faint glow of a shaded lantern at our feet when he arrived. He flung himself on to the canopied garden seat with a sigh and covered his face with his hands for a minute. 'It is this headache—when I am worried I have it for days.'

'The news is bad then?' I asked.

'I have just been talking to someone who has come from the Yemen. I think it is good you are leaving tomorrow, sad as we are to see you go.'

'What will happen here?'

He took off his turban with a characteristic gesture and ran his hand through his hair which glistened short and fine like the fur of a black cat. The lamp threw a thin gold tissue of illumination up over his features, darkened the shadows around his eyes, as he leaned forward. 'Some things become very difficult for me to understand. Why for instance your Government refuses to take direct action against the Yemen. Air action. You have the 'planes in Aden. And it would mean the end of all my troubles. No more attacks, no more sanctuary and rewards for those of my own tribesmen they persuade to turn against me, to raid their own country at night and return back over the Yemen border before dawn.'

I murmured the usual thing about world opinion but it sounded a feeble reply and Saleh ignored it. 'You know I am not one of those rulers who shelter behind the British to keep themselves in office,' he went on. 'All I want is that my people should be shown clearly which side you are on. Let them have a good answer to those Egyptian lies that the British are leaving us, too, now to the mercy of our enemies. My people are a primitive people and they believe only what they see. When they see no direct action they think you are either afraid or that you don't care. And if you can't do this thing at least give us some arms to fight in our own way.'

'But you have told them all this—you have told the Government?' I asked. He nodded and suddenly grinned at me. 'But you can tell them too. Perhaps you can prove that women have some power in the western world as you always say!'

Then he brought out farewell-presents for us both—an embroidered scarf for Fatima and something wrapped in a shawl for me. I hesitated before unfastening it but he stepped forward impatiently and did it for me. Inside was a beautiful length of black Persian lamb stitched casually to form the lining of a coat of rough blue serge.

Imagining the fur coat it would make in its own right I was overcome. 'These skins I asked a man on the Yemen border to get for me two weeks ago,' he said with pride. 'Please put it on.' He stepped back and surveyed the result with a delightful pleased smile. 'This is good.'

But he waved aside all thanks for the gifts and any gratitude for the time we had spent in Audhali. To me he said, 'I would like to come to the airport tomorrow. If it was Aden I could do so but you understand here among my people it would not be looked on as correct procedure. So I say goodbye now—but not really goodbye. Friendship is not made to be broken. We shall meet again often—if not in Aden, then in London—anywhere in the world, in fact.'

He turned to leave and added from the doorway, 'And did I not keep you safe in my Land as I promised? Then this promise shall also be kept—that we shall be meeting again. Also, you will see how well I am learning to write English!'

Then he was gone. . . .

When we went to bed, there was no rain, only the patter of drums coming over faintly from the Yemen hills. From the watch-tower behind the Palace a message was being flashed out with a hooded lantern to some unknown sentry on the border and the lamp was still alight in the window of the Sultan's room.

Mohamed came for us in the jeep soon after dawn the next

morning. At the airstrip a crowd of people were already waiting. They gave every appearance of having happily spent the night there. Some were sitting on large tin trunks gaily painted with pink and blue flowers. Others were making a leisurely breakfast, reclining against the sacks of vegetables which were to be taken to Aden. The sun was shining with crystalline brilliance through the early mists.

When the flare was eventually sighted, a tiny speck over the distant mountains, it was only ten minutes after time. As it circled overhead and roared up the rough turf of the runway it was greeted with a fusillade of welcomes, exclamations, farewell blessings and embraces between friends and relations. But once the engines were turned off the atmosphere became placid again and we did not leave for at least another half-hour. The coolies went on standing around in restful attitudes, gossiping, until someone remembered to remind them about loading the baggage. This they did in an unhurried enjoyable sort of way, while half a dozen people in various positions of authority wandered around ticking off crumpled lists of goods and delicately painting letters and numbers on to wooden boxes with long sticks dipped in ink.

Just as we had hauled ourselves on to the 'plane we saw someone jolting at top speed astride a donkey along the track to the airstrip. The figure waved urgently in our direction and as he drew closer we saw it was Awadh. He flung himself off his mount and sprinted the last fifty yards on foot, panting as he came up to the 'plane—'Mrs Knox—my chit! Your report for my cooking —you forgot to give it me—you remember?' With tremendous winks and grimaces he mouthed the word 'Rifle'. I nodded conspiratorily and, surrounded by interested onlookers, sat down in the 'plane to scribble a positive paean of praise about Awadh's curries on the back of an old bill I found in my handbag.

My last glimpse of Mukeiras was the beaming figure of Awadh triumphantly waving his scrap of paper as we rose into the air. We held our breath as we skimmed up above the steep range of hills in front. Then we were safely over the edge of the plateau and all the mountains far below so many wrinkles on an elephant's hide.

Back in Aden the pre-monsoon atmosphere descended on us again like a wet blanket in a steam laundry. Only twenty-four hours later the news came through that the following morning's 'plane from Mukeiras was fired on by Yemeni troops while flying near the border and the pilot was shot through the neck. The order was issued: 'No one to land in Audhali unless under Government or Military orders.' I was right—it had been my last chance.

Sultan Saleh bin Hussein of Audhali wearing a khaki jacket, *futah* and solid gold *jambia*

Lunch party at Sheikh Mohamed Omar's

After the picnic in the Husseini Gardens, Lahej. The Author, Sultan Ali and Sheikh Ali

Sultan Ali of Lahej wearing an English sports jacket, Arab sash
and *jambia*

Sultan Ali with Sayid Mohamed Ali Jifri

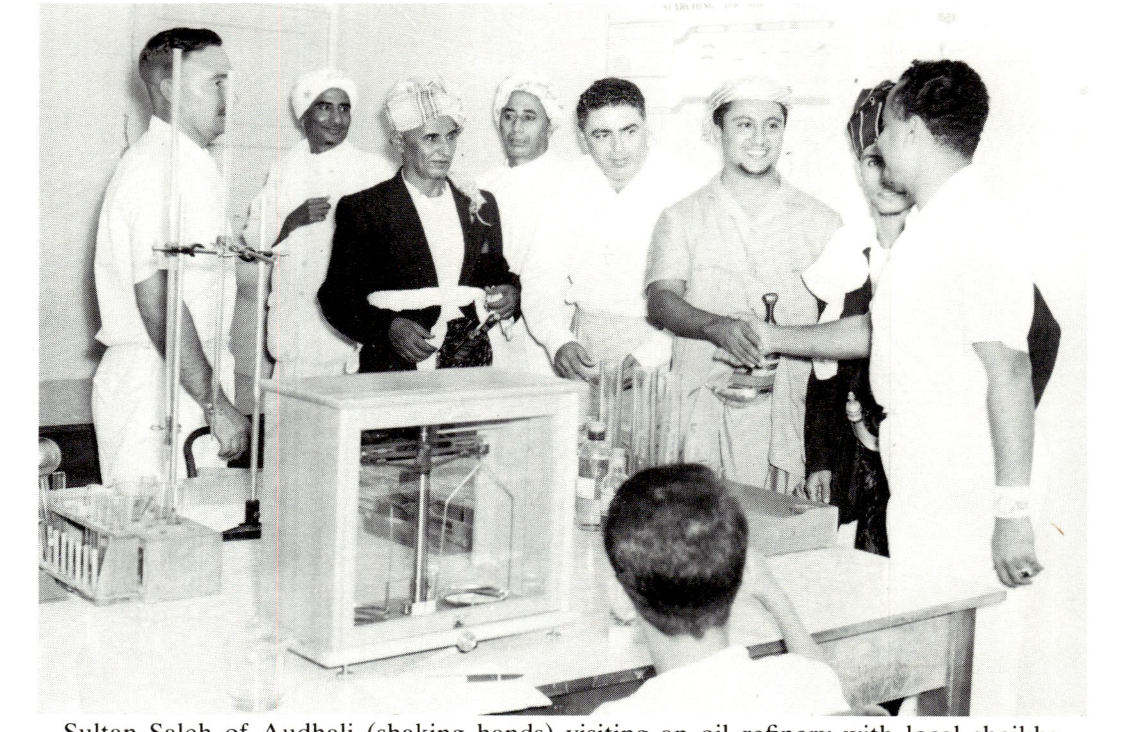

Sultan Saleh of Audhali (shaking hands) visiting an oil refinery with local sheikhs

Sultan Ali on tour in Subeihi country, greeted by a procession of villagers

Small boy of Mukeiras

Small girl of Mukeiras

Two unveiled women at Kirsh

Bedouin women of the Lahej desert, on the way to Kirsh.

The Author with a bodyguard of six warriors at Kirsh

12

Last View from the Palace

I had just started on the task of packing the glass and china one morning when the 'phone rang and Farid let loose a torrent of talk at the other end which finally resolved itself into an invitation to travel with him to Kirsh the following day. Kirsh was a village in Lahej State on the Yemen border. He was taking a party of road engineers there to pay a courtesy visit to the local Naib.

We were leaving Aden in a week's time and I knew this was my last opportunity of seeing something new in the Protectorate so I said thank you very much, I would be ready at 5 a.m. the next day.

It was still pitch-dark when Farid called with his party in a Lahej government land-rover. By the time the winding, rutted track of sand and stone began to climb out of Lahej the first light was breaking and we stopped for a picnic breakfast. Around us was a harsh, barren land to which the haggard little villages clung in clusters along the way. Some of the houses were tall and built of stone, others were mere mud-huts thatched with straw. Each village had its white-domed tomb of the local saint and a small mosque with the traditional crescent moon glinting like a weather-cock from the topmost spire. The one at Zaid, just outside Lahej, looked almost like an English village church in outline except for the bubble-shaped roof of the square central tower.

Whenever we approached a village squads of small boys would rush out waving bottles of fizzy lemonade and bottle-openers as though we were marathon runners to be refreshed as we went along with the greatest possible speed.

The *suks* of the villages we passed through varied from a string of tiny, open shop-fronts crammed with kettles, pans and tinned food, to mere squares of cloth laid out along the verge of the road displaying with careful artistry a few bunches of bananas and some battered packets of cigarettes.

The engineers who were travelling with us had come to make preliminary surveys for a new road. It would eventually cut across the whole of the state of Lahej from the Yemen border to Aden. They were four brawny South Africans and they seemed giants even in this country of gigantic landscapes with their laconic talk of, 'We'll have to shift that bit of a rise of course,' pointing to a rearing craggy hill on our right, 'and perhaps fling some sort of bridge across this gap'—a lunar chasm yawning in a dried river bed beneath us—'instead of going all the way round it.'

In between the scattered villages life would seem extinct until, as we drew nearer in our bouncing, rattling, snorting box of a vehicle, a group of slight, black-robed figures would suddenly appear out of nowhere. Carrying small babies and surrounded by older children and flocks of goats, these Bedouin women greeted us with welcoming smiles and shy cries of surprise. One looked closer and saw in the background the homes of these families, tiny wigwams of woven branches, twigs and dried grass which could be left behind for the desert winds to scatter when the tribe moved on in search of fresh pasture grounds for their flocks.

Even here Farid was a familiar figure. He had travelled this way with the Sultan often before. There was always a short preliminary exchange of chaff and laughter, Farid exuding beaming compliments and improper suggestions in the direction of the family beauties. Then the younger women disappeared into the tents to return with offerings of goats' milk and fresh eggs for us. The old ones, bent and witchlike in their rags, hovered in the background with expressions of disapproval on their faces. But they brightened up considerably at the sight of coins changing hands. One of them, a tiny withered creature with blue tattoo marks on her face and that terrible appearance of extreme age which is only seen in primitive people, hobbled forward with a grin to request the favour of a few cigarettes. She told us that smoking was now her greatest pleasure in life but it was a luxury rarely to be had. Farid lit one for her and, puffing away like a 1920's vamp, she regaled us with the gossip of the tribe. The old man standing in the doorway of the first tent—he had had four wives and killed them all off. Everyone knew that the prettiest of the young girls was really a *jinn*—it was said she could turn into any animal during the hours of darkness—and of course she would get no husband. No man would have the courage to take on that. The young fellow sitting under the thorn tree—he was not left behind by the other men because he was lazy but because he had sickness of the eyes. He was so frightened of blindness he had asked some wise man of another tribe to save him. She called him over to us and pointed out the scar of a deep cut across each cheek—'But it did no good.' The man's eyes were red and inflamed as were those of many other Bedouins we saw, and Farid promised to bring ointment next time he passed through this way.

Among the sparse greenery of the river banks a tribal encampment presented an idyllic scene, the smoke rising unruffled from a wood fire, the men straight and bare to the waist setting out with their rifles and their flocks, the women small and lithe in their flowered shifts, bound with a scarf at the hips, black turbans swathed around their heads, as they spread out their washing on the rocks. They straightened up, shading their eyes, and waved to us as we whirled past, visitants from another world. Their exclamations, shrill as birds' cries, echoed after us across the valley.

How different were the valleys, over which a deadly, hopeless air of lethargy often seemed to brood among details of squalor which recalled the drawings of Hogarth. Here the villain was not gin but *qat*, which stupefied rather than excited its addicts. And so we saw no scenes of violence. Instead there was this strange feeling everywhere of sapped energies, of will-power vitiated by a drug which served to dull the harshness of life in such a climate and setting. The low-roofed interior of almost every hovel seemed crowded with the reclining figures of men chewing the green leaves, for *qat* is not a private but a social pleasure. In other doorways were young girls with babies in their arms—'The mothers are working in the fields,' said Farid. 'The women do most of the work in this part while the men take their ease.' One of the huts seemed to be turned into a communal *crèche*. Inside we could glimpse a pair of rough swinging cots, suspended by ropes from the rafters, in which a number of babies were sleeping or crying, while toddlers ran around the floor. A pregnant woman sat watching them with an expression of placid resignation.

Kirsh was the biggest village and here there was a more prosperous air with many stone houses and the surrounding fields thick with crops. From a towered stone building, like a miniature fortress ahead of us fluttered the red-and-white Lahej flag. 'The house of the Naib,' said Farid.

We got out stiffly, brushing the layers of dust off our clothes and walked across the courtyard. A row of spectators decorated every wall. There were shouts of welcome and enquiries as to who the unknown Englishwoman was. The Naib, a small wiry man in a clean white shirt and *futah* and russet-coloured turban, a dagger studded with cornelians in his belt, waited to greet us in the doorway. He was also a little surprised to see me but said gruffly, with an encouraging nod in reply to my greeting, 'Eh!— She speaks our language well.' I remained mostly silent for the rest of the visit, to keep up my reputation. This, however, was not difficult with Farid in the company.

The Naib's room was at the top of the tower. It was small with whitewashed walls and furnished with an iron bedstead and cane chairs from Aden. Black-and-white checkered lino covered the floor with two or three strip rugs around the walls. The Naib proudly pointed out that the place had been re-roofed recently with corrugated iron and—*pièce de résistance*—the beamed chassis end of a wrecked lorry. There were the inevitable rifles in the corner and it all reminded me a little of the Sheriff's room in the shanty town of an old-fashioned western.

Over the Naib's bed hung a torch, a mirror and a faded snapshot of the village. He had thrown his jacket over the long bamboo pole which was strung like a clothes line from one wall to another. The ancient centre table was cluttered with magazines from Cairo, and an office diary.

'How was Lahej when you came through?' was the Naib's first question. He told us that he and most of his soldiers came from the town of Lahej. But Kirsh was a frontier outpost and their wives had had to remain behind until the spell of duty was completed. 'And our Lord the Sultan? The blessings of Allah upon him.'

Then he showed us the view through the narrow window. 'This is the best thing we have,' he said, pointing to a brand-new petrol station on the other side of the dusty track. Spick and span under its red-and-yellow paint and glistening pumps, it could have taken its place in any modern city. Here, among the mud houses, the miles of barren desert and the flocks of goats, it was an incredible sight. The Naib told us it was the last stop for all the lorries passing through on their way to the Yemen. 'The frontier is only three miles away.'

I was eager to drive up to it and perhaps put one foot on the forbidden territory but the Naib shook his head. 'It would not be safe—for you, that is.'

'And do the Yemenis ever make any attacks on your people?' I asked.

'*Abadan!*' He shook his head emphatically. 'We are all brothers, are we not?'

Two boys brought in a meal of rice and mutton and the Naib opened a cupboard in the wall to bring out glasses for the fresh lime-juice. He also took out a roll of tobacco, carefully tied up in an old towel, and filled the hubble-bubble to hand it round to the guests. Inside the cupboard I glimpsed a tin of English biscuits, a doormat with 'Welcome' on it, half a dozen Thermos flasks and other treasured possessions of the Naib's.

After we had eaten I said I would like to look around the village. The Naib hesitated for a moment until I added that I swore on the life of his father not to stray in the direction of the Yemen border. He grinned and said he would give me a bodyguard. They would show me anything of Kirsh I wished to see. He went out of the room for a moment before calling me down the twisting stone stairway again and through the doorway. Outside in the courtyard six stalwart warriors stood in line, rifles held stiffly before them. They relaxed to shake hands and be introduced. Then off we set, leaving the Naib behind with an amused expression on his face.

There was not very much of Kirsh to be seen, and the expedition was a short one. We inspected the petrol station, the local mosque and the coffee-house kept by a pretty young woman in a red shift and a black shawl. The narrow laneway between the houses was full of dust and rattle of loaded lorries making for the Yemen. They were more like huge motor-driven farm-carts than anything else, these lorries, the wooden beams crudely painted in red and yellow, the bales of goods topped with the swaying figures of travellers getting a cheap lift over the border. They kept their faces swathed bandit-style with pieces of wet cloth against the clouds of sand which rose from under the wheels. But these jolting caravans were the only signs of activity about the place. Otherwise the air of drowsy lassitude was the same as in the other villages we had passed. *Qat* was being chewed everywhere, though the fields outside were heavy with crops and the soldiers told me that practically all the people of Kirsh were small farmers and land-workers.

In the middle of this wilderness the tiny shops were selling among other things, tinned pineapple and washing powder. I bought myself a sample of each. When we stopped to talk to a family outside one of the wigwams of branches and dried grass on the edge of the village, these purchases were eyed with such admiration that, although I could imagine a dozen things more useful to her, I presented them there and then to the young wife. These people were living in the extremes of poverty, yet hardship had failed to blunt either the fine edge of their courtesies or the shy grace of the young women and the beauty of the children. Many of the small girls we saw had decorative patterns painted in indigo on their faces, usually a narrow line running down the centre, with 'beauty spots' on the chin and each cheek.

Though they were unveiled, the women were as shy of the camera as they had been in Mukeiras. Before we left the guards took us in a jeep to see some hot springs nearby. Farid, however, was far more interested in the three shepherdesses who were watching the flocks of sheep in a field on the other side of the stream. And despite the orders of the soldiers telling them to come up to the water's edge to be photographed, there they remained, clustered together in their black Greek draperies under a far-off tree, fiercely cherishing their modesty and calling down in shrill voices the curses of Allah on any who tried to rob them of it. Even Farid would not brave the water between, which gushed out of a hole in the ground at a temperature a little below boiling point. 'Besides, they look very cross,' he added nervously.

Then we drove back to take our leave of the Naib. He gave us half a dozen messages of loyalty to take to the Sultan and stood in the sun waving goodbye to us with the six soldiers and a crowd of villagers until we turned the first bend in the long dusty track home.

Soon after we made our last visit to Lahej. This time Ali received us in the old Palace which had just been re-designed throughout. It was in the evening and supper was served on small tables in what a luxury hotel would undoubtedly call the 'Arab Room'. Before, this had been a long strip of verandah. Now, it was lavishly furnished with striped ottoman couches, brass hookah stands and tables, Persian rugs, with a series of dividing half-walls in scrolled Moorish lattice-work. Yet the whole effect was somehow false—it was too much the Hollywood version of Arabia, had too much the air of a fashionable restaurant.

'This is where I shall receive my Arab visitors,' said Ali. I imagined some travel-stained Sheikh resting his weary limbs on the silk cushions and thinking himself in Paradise itself among such luxury.

On the walls hung a collection of family swords and daggers, surmounted by an enormous gold scimitar which had been presented to Ali's grandfather by the Imam of Yemen at that time.

The women's quarters were at the back, and the servants' on the ground floor. Amongst the grandeur of the entrance hall two workmen were squatting by lamplight putting the finishing touches to a plaque of electric switches—the Palace had its own generator in the grounds.

After supper, Ali took us through some of the other rooms. The main reception-room was unrecognisable. Gone was the fumed oak, the chocolate paint, the red plush, the Harrods' suites of his father's choice. Instead, the black marble floors reflected pillars and walls of a pale grey-green—Ali's final choice after weeks of deliberations and consultations over shade charts and scraps of material. The long windows were vogueishly veiled in drifts of white muslin with side drapes of pale green brocade.

'At what height should the loops be to hold them back do you think?' Ali asked anxiously, draping his handkerchief at an experimental angle round one of the curtains. 'This is something I do not know.'

The furniture was his favourite French and Italian eighteenth-century—all carved gilt and stuffed tapestry, with ormolu mirrors on every wall, except in the dining-room where the familiar sepia-tinted ancestors brooded among crimson morocco and mahogany and the glitter of crystal chandeliers.

'And here I would like a Constable, I think,' he said, indicating a bare expanse of wall at the far end of the main reception-room.

'A Constable?' I asked. 'Something so English?'

'Well, what can one do?' he said with resigned regret. 'Our own people do not produce paintings and I would prefer to have an English scene by an Englishman than his version of an oriental one—don't you agree?'

I said yes and promised to look out for something suitable in England—not the real thing—all those were already in the art galleries. But something that looked just as good from a sale room.

'A sale room,' he repeated dubiously.

'It will be much cheaper. . . .'

He nodded in acceptance. 'You are right—and after all neither I nor anyone else here would know the difference.'

Back in the 'Arab Room' we found a figure from the past waiting by the window for us—Mohammed Ali Jifri, exiled from the Colony and now living half in Cairo and half in Lahej. He was plumper than when I had last seen him in Aden, but flashed the same charming smile at us as he stood up to greet us.

Then we all sat down together.

There were no signs of bitterness in his conversation. He talked of the glorious future of a free and united Arabia with all his old fire and enthusiasm. Once or twice at the height of a discussion he forgot himself. His voice lost its note of control, and an odd disparity of focus became noticeable in his eyes as he spoke. At these moments he became a fanatic and the hand he laid on Ali's shoulder in argument seemed a reminder to his ruler of some powerful obligation rather than the easy bond of friendship.

Half-way through a sentence he suddenly remembered something and sprang to his feet to turn on the radio. The voice that came through was that of Colonel Nasser speaking at Alexandria on the anniversary of the Egyptian seizure of the Suez Canal. The roars from the massed crowds of his audience, the ranting torrent of gutteral-sounding language had an uncanny flavour of the pre-Munich broadcasts from Berlin. Through the crackling of the set the bitter edge to the often-repeated word 'Israeli' pierced like acid.

Everyone in the room was listening with the closest attention. The atmosphere was startlingly transformed. Farid was sitting next to me a little apart from the others and to ease my own tension I murmured a joking remark to him under my breath, linking the speech with some little thing that never failed to make us all laugh. But he remained intent, gazing at the radio, as though he hadn't heard. It seemed that now he too was involved. I felt like someone who sees the ice begin to crack under his feet in all directions.

Then Ali, sensing the strain, quickly got up and snapped the voice off again. From the table he picked up a photograph album and sat next to me with it. 'There are some things here that might interest you.' He turned over the pages pointing out the people

I knew. When he came to a picture of two men in elaborate turbans and gowns sitting together heads bent in laughing conversation, Ali stopped and remarked with a harshness in his voice —'This is my step-brother, the former Sultan, with a friend. This same friend he had murdered in his own house by a firing squad only two months later.'

When he replaced the book on the table I noticed an elaborately-carved antique silver box underneath and went over to look at it closely.

'What does it hold?' I asked.

Ali picked it up and opened it. Inside was a very old and beautiful Koran bound with ivory-coloured doeskin and printed in gold. I instinctively put out my hand to it but a curious hesitancy in Ali's manner restrained me.

'You see, it is forbidden for any but a believer to touch it,' he said awkwardly. 'This is an old law—something very sacred— you understand.'

There was a second's silence of embarrassment. We were standing with our backs to the others some distance away. Then he said quickly in a low voice, 'But I would like you to touch this Koran.'

I was still unsure. He nodded. 'Please take it in your hands and look at it. It has been in my family for many many generations.'

The pages inside were of doeskin too, tender as rose petals. They gave up a scent of musk and incense and of piety itself, The printing was in black and gold—it had been done by hand. lovingly, and it was fading now.

'These old words and the words of Nasser—they are all part of the same Islam,' he said, taking the book back from me and locking it in the silver box again. 'This is something you must remember.'

Before we left he took us on to the flat rooftop of the Palace, leading the way up the narrow staircase with a lamp in his hand. Building materials were still littered everywhere. We leaned over the carved breast-high parapet. In the distance we could see the sparkling fringe of the Aden lights. 'And on a clear morning, the sea.'

Ali asked us whether it had been awkward for us to meet Mohammed Ali again now he was exiled by Government. He hoped we didn't mind but Mohammed Ali had been anxious to see us once more before we left. 'It is a difficult time for both of us now,' he said. 'Government would like me to ban him from Lahej too—this is their wish, I know. He is still too near to Aden for their comfort with his speeches and the following he has. But they must realise this is impossible—to tell a man to move from his own country where his people have lived for generations. Besides the Jifris have always been the closest friends of the royal family. The British cannot understand that to an Arab, friendship such as this comes above any other thing in the world.'

He turned with a sigh and looked around the shadowy rooftop. 'This place always reminds me of when I was a child. On hot nights in the summer, like tonight, the men of the family would come up here to sleep sometimes. I always slept next to my father and I can remember his standing over me, shaking me hard to rouse me for morning prayers before it was light. If I turned over and went to sleep again I got a whipping and no breakfast.'

After a moment the moon came out from behind the clouds. A hot wind flickered across our faces with the smell of dust in it, dry and prickling to the throat. 'I think there will be a sandstorm tonight,' he said. Beyond the dark belt of the gardens below the Palace walls a veil seemed to hang over the furthest dunes as though the sand was white-hot and smoking from some strange subterranean fire. The impersonal vastness of the desert seemed suddenly to be closing in on us. Its hugeness seemed to menace the fragility of the toy civilisation beneath our feet—the gilded cabinets, the rococo mirrors and the chandeliers. The last two lines of some poem I had forgotten came into my mind:

> Outside, the hourglass earth and sky lie tilted;
> Slow grain by grain the desert sands advance.

Our goodbye to Ali was only a goodbye to the Ali of Lahej.

He was leaving for Europe himself the following month, for his yearly vacation. We were to meet him again in Italy where he had asked us to stay at his villa at Rapallo for a few days.

As we walked out through the gardens for the last time, through the scent of jasmine and frangipani, from the roof-top a lantern waved slowly backwards and forwards then was extinguished.

The last week was an unreal round of packing and goodbyes. The final items to be packed were two superb Persian carpets which arrived from Lahej, a farewell gift from Ali, the day before we left. The final farewells were to Aboker, who cried a little then cheered up to announce if we didn't come back he would become a wealthy sheep-trader; to So-help-me who pressed into our hands a carefully prepared package of sandwiches to sustain us between Aden and Britannia; to Abdu-Sweeper who was engrossed in inspecting his own share of farewell presents—a collection which had been regrettably depleted by one shirt at the last minute when Ronald discovered he had packed all his own.

Or almost the final farewells. When we arrived at the airport as dawn was breaking we found Farid there before us. Under his own highly personal system, every airport resource was summoned into organising our successful departure, extra pounds of baggage were dismissed with a knowing wink of his eye, passports and documents taken over and stamped with startling speed. 'You see, everyone knows Farid,' was his by-word. Only the roar of the engines and the desperate admonitions of the stewardess eventually removed him from the seat alongside ours. He had bustled us into them ten minutes ago—'The best in the whole 'plane.' 'Don't forget to send those things to Mukeiras for me,' I said from the doorway—I had bought a musical box for the harem at Ariab and the promised red velvet for Nur. 'And don't forget us either.' I suddenly had a lump in my throat. 'You will be back,' was his farewell, as he stood waving with his shock of grey hair blowing in the wind, the familiar horse-bag face half cheerful, half distressed. 'You will be back.'

The 'plane turned up the runway and we left Farid behind, an ever-diminishing figure, still waving until we roared into the air and lost sight of him. For a moment the whole of Aden, the Khormaksar isthmus and the desert beyond lay beneath my window in the sun. I stared down at it trying to preserve in my memory this final fragment of past happiness. But from the air, my Arabia Felix meant no more than a relief map in a glass case. Besides it was all going by now too fast, and I knew that however often I might be drawn back, I had lost that part of it, the freshest and the best, for ever.

We didn't go back to Aden . . . A new posting came through for Ronald from the Colonial Office. It was to Fiji in the South Pacific—the greatest contrast imaginable to Aden.

But this was later. First we had our holiday in Italy.

The Ali of Rapallo was an overwrought depressed young man who tried to bury his anxieties about the future in a round of night-clubs, speed-boats and new sports cars. He told us that Government was pursuing a policy 'harassing' him at every turn. Also that increasing pressure was being put on him to banish Mohammed Ali. 'They would be happy to get rid of us both. But I will never abdicate. They may push me off the tightrope or I may fall but I will never jump off of my own accord.'

'But perhaps you are harassing them in turn?'

'I myself am no trouble-maker,' he said. 'But can I help having the ideas of a civilised man? I am well-educated, I have travelled, I have more knowledge of the Yemeni background than any other ruler—surely I could have been of use to Government. How has it happened that things have come to this?'

We said goodbye to him outside the Casino at Monte Carlo, a lonely incongruous figure in his beloved Thunderbird among the crowds of holiday-makers. It was not to be foreseen that in less than a year he would be once more in Europe—this time as an exile, forbidden by the British to return again to his own country.

Events unfolded in this way. In April an order was issued by the Governor for the arrest of the three Jifri brothers. Abdulla bin Ali was taken in Lahej, but after a search had been made of every building including the Palace, it was discovered that Mohammed Ali with his other brother Alawi had succeeded in escaping to the Yemen.

Sultan Ali then left Aden for consultations with the Colonial Office. He was greeted in London with the usual T.V. interviews and pictures in the popular press of the 'young Arab ruler' taking tourist snapshots of the city. Shortly afterwards it was reported that the Commandant of the Lahej Army had fled to Yemen with most of his troops and a large sum of money from the State Treasury. Also a secret store of arms and ammunition was discovered on the Colony border of Lahej. Sultan Ali denied knowledge of either of these events.

All this we were gathering in fragments from newspaper cuttings and letters. It was a few weeks later that through the cracklings of a portable radio on a sunny South Sea beach I heard the news that while in Milan he received official notification of his deposal. Her Majesty's Government withdrew recognition from him as Sultan of Lahej. There was an unenthusiastic column of editorial comment in *The Times*, which suggested that stronger proof of the Sultan's implication would have to be brought forward by the Colonial Office to withstand the scrutiny of anti-British propagandists. In Parliament questions were asked but there was no organised objection to the deposal by the Opposition. There have been numerous rumours of an appeal on his behalf before the United Nations to be sponsored by Yemen's chief delegate, H.R.H. Seifal-Islam al Hasan but so far nothing has materialised.

Ali is now living in Cairo where he has made a number of broadcasts on behalf of the U.A.R. He is still known as the Sultan of Lahej, but his title as Knight of the British Empire, I hear, has tactfully fallen into disuse.

In his place at Lahej is his uncle, the enigmatic Fadl of the noble profile and distinguished moustache, the Fadl whose rather colourless personality I had heard well described by the Arab simile 'a man like glass'. Unlike his nephew, Fadl obviously had no ideological objections to joining a Federation of Protectorate States. The final arrival into the fold of the black sheep, Lahej, most powerful state of them all, was a political triumph for the British Government.

Sultan Saleh flourishes. In addition to the award of C.M.G. last year, he now bears the impressive title of Federal Minister for Internal Security. It was in this rôle that he arrived last May for talks with the Colonial Office in London where we were able to see him for one evening before we flew to Fiji again. He was to have been our guest in North Wales for a fortnight's stay and we had been painting the attic a striking shade of blue in honour of the forthcoming visit. This was the only accommodation available in our flat and Saleh had written to say he would be very pleased indeed to share the three small top-storey rooms with his entourage. But, sadly, the Sultan-in-the-Attic episode was not to be. Our leave was unexpectedly cut short and a meeting in London was all that could be arranged.

We had arrived at our hotel that afternoon. Ronald had rushed off to see about ticket arrangements and I had been walking in St James's Park. As I pushed through the revolving doors into the lobby again, the commissionaire pointed out a group of three men standing at the far end of the maroon-carpeted expanse. One of them came forward to meet me, a shortish, immaculate figure in a dark-blue suit with the grinning, bearded face of Saleh of Audhali.

Shaking hands excitedly, we were both stricken with the terrible shyness of all reunions in formal settings. It was rather like one of those dreams where familiar things are inextricably jumbled up with incongruous details from another context altogether.

'*Kef halek?*' he asked laughing, and the spell was broken.

'*Salaam aleikum,*' I replied, and we were almost in Mukeiras again.

'You have increased weight,' said His Highness with the familiar twinkle.

'And you are slimmer,' I said, and he was, and not so tall as I had remembered without his turban, and above all, disconcertingly urbane-looking. Before an interested audience of hotel staff he introduced me to the Federal Minister of Finance, a dashing slickly-spoken personage, and a quiet young man who was the Sultan's travelling secretary. The only polite procedure in Arab eyes was, of course, to invite them up to our room for tea. Nevertheless the chambermaid's expression as she unlocked the door for me and my oriental delegation—Ronald having gone off with our own key—remains an unforgettable memory.

For the next half-hour, messages, photographs and gifts were duly exchanged. And then '*hashush*'.

'I have just bought a Mercedes. It is beautiful,' said Saleh with a gesture of pride.

We both smiled, remembering Ali.

Almost apologetically, he added, 'You see, I am staying the majority in Aden now I am Minister. I have new house in Khormaksar. I would be neighbouring you.' His English was now quite fluent though he steered his sentences along with the tender caution of new ownership.

After dinner that evening, slightly restricted by the Cathedral hush of the hotel lounge, we discussed the present situation in Aden, while an elderly waiter renewed glass after glass of iced water in front of His Highness with a look of awed disbelief.

Saleh said that life in the Protectorate had decidedly become more peaceful. In the Colony, too, there had been no further bomb incidents, only labour troubles and a dock strike from time to time. But he could not say how long this calm would last.

'You must come back to Aden soon,' he said. 'Please come again and stay with us all.'

But as they talked, the present Aden seemed blurred and unreal. Far sharper and more luminous than ever before were the images I carried with me, those things that had become a part of myself —the songs and the dancing, three horses on a beach, a necklace of coins strung from a nail in a bare room. Some day I would add to these and all the rest a new gallery. But that would be another time, another place . . .